THOR

Thor

Myth to Marvel

Martin Arnold

continuum

Continuum International Publishing Group

The Tower Building	80 Maiden Lane
11 York Road	Suite 704
London SE1 7NX	New York NY 10038

www.continuumbooks.com

First published 2011
Reprinted 2011

British Library Cataloguing-in-Publication Data
A catalogue record for this book is available from the British Library.

ISBN: HB: 978-1-4411-3715-9
PB: 978-1-4411-3542-1

Typeset by Pindar NZ, Auckland, New Zealand
Printed and bound in Great Britain

Contents

For Nils Ralph Arnold

Acknowledgements

Formal acknowledgements and thanks are due to Cambridge Scholars Publishing for permission to reproduce material from my essay, "'Strength, Work, Duty, Truth, Honor Bright": Pan-Scandinavianism, Pan-Germanicism and the Myths of Thor the Thunderer', in Paul Hardwick and David Kennedy, eds, *The Survival of Myth: Innovation, Singularity and Alterity* (Cambridge Scholars, 2010); Brepols Publishers for permission to reproduce material from my essay, "'Lord and Protector of the Earth and its Inhabitants": Poetry, Philology, Politics, and Thor the Thunderer in Denmark and Germany, 1751–1864', in Andrew Wawn, ed., *Constructing Nations, Reconstructing Myth: Essays in Honour of T. A. Shippey* (Turnhout, Belgium: Brepols Publishers, 2007); Leifur Eiríksson Publishing for permission to reproduce material from Viðar Hreinsson, ed., *The Complete Sagas of the Icelanders.* Volumes I-V (Reykjavík: Leifur Eiríksson Publishing, 1997); and Oxford University Press for permission to reproduce material from Carolyne Larrington, trans., *The Poetic Edda* (Oxford University Press, 1996). I am grateful to the Faculty of Arts and Social Sciences at the University of Hull for the support I have received for the writing of this book. In particular, I would like to thank my immediate colleagues in the university's Andrew Marvell Centre for Medieval and Early Modern Studies. For giving me the benefit of their expertise at various points in this study, thanks are due to Professor Emeritus Andrew Wawn (University of Leeds), Professor Jonathan GoldbergBelle (University of Illinois Springfield) and Professor Emeritus Tom Shippey (Saint Louis University). Any errors of judgement are entirely my own responsibility. I have also been fortunate in having the encouragement and, it should be said, toleration of my children and many friends. Finally, as always, it is to my wife, Maria, that my debt is the greatest.

Note on proper nouns

In this book, the practice has been to anglicize proper nouns from medieval Scandinavian sources, but to give titles of works in the vernacular with an English translation after the first mention in each chapter. This practice has not been applied to the spelling of personal names derived from post-medieval European languages.

Introduction

The Norse god Thor has variously been depicted as a sky god, a thunder god, a god of the seas and the winds that govern them, a fertility god, a god of war and as the god who was the ultimate bulwark against monstrous evils. He has been expressed as the essence of Denmark, Sweden, Germany and, as a comic-book superhero, the United States. He has been labelled the enemy of Christ and depicted as Satan, and the enemy of Rome and Roman Catholicism and, therefore, the salvation of Protestant Europe. He has been perceived as the almighty god, condemned for having 'no guts', lionized as the epitome of good, criticized as being 'boorish and uncouth', celebrated as the 'guardian genie of the Fatherland', recommended as the friendliest and most good-natured of the gods, sought out in order to discover the technology to harness cosmic energy and summoned as the awesome Mighty Thor. Yet, save for the fear he provoked among Christian missionaries over 1,000 years ago, the one characteristic of Thor that has been consistently recognized is his devotion to protecting humanity from ill, however that ill might be defined.

Among all the Norse gods, Thor is unique in having this particular mission and in having human company at his bidding on many of his perilous mythological adventures. These days, he might well be called 'the people's god'. The problem here is the failure of the people to agree on what his service should be and against whom his powers should be directed. In this respect, he has been enlisted to promote regional and national causes for the last 1,000 years, conspicuously so for the last 250. No other god from Norse mythology has had such a controversial and prominent history, not even Thor's father, Odin.

This study begins with an exploration of Thor's appearances in the earliest known sources, chiefly those preserved in medieval Iceland in the *Poetic Edda* and the *Prose Edda*. Questions are then considered as to why and how such a complex mythology ever came into being and why it is the case that very Thor-like gods doing very Thor-like things are recorded in ancient myths from the Mediterranean, Iran and India. These similarities among mythological systems are beyond coincidence and take us back thousands of years BC to who was, in all likelihood, the original god of thunder. But it was the old northern Thor, the hammer-wielding ally of ordinary folk, who was worshipped by Viking foot soldiers and seafarers and remembered in Icelandic sagas and Scandinavian histories set down during the Middle Ages, and it was this Thor who was the target of ruthless kings seeking to expand their influence in Christian Europe. It was at the temples of Thor, where bloody human sacrifices were performed, that these kings and their missionaries sought to eradicate all traces of the god, typically with threats of steel, fire and dispossession to those who failed to accept the new order.

With the demise of paganism and the spread of Christianity, Scandinavian countries rapidly sought out new identities in wider Europe, but the extraordinary legacy of the pagan past continued to have its uses, and Scandinavian monarchs handsomely paid those who could research their countries' ancient histories and establish their right to rule over their neighbours. In this way, Old Norse myths and legends were preserved. When, during the latter part of the eighteenth century, a new spirit of Romanticism began to dawn across Europe, the collected knowledge of that self-same past was suddenly, even shockingly, released from the confines of court historians to become an inspiration to patriots, poets and dramatists. For many, it was Thor who, like no other, focused the need to recover the traditions of national identity and to shrug off foreign influences. Exactly where this led the god is the subject of the latter half of this study. It is tale of greed, jealousy, belligerence, prejudice and eventually world war. It is also a tale of Thor being drawn south out of a purely Scandinavian context and into the ranks of Nazi ideologues in Hitler's Germany.

The taint Norse mythology picked up after its abuse by the Nazis has never quite gone away, nor has the distrust of high-culture elitism that attended it. However, in the United States, the answer to high culture that was formulated during the course of the twentieth century was mass culture. Once paraded in three dimensions as a champion of the 'master race', in the United States we find Thor in two dimensions as the troubled superhero The Mighty Thor. From myth to Marvel, Thor's story is about the formation of modern Europe and the rise of mass consumerism. It is a story of mythological proportions.

The Giant Killer: Thor in Old Norse Mythology

THE EDDAS

Our understanding of Old Norse mythology would be vastly impaired were it not for the preservation instincts of the brilliant Icelander Snorri Sturluson. Born in 1178/9 into one of the most powerful families in Iceland, whose lineage can be traced to the disaffected, anti-monarchic Norwegians who settled Iceland from the 870s onwards, Snorri's life epitomizes the complexity and contradictions of his age. Twice elected to the country's highest office of law speaker at the Icelandic parliament, the Althing, and feted at the royal courts of Norway, Snorri's political ambition brought him ownership of huge estates and greater wealth than any of his countrymen. It also brought about his death at the hands of the agents of the Norwegian king Hakon Hakonarson (r. 1217–63), whose interests in Iceland Snorri had sworn to promote. From Hakon's point of view, Snorri had not only disappointed, but also appeared disloyal and, finally, defiant. It therefore came about that on the night of 22 September 1241, a posse of 70 armed men led by the king's representatives, two of whom were Snorri's former sons-in-law, descended on Snorri's comfortable estate at Reykholt. Five of them pursued the defenceless chieftain to his hiding place in the cellars and hacked him to death. It is said that Snorri's pathetic last words were 'Eigi skal höggva!' ('Do not strike!').[1]

As Snorri's brutal ending illustrates, thirteenth-century Iceland was a place of great turbulence, wherein self-interest and greed precipitated civil war, a circumstance that the Norwegian king did much to encourage. As a key figure in the power politics of his day, Snorri's actions did little to ameliorate the violence. Iceland was a 250-year-old oligarcho-republic, the like of which was unknown anywhere else in Europe, but some 20 or so years after his death, Icelandic independence was no longer viable and the Icelandic parliament willingly submitted to monarchic rule from Norway. Yet in this same century, Icelanders produced a body of literature that will forever rank as one of the greatest cultural achievements at any time and place in the world. Snorri was central in this, too.[2]

Whatever leisure Snorri's fortune brought him was not wasted. Three masterpieces of medieval literature have been credited to him: *Heimskringla*, a voluminous history of the Norwegian kings; *Egils saga*, the compelling tale of Snorri's tenth-century warrior-poet ancestor; and the *Prose Edda* (in this case the term 'edda' obscurely signifies an explication of Norse mythology and the traditional poetry associated with it). It is in this latter work, written during the 1220s, that the world of the Norse gods is more lucidly described than in any other medieval source. Presented in a style that combines the structural features of the European folk tale, Graeco-Roman literary motifs and learned Christian commentary, Snorri's compositional technique is indicative of both the refined and the popular tastes of his contemporary audience. The *Prose Edda* is not, however, presented as an advert for paganism, at least not in any ideological sense; indeed, he is explicit in cautioning his readers that 'Christian people must not believe in the heathen gods, nor in the truth of this account . . .'[3]

Although Iceland was one of the last European countries to adopt Christianity, in AD 1000, by the thirteenth century, Christianity was fully embedded in Icelandic culture, even though many in authority resented foreign pressure that threatened the independence of the Icelandic church's ministry and revenue. Not least among the defenders of the autonomy of the Icelandic church was Jon Loftsson (d. 1197), a pre-eminent chieftain and church deacon, and foster father to Snorri. Whilst it is beyond doubt that Snorri's upbringing was imbued with Christian teachings and values, it is equally beyond doubt that Snorri was deeply influenced by his foster father's chauvinism. Pride in Icelandic traditions and culture and in contemporary Christian beliefs could not always sit comfortably together, especially when that pride extended to the worldview of pre-Christian Icelanders. This potential conflict of interest is something that Snorri tries hard to reconcile in the *Prose Edda*.

The *Prose Edda* is divided into three main sections: 'Gylfaginning' (The Deluding of Gylfi), 'Skáldskaparmál' (The Language of Poetry) and 'Háttatal' (List of Verse Forms), which are preceded by the Prologue. The most explicit attempt to provide a Christian perspective on Norse paganism is made in the Prologue through the principles of euhemerization, whereby in the passage of time mortal rulers were believed to have been deities. In this way, Snorri rationalizes the error of pagan beliefs as a consequence of Scandinavians' reverence of descendants of warriors from Hellenic Greece who conquered and settled in the far north after the Trojan War at around 1200 BC. Thus the collective name for the gods, the Aesir, is etymologized by Snorri as 'men of Asia', a euhemerist value that Snorri also employs at later points; for instance, in his assertion that the name Thor is a corruption of Hector, the Thracian hero. Having thus framed the origins of the mythology as rooted in misunderstanding and ignorance, Snorri is at liberty to recount what these fancies entailed. He remains careful, however, to keep his distance from any endorsement of their truth value. In 'Gylfaginning', Snorri contrives a Swedish king, Gylfi, who assumes the name Gangleri (perhaps meaning 'the one weary of walking') and goes in search of the gods to question them about the nature of things. As a result, Gylfi is left with the delusion that his informants actually are divinities, whereas it is made clear to the reader that they are fraudsters.

The remaining two sections are given as copious technical glosses on what mythological meanings lay behind the use of traditional poetic collocations, the latter of which consists of an annotated poem in praise of King Hakon and the king's regent and uncle, Earl Skuli. By these methods, and with considerable panache and wit, Snorri offers a comprehensive account of Norse mythology without risk of censure. Nevertheless, at a point in history when memories of the old faith were beginning to fragment and fade, what Snorri in effect achieves is their rescue and repair. Along the way, he sets down in writing numerous tantalizing extracts from the oral literature sacred to Norse paganism. As already remarked, Snorri was not in the business of posing a challenge to prevailing tenets of faith; rather, he is motivated by the desire to conserve a literature in danger of extinction. Even so, what the *Prose Edda* does do is provide a cultural continuity between the pagan past and the Christian present, a line that had been severed when Iceland abandoned the old ways and conformed to the religion of wider Europe. Snorri's work is, in this sense, one of the earliest affirmations of Nordic cultural identity. Much of what he records can be corroborated, not only by manuscripts that may well have been his sources, but also archaeological evidence that pre-dates Snorri's edda by hundreds of years, such as graven images found in Sweden and Denmark depicting Thor overcoming the monstrous Midgard Serpent in precisely the manner he describes.

Nevertheless, it should be borne in mind that, for all Snorri's efforts, Norse myth is not in all respects a coherent narrative and that even in Snorri's time much was either lost or simply no longer understood. Besides this, one can reasonably surmise that during the centuries that the myths were evolving there were many variants in their telling, as well as variants in religious practice. Inconsistencies, contradictions, the blurring of creature categories and the obscurity of the original functions of the gods are matters that Snorri was in all probability keen to rectify, where possible. While our debt to Snorri is incalculable, many scholars have regretted that he did not leave a full account of all the sources at his disposal. So complex is the material that Snorri is dealing with, and so subtle is his procedure, that in his extemporizations on the raw material he can scarcely avoid adding to the problems of those who have since sifted through the myths in an attempt to recover mythological authenticity.

The verse forms that Snorri cites in the *Prose Edda* consist of two types: eddic and skaldic. Many eddic lays were composed before the coming of Christianity to the north and these may well have been recited in some form for many centuries prior to the conversion. Others post-date the conversion but have developed out of mythico-legendary material since lost in its original form. Eddic lays employ a number of different forms of alliteration and, generally speaking, take as their subject matter the intrigues of the Norse gods or human heroes with extraordinary attributes who strive to fulfil their destinies, often according to the grand plans of the gods. The legendary material includes a number of lays concerning the early Scando-Germanic Niflung and Volsung dynasties, and the ill-fated love triangle involving Sigurd Fafnisbani, slayer of (the dragon) Fafnir; the outcast valkyrie Brynhild; and the Burgundian princess Gudrun. These lays and their saga derivatives would go on to occupy a central place in European art and literature during the nineteenth century. Eddic verse is often quite lengthy but is relatively easy to read, despite the fact that there are many allusions to episodes and ideas that are cryptic to us.

By contrast, skaldic verse is usually shorter and is famously difficult to decipher, being densely configured with strictly wrought 'kennings', which are compound expressions with metaphorical meaning. For example, a warrior may be described as 'helm tree', a battle as 'shower of arrows', blood as 'dew of wounds' and a prince as 'reddener of swords'. Personal names are also substituted by kennings; for instance, one kenning for Thor is 'breaker of giant heads'. Skaldic verse usually takes the form of praise poetry composed in honour of illustrious patrons. Icelanders were the acknowledged masters of skaldic poetry and were sought for service in royal households across mainland Scandinavia, as is apparent from Snorri's historical work *Heimskringla*. Because of its metrical complexity, and thus the virtual impossibility of altering it without ruining its structure, much skaldic verse is considered to have survived intact in oral transmission from the ninth and tenth centuries. Skaldic codifications and paraphrases constitute a treasure trove of information about mythological subjects. And, unlike the anonymous eddic lays, the authors of skaldic verse can very often be reliably identified.

As previously mentioned, exactly what sources or which informants Snorri used cannot be known in all cases, although it is evident that scattered citations of eddic and skaldic verse in twelfth-century works and access to expertise on oral traditions were readily to hand. It is clear, however, that Snorri knew material that has not survived. Fuller details of much of what Snorri knew became apparent in 1643, when a sheaf of manuscripts in an anonymous hand on which were copied 34 eddic lays were recovered from a farmhouse in Iceland and given to an Icelandic bishop, Brynjólfur Sveinsson (1605–75). In 1662, the bishop presented them to Iceland's colonial monarch, King Frederick III of Denmark and Norway (r. 1648–70), and the collection thus became known as the *Codex Regius* (King's Book). The *Codex Regius* collection cannot itself have been Snorri's source, as the eddic lays it contains would first seem to have been set down in writing in the late thirteenth century and so some time after Snorri's death. Nonetheless, there is an exact match between the *Codex* lays and many of Snorri's citations. Supplemented with certain other surviving eddic verses, this collection is now most commonly known as the *Poetic Edda*. Set together, the *Prose Edda* and *Poetic Edda* provide an extraordinarily revealing window onto the world of Norse paganism. As such, they are the inevitable starting point in the search for the mythological Thor.

THE MYTHOLOGICAL CONTEXT

The nearest we get to a chronology of the genesis, lives and doom of the gods in the *Poetic Edda* is given in the 66 stanzas of the ancient eddic lay 'Völuspá' (The Seeress's Prophecy). This lay tells of Odin, the chief of the gods, summoning a prophetess, who then recounts the origin of the gods, their tribulations and their eventual demise and subsequent renewal. Although sometimes confusingly allusive and obscure, 'Völuspá' provides a linear structure from Creation to Ragnarok, the doom or twilight of the gods, and is, in this sense, a spine around which all the other mythological lays can be placed and from which Snorri seeks to systematize the whole mythology, most notably in 'Gylfaginning'.

The cosmos of Norse mythology is comprised of ten worlds, nine of which are located on three tiers or planes of existence. Encompassing and unifying these tiers are the roots of the sacred tree Yggdrasil, the Guardian Tree, whose branches are home to a riot of animals. Around the tree sit the three Norns, mysterious female agencies who weave the fates of all living things. In the upper tier is Asgard, the home of the warrior gods, the Aesir; Vanaheim, the home of the fertility gods, the Vanir; and Alfheim, the Land of the Light Elves. Also within this tier is Valhalla, the Hall of the Slain, where those who have died in battle ready themselves for Ragnarok as the chosen army of the Odin. In the middle tier are Jotunheim, Giantland; Nidavellir, the Land of the Dwarfs; Svartalfheim, the Land of the Dark Elves; and Midgard, Middle Earth, where humans dwell. In the oceans encircling this tier lives the gigantic venomous snake Jormungand, otherwise known as the Midgard Serpent, which circumscribes Midgard. Connecting the upper and middle tiers is Bifrost, the Flaming Bridge, guarded by the god Heimdall, who sits in readiness to sound his horn to warn of the coming of monstrous armies intent on the destruction of the gods and the world at Ragnarok.

In the lower tier, at the remotest roots of Yggdrasil, is the dreadful goddess Hel, who presides over both the frozen region that bears her name, and Niflheim, the Land of the Dead, where those who have not died in battle, and are therefore excluded from Valhalla, reside. The fearsome dragon Nidhogg, the Corpse-Tearer, stalks this realm devouring the dead and gnawing at the roots of Yggdrasil. Spanning the abyss between Hel and Midgard is Gjallabru, the Echoing Bridge, guarded by the giantess Modgud, who is set on deterring those who wish to cross into or out of the frozen gloom of Hel. Imprecisely located to the south is Muspelheim, the Land of Fire, ruled over by the giant Surt, who will eventually bring his conflagration to bear at Ragnarok. Although gods and giants traffic freely between the upper and middle tiers, none but the god Hermod is recorded as visiting and returning from Hel in his failed quest to recover the god Baldur, the pride of Asgard (see 'The death of Baldur' in this chapter).

As the seeress tells Odin, this intricate cosmos is the product of evolutionary forces beginning with the creation of the world from the body of the evil frost giant Ymir, and the gradual emergence of the various races from his dismembered corpse. As the world is thus materially evil, its inhabitants are fated to chaos and conflict. The first war is between the fertility gods and the warrior gods, the Vanir and the Aesir, which is resolved in the triumph of the Aesir and the eventual union of all the gods under their aegis. Thereafter, it is the cold and implacable enmity of the gods and the giants that steadily escalates. At the end, the seeress reveals the future in her grim vision of Ragnarok, followed by the renewal of the gods and thereafter a seeming return to a pattern of conflict and destruction. The cunning calculations of Odin, the heroic defence of Thor and the rejuvenating magic of the fertility gods and goddesses – significantly, Frey and his sister Freyja – can ultimately do nothing to deflect inexorable fate and their doom. Chief agent in the undoing of the Aesir is Loki, who, according to the custom of judging kinship with regard to paternity, is himself of giant stock. It is Loki's indiscriminate sexuality and perverted intelligence that leads to the spawning of the monstrous brood – the Midgard Serpent, the apocalyptic wolf Fenrir and the goddess Hel – and it is Loki's malice that brings about the death of Baldur, the most beloved of the gods and their prospective saviour. If one myth in the eddas exceeds all others in importance, it is that telling of Baldur's death, for it is on this that the future of the gods turns.

THE DEATH OF BALDUR

The myth is given in its fullest form in Snorri's 'Gylfaginning'. Baldur is disturbed by dreams that bode ill for his life. When he tells the Aesir of this, they determine to ensure his invulnerability, for Baldur is the wisest and purest of their kind. His mother, Frigg, Odin's wife, successfully requests his immunity from all living things and all the elements. With Baldur now impervious to harm, it becomes the entertainment of the gods, seemingly with Baldur's approval, to assault him with stones and spears at their assemblies. Only Loki regrets that Baldur remains unharmed. Disguising himself as an old woman, he pays a visit to Frigg, whom he questions about Baldur's immunity. Frigg tells her visitor that the only thing she did not bother to ask for cooperation from is the mistletoe, as she considered it harmless. Loki now goes and plucks a stick of mistletoe, fashions it into an arrow and takes it to the assembly. Here he finds the blind god Hod, who because of his impairment cannot join in the fun with Baldur. Loki hands him the arrow and directs his fire, so killing Baldur in an instant. No vengeance can be taken in the sacred precincts of the assembly. The grief of the gods, particularly Odin's, is unparalleled. The god Hermod is dispatched to Hel to request Baldur's release, which is granted on the condition that all things living or dead must first cry for him. Only a cave-dwelling giantess refuses to do so and so the mission fails. The giantess is believed to have been Loki in disguise.

Baldur's death marks the beginning of the end for the gods. As the only one of them without vice has gone from their ranks, their situation now seems hopeless. Punishment is duly meted out to Loki, who, having returned to harangue the gods (as is told in the eddic lay 'Lokasenna' [Loki's Quarrel]), is bound in fetters from which he will escape at Ragnarok to help his giant kin besiege his one-time companions in Asgard. According to the lay 'Baldrs draumar' (Baldur's Dream), in which Baldur's death is prophesied to Odin, harsh vengeance is taken upon Hod by Odin's day-old son Vali, who would seem to have been produced for this very purpose.[4] Aside from the cosmic implications of Loki's spiteful and wicked actions, the true colours of this most disruptive of gods are thus revealed and his giant nature is now clear. Although frequently ingenious and creative, and even on some occasions a helpmate to Thor on his travels, Loki turns out to be the enemy within and, in this respect, the antithesis of Thor. Indeed, the enigma that is Loki lies at the heart of the unstable world of the mythology.

The characteristic features of Norse myth, then, are ubiquitous violence and the ravelling of fate. While in the enemies of the gods there is clearly a depiction of evil life-denying negativity, with the exception of Baldur – whose death is a catastrophe, but whose role is otherwise passive – there is no depiction of absolute good. Instead, the moral ideal is given as a practical code of conduct, which is most fully put forward in the eddic poem 'Hávamál' (The Sayings of the High One). Given in this poem is Odin's wise advice to heroes on topics ranging from matters of trust to the right manner in which vengeance should be sought. Almost all the gods, including Odin, frequently fall short of these standards and are shown to be treacherous, licentious, vain and impetuous. In 'Lokasenna', Loki pointedly identifies the shortcomings of each of the gods and, as Ragnarok approaches, their moral turpitude is reflected in the disintegration of the most intimate of social bonds. As 'Völuspá' predicts:

Brother will fight brother and be his slayer,

brother and sister will violate the bond of kinship;

hard it is in the world, there is much adultery,

axe-age, sword-age, shields are cleft asunder,

wind-age, wolf-age, before the world plunges headlong;

no man will spare another.[5]

In the doom-laden journey from Creation to Ragnarok, Thor is the only one of the chief gods who consistently fulfils their duty to vanquish the forces set on their extinction. Unencumbered by emotional or intellectual complexity, Thor is unfailing in his determination to confront danger. He is the hero's hero, who in an authoritarian patriarchy is an ideal of aggressive masculinity.

THOR IN THE EDDAS

THOR'S FAMILY

The eddas are consistent in naming Thor, or Asa-Thor (Thor of the Aesir), as the eldest son of Odin.[6] Perhaps his most prominent brother, or, rather, half-brother, in the mythology is the ill-fated Baldur, although the guardian god Heimdall, Baldur's unwitting slayer, Hod, and the so-called silent god Vidar, all have significant functions. Thor's mother is the giantess Jorth, sometimes referred to as Fjorgyn; both names signify 'Earth' and 'Land'. This maternity may indicate an ancient tradition in which Thor was originally associated with a fertility cult. According to Snorri, Jorth is reckoned among the Asynjur, the most powerful of the goddesses. An obscure reference in Snorri's 'Skáldskaparmál' alludes to Thor as having been fostered by Vingnir, who is perhaps the giant of the same name, and Hlora, who may be cognate with 'Glora or Lora',[7] the foster mother killed by the Thracian Thor alongside his foster father Loricus in Snorri's Prologue.

Thor's wife is Sif, a name signifying kinship by marriage rather than by blood, thus embodying the concept of wifely 'affinity'.[8] Sif has a son named Ull from a previous relationship about which no details are known. Ull is athletic, warlike and a fine archer, and it is therefore apt that according to the eddic lay 'Grímnismál' (Grimnir's Sayings) that he lives at Ydalir (Yewdale). He is, Snorri tells us, the god of skiing and skating, and he has a particular relationship with the sea, which he skims across on a shield; hence, a kenning for shield is 'Ull's ship'.

According to the eddic poem 'Atlakviða' (The Lay of Atli), vows were made on Ull's ring. On the chape of a sword sheath, found in a second-century AD weapon deposit at Torsberg in Slesvig, the word *Wulþuþewaz* is inscribed, which is believed to mean 'servant of Ull'.[9] In Danish tradition, as set down in the late twelfth-century *Gesta Danorum* (History of the Danes) by Saxo Grammaticus, Ull temporarily displaces a disgraced Odin, who later returns and kills him. Much suggests, therefore, that he may once have been an important Norse god whose lustre had waned.

Although little is known about Sif, the probable importance of Ull suggests that she is an important goddess in her own right. A kenning for gold is 'Sif's hair' and this has led some scholars to speculate that she had an association with ripened cornfields, and so is in all likelihood a figure derived from a vegetation or fertility cult.[10] One tale – concerning the theft of Sif's hair by Loki and its eventual replacement – is told exclusively by Snorri (*see* 'Mjollnir' in this chapter). Presuming that the story is not a fabrication by Snorri to account for the kenning, then the possibility that Sif had cultic origins is strengthened. Apart from this there is Loki's vulgar claim in 'Lokasenna' that he cuckolded Thor, but this might well be disregarded as mischief-making, although some support for the claim could be derived from a cryptic remark made in the eddic lay 'Hárbarðsljóð' (Harbard's Song), where Harbard, who is in fact Odin, tells Thor that 'Sif has a lover at home . . .'.[11]

Thor has two sons, Magni (Angry One) and Modi (Strong One), and a daughter, Thrud (Mighty Woman). Magni is said by Snorri to be the product of Thor's relationship with the giantess Jarnsaxa, who is thus named as a rival to Sif, but it is unclear whether Modi is also a product of this same relationship. Depending on how one interprets the lines referring to Sif's characteristics in 'Skáldskaparmál', Thrud could either be the daughter of Sif or Jarnsaxa, although the balance of probability is that her mother is Sif. All three children exemplify aspects of Thor's character and strength. Thrud, though, is a relatively unknown personage and plays no explicit part in the myths that have survived. Nevertheless, in the eddic lay 'Alvíssmál' (All-Wise's Sayings), she would appear to have been betrothed to the dwarf Alvis without Thor's prior approval. Thor, however, displays quite uncharacteristic cunning in his encounter with Alvis and manages to extend his interrogation of the dwarf's wisdom until the sun rises, the consequence of which is that the dwarf is petrified. This source may well be thirteenth-century, which would account for Thor's anomalous characterization, but this does not discount the likelihood that some of the raw material of the poem is much older. Thrud's sexual vulnerability is also suggested in a kenning dating from the ninth century, which is cited by Snorri from the skaldic poet Bragi Boddason. The kenning denotes the giant Hrungnir as 'the thief of Thrud' and so suggests a lost myth in which Thrud is abducted and perhaps violated by the giant. If so, this would add further motivation to her father's struggle against him (*see* 'Hrungnir and Geirrod' in this chapter). Thrud was clearly an important figure and, like Thor's mother, is listed by Snorri among the elite group of goddesses, the Asynjur.

As regards Magni and Modi, the eddic lay 'Vafþrúðnismál' (Vafthrudnir's Sayings) relates that on Thor's death they will inherit the sacred hammer Mjollnir, Thor's chief weapon, and will be among the few to survive Ragnarok. Snorri tells how the 3-year-old Magni plays a helpfully supportive role beside his father in his battle against Hrungnir. For this Thor gives Magni his adversary's horse, Gullfaxi, a gesture that Odin disapproves of on the grounds that Magni is the son of a giantess and that he himself would be a more deserving recipient. Apart from this, there are few other mentions of either of Thor's sons in the eddas, other than in relatively transparent kennings, which nevertheless confirm that they were well known in the heathen period. Some confusion concerning the parentage of Magni and Modi arises again as a result of Snorri's obfuscatory Prologue, where the Thracian Thor travels north and meets a prophetess named Sif. Their descendants are described through numerous generations and include at a relatively remote point of descent Magi and Moda, whose names readily suggest Thor's sons in the myths.

According to Icelandic saga tradition, Thor has fiery eyes and a great red beard and is often invoked by his devotees under the name Redbeard. Thor's realm is Thrudheim (The Mighty Abode) or Thrudvangar (The Mighty Fields), and his great hall is called Bilskirnir (Flashing of Light), which according to 'Grímnismál' has 540 apartments. The chief practical role of Thor in the eddas is as 'enemy and slayer of giants and troll-wives'.[12] Armed with Mjollnir, which he brandishes in iron gauntlets, and his girdle of strength, he traverses the sky in a chariot drawn by two he-goats, which, says Snorri, are named Tanngrisnir (Teeth-barer) and Tanngnjost (Teeth-grinder). As a charioteer, Thor is also known as Oku-Thor (Driving-Thor). Master of both thunder and lightning, Thor is almost permanently preoccupied in defending the gods' domain, a task that routinely requires him to cross rivers to sit in judgement beneath Yggdrasil or to enter Giantland and boldly challenge the giants, either in high-stake contests or through direct assault. As the basic narrative of Norse mythology suggests, no role is more vital than this, for the tenancy of the gods depends upon Thor's single-minded mission to keep it secure. The broad mythological context for Thor's mission, though, is far from secure, and it is one that ultimately prevents the god from achieving his ends. This is foreseen almost from the outset of the mythological cycle.

THE MASTER BUILDER TALE

Myths concerning Thor's battles against the giants defy any strict chronology, save that which is indicated in the eschatological move from Creation to Ragnarok. Some seem retrospective, for, as might be expected, the mythology as it has survived does not readily conform to narrative logic. However, one candidate for being the first myth in which Thor plays an important giant-killing role is that known as The Master Builder Tale, as it is in this myth that the conflict between the gods and the giants could be seen to originate. The tale is only fully recounted in 'Gylfaginning', where the pretext for relating it to Gylfi is to explain the origins of Odin's horse Sleipnir.

The episode takes place shortly after the Aesir–Vanir war, when the gods plan to fortify their home in Asgard. Significantly, Thor is away on a troll-killing campaign when the gods employ the services of a giant stonemason. The stonemason demands his payment be the sun, the moon and the fertility goddess Freyja, a price that would bring about the end of all life. Believing that these consequences can be avoided, the gods set a penalty clause of forfeiture of payment should the stonemason fail to complete the fortification within one winter. He also must complete the work without help from any man. By way of a concession, Loki agrees to let the stonemason use a horse. Great oaths are made guaranteeing the giant's safety should Thor return home. Worryingly, however, the giant's horse turns out to be the huge stallion Svadilfari and it soon becomes apparent that the work will be completed on time. The gods convene and lay the blame for every aspect of the deal on Loki, demanding that he find a solution on pain of death. In desperation, Loki transforms himself into a mare and lures the stallion away, one outcome of which is that Loki will give birth to the eight-legged foal Sleipnir. Realizing that the work will not now be completed on time, the stonemason flies into a great rage, which reveals his true mountain-giant nature. Somewhat oddly, the gods appear to have failed to perceive the stonemason's racial identity up until this point, but now they consider their oaths and the contract made with him to be void. Thor is thence summoned and he returns to raise Mjollnir and pay out the giant with a fatal blow to the skull.

It has been argued that The Master Builder Tale owes more to European wonder-tale traditions than to myth. In support of this argument, two thirteenth-century Icelandic saga episodes are adduced that tell of the fractiousness caused in farming communities over issues of wall building.[13] While this is probably true in some respects, elements of the myth were evidently well known before Snorri's time. The curious twelfth-century poem 'Hyndluljóð' (Song of Hyndla), which contains the so-called 'Short Völuspá' but is mostly concerned with genealogical lore, remarks that Loki 'got Sleipnir by Svadilfari'. Moreover, the antiquity of the notion that the enmity between the gods and the giants is associated with a broken contract concerning the goddess Freyja is indicated in two allusive verses in 'Völuspá':

> Then all the Powers went to the thrones of fate,
> the sacrosanct gods, and considered this:
> who had mixed the air with wickedness,
> or given Od's girl [Freyja] to the giant race.

> Thor alone struck a blow there, swollen with rage,
> he seldom sits still when he hears such things said;
> the oaths broke apart, the words and the promises,
> all the solemn pledges which had passed between them.[14]

Here we can assume that the 'them' of the last line refers to the gods and the giants, and that the contract made with the Master Builder had implications for all future relations between the two races. Whatever the case, the gods' recklessness, Loki's nefariousness and Thor's pre-emptive strike guarantee hostility for all time. The pretext given in 'Gylfaginning' for telling the tale is also significant, for certain eighth-century picture stones found on the island of Gotland, Sweden, depict an eight-legged beast and rider. These images have been interpreted as a mythic symbol of a coffin stand borne by four men (hence the eight legs).[15] If Odin on Sleipnir is a symbol of death, particularly his death, as chief among the gods, Odin's extinction would precipitate the extinction of all associated with him.

It is also the case in 'Baldrs draumar' and in 'Gylfaginning' that Sleipnir is ridden to Hel, the realm of the dead, in the failed effort to recover Baldur, a failure that betokens the desperate vulnerability of the gods. Indeed, vulnerability is also at the symbolic heart of The Master Builder Tale, for the fortification of Asgard is never completed. This idea of a permanent breach in the defences can be found in Icelandic folk tale traditions purporting to explain why a church wall is in disrepair, where the reason given is that a ravening troll, or even the devil, had invaded the sacred space and demolished the wall fleeing from the horrible sound of the church bells.[16] The church is therefore susceptible to further trespass from wicked interlopers. As for the gods, their futures are now finite, as not only are the giants set on their destruction, but also their capacity to defend themselves is compromised. Thor's role is thus defined, and in these intimations of the mortality of the divines, The Master Builder Tale could be taken to signify the first step towards Ragnarok.

MJOLLNIR

If a chronology of Thor's role in the mythology were wholly possible, then one obvious objection to The Master Builder Tale arises from the fact that Thor is already in possession of Mjollnir, for another myth tells how he comes by it and that its primary purpose is to vanquish giants. The myth of the origin of Mjollnir is told at length in Snorri's 'Skáldskaparmál' but is not supported in any of the surviving eddic poems. In a typical act of mischief, Loki has cut off Sif's hair. Confronted by a murderously irate Thor, Loki has promised to get Sif a replacement head of golden hair that will grow like any other. So it is that Loki commissions certain dwarf brothers to smithy the hair, and they not only do this, but also make the magic ship Skidbladnir, which is large enough to accommodate all the Aesir but can nevertheless be folded to fit in a pocket, and the spear Gungnir, which can determine the outcome of battles and is later given to Odin. Loki, however, wants more and wagers his own head in a bet he makes with two different dwarf bothers that they cannot make three things even more precious. The wager is accepted and the three objects that are crafted are the gold ring Draupnir, which every ninth night drips eight more rings of equal worth, a gold-bristled boar that will transport the god Frey across sea and sky, and the hammer Mjollnir, a weapon of great potency that when thrown will always return to its owner's hand. Yet, in the manufacture of these things, the brother charged with blowing into the forge is distracted by a troublesome fly, the consequence being that Mjollnir's haft is rather short. Even so, it is deemed to be the finest of all weapons and the gods decide that only Thor, the bulwark against the giants, should be its owner. When Loki subsequently tries to escape his debt to the dwarf brothers, he ends up saving his neck but is punished by having his lips stitched together.

A sceptical view would be to regard this myth as largely the creation of Snorri. Yet the intricate detail of the myth is convincing, even to the point of giving names to the instrument, personified as another dwarf brother, used to pierce Loki's lips and to the thong used to stitch them up. As for Mjollnir's defectively short haft, this was clearly a widely held belief, for it is found in a separate Danish tradition, as given by Saxo Grammaticus, where the defect is explained as a result of damage sustained to the hammer in a battle between the gods and men. As for the name 'Mjollnir', a number of explanations have been offered: one is that it derives from the Old Norse word *mjöll*, meaning 'new snow'; another, particularly attractive explanation, is that it is a corruption of the Old Slavic word *mluniji* (Russian *molnija*), meaning 'lightning', a defining characteristic of Mjollnir.

Mjollnir is the subject of one other myth in which its sacred ritual function is indicated, but, again, doubt has been cast regarding the myth's authenticity. In this case, however, the problem is in reverse, for this myth only appears in a single eddic poem and is not mentioned by Snorri. 'Þrymskviða' (Thrym's Poem) tells of the theft of Thor's hammer by a giant and the stratagem devised by the gods to recover it. It is an explicitly comic tale, during which Thor is deeply humiliated. This irreverence has prompted one scholar to suggest that it is a lampoon of Norse myth by a Christian author, who may well have been Snorri himself.[17] Contesting this hypothesis, it has been argued that regard for the gods in the heathen period was not necessarily limited to the solemnity and seriousness that characterizes Christian belief; indeed, that mockery in Norse myth could, in itself, be regarded as reverential. Certainly, comically disrespectful behaviour among, and by, the gods is a feature of several eddic poems deemed to have been composed before the conversion.

In 'Þrymskivða', Thor awakes to discover his hammer missing, which prompts Loki to borrow a magic cloak from the fertility goddess Freyja, so allowing him to fly. In Giantland he comes across Thrym, who admits to having stolen Mjollnir and buried it eight miles beneath the earth's surface. For its return, Thrym demands Freyja as his bride, a proposition that, on Loki's return to Asgard, the goddess angrily rejects. The gods now convene to decide what to do and Heimdall suggests dressing Thor as Freyja so that he can recover his property and take due vengeance. Thor is less than enthusiastic about the scheme but, reminded by Loki that 'The giants will be settling in Asgard/Unless you get your hammer back', he relents.[18] So, with Thor attired as Freyja and Loki accompanying him dressed as a maid, they set out in Thor's chariot. Their arrival is signified by a burst of flames and earth-shattering noise, prompting the excited Thrym to believe his bride is approaching. At Thrym's court, Thor is honoured with a pre-nuptial feast, during which his astonishing appetite draws Thrym's attention. Assured that Freyja has been too excited to eat for several days, Thrym now questions her terrifyingly fiery eyes, and is reassured that neither has she slept for some time. Thrym's sister now enters and demands a wedding gift from the bride-to-be, at which point Thrym insists that Mjollnir be set on Thor's lap to consecrate the marriage and so, presumably, to bring fertility to the bride. Thor, however, has in mind a different use for Mjollnir and duly wreaks havoc, killing Thrym, his sister and all their kin.

Although this farcical tale is unreferenced elsewhere, the existence of a giant named Thrym is almost certainly not of Snorri's invention, for Thrym is mentioned in the list of giant names in 'Skáldskaparmál', and the existence of a place known as Thrymheim (Thrym's Home or, more literally, House of Thunder) is mentioned in both 'Gylfaginning' and the lay 'Grímnismál', albeit in all these cases it is said to be the residence of a giant named Thiassi. One possible and tantalizing reference to Thrym may lie beneath the kenning used by the poet Bragi Boddason in the ninth century and cited by Snorri in 'Skáldskaparmál'. In this kenning, Bragi refers to Thor as 'the cleaver apart of Thrivaldi's nine heads', about which we know nothing else, and then congratulates Thor for having 'held back your steeds with notorious giant-feast drinker'.[19] If 'giant-feast drinker' is taken to mean Thrym, a name that could also mean 'thunder', and the allusion is to the god of thunder arriving at Thrym's court, then Bragi is subtly, if rather opaquely, conflating names, actions and scenes from 'Þrymskivða'. Not surprisingly, some have considered this speculation a little too bold.

HRUNGNIR AND GEIRROD

Two tales of Thor's encounters with giants are told in sequence in 'Skáldskaparmál', ostensibly to explain the background of certain kennings. Both of these myths are substantiated by pre-Christian skaldic verses.

Hrungnir

In the first of the sequence, Thor, as is often the case, is initially absent and has 'gone to eastern parts to thrash trolls'.[20] Odin has chosen this moment to ride to Giantland on his eight-legged steed, Sleipnir. Arriving at the home of the giant Hrungnir, Odin quickly causes irritation by boasting about his horse. A pursuit follows with Hrungnir mounted on his horse Gullfaxi chasing Odin out of Giantland and then straight through the gates of Asgard. The other Aesir deem it wise to offer the giant a drink, but he consumes such a large quantity of ale that he becomes drunk and blusters that he will remove Valhalla to Giantland, destroy Asgard and abduct Freyja and Sif. Perturbed by all this, the gods summon Thor who arrives in a trice. Thor's instinct is to make short work of Hrungnir, but the giant protests that he has Odin's protection and does not have his weaponry – his whetstone and shield – with him. Instead, he offers to meet with Thor on the frontiers of Giantland for single combat. Thor eagerly accepts, for no one had ever before dared challenge him in this way.

As Hrungnir is the most powerful of their kind, the giants are keen to ensure that he will be victorious. They build a vast clay giant named Mokkurkalfi (Fog-Leg) and invest it with life by inserting in it the heart of a mare. They position it beside the stone-hearted Hrungnir, who is awaiting Thor's arrival with his whetstone and shield at the ready. But Thor's manservant, Thialfi, goes ahead of his master to tell Hrungnir that Thor will arrive from underground, whereupon Hrungnir stands on his shield. This, however, is a cunning deception, for Thor duly arrives from the sky amid thunder and lightning and hurls Mjollnir at his opponent's head. While Mokkurkalfi stands by so fearful that '[t]hey say he wet himself when he saw Thor',[21] Hrungnir responds by hurling his whetstone at the god. The two projectiles meet in mid-air and the whetstone breaks in two, one part becoming lodged in Thor's head. Yet Mjollnir is not deflected and explodes into Hrungnir's skull, shattering it. As Thialfi demolishes Mokkurkalfi, the dead Hrungnir topples forwards, his leg pinning Thor to the ground. None among the gods is able shift it save Thor's prodigious infant son Magni. Magni is rewarded by his father with the gift of Hrungnir's horse, a gesture that Odin considers inappropriate, as Magni is the son of the giantess Jarnsaxa. Thor, meanwhile, is in need of medical attention and the sorceress Groa arrives to extract the whetstone from his skull using incantations. Pleased with the progress of her work, Thor tells Groa that he recently assisted her husband, Aurvandil, by carrying him in a basket across a great river, but one of Aurvandil's toes froze and he, Thor, snapped it off and cast it into the sky to become a star. Delighted that her husband will soon be home, Groa forgets her spells and so the whetstone remains forever lodged. It is therefore taboo, says Snorri, to throw whetstones across the floor, for this causes the whetstone in Thor's head to move.

Snorri's lucid account of this myth is followed by what would appear to be his chief source: an extract from Thjodolf of Hvin's poem 'Haustlöng' (Autumn Long). This poem is known to have been composed in Norway at some point between the late ninth and early tenth centuries, and is, therefore, one of Snorri's oldest extant sources. It celebrates the gift of a shield to the poet by his patron Thorleif the Wise. On each quarter of this shield certain mythological scenes were depicted that inspired the poet – among the scenes, that of Thor's encounter with Hrungnir. The myth clearly played a central role in beliefs about Thor, and Hrungnir is mentioned in five other eddic poems, as well as being widely referenced in kennings used by other skalds, such as Bragi Boddason's early ninth-century allusion to Thor as 'Hrungnir's skull-splitter'.[22] Nevertheless, while the efforts of Groa to remove the whetstone from Thor's skull are present in 'Haustlöng', where it is suggested that the operation was a success, the tale told by Thor regarding Aurvandil's toe is uniquely Snorri's. It is probably right to conclude that this is Snorri's extemporization, perhaps based on a medieval folk tale that sought to explain why a star was named Aurvandil's Toe. The related Old English word *earendil*, meaning 'ray of light', supports this possibility.[23]

Geirrod

The second myth of the sequence concerns Thor's encounter with the giant Geirrod, and, once again, Thor is inveigled into dangerous dealings with the giants by Loki. As a result of sheer recklessness and bravura, Loki, in the form of a falcon, has managed to get himself imprisoned in a chest by Geirrod, where he is left without food for three months. Brought forth for interrogation by his captor, Loki trades his freedom in exchange for the promise to bring Thor to Geirrod's court, without either his girdle of might or Mjollnir. How this is achieved is not told, but on his journey to Giantland with Loki, Thor has the good fortune to take lodgings with a helpful giantess named Grid, daughter of the god Vidar the Silent, who is himself a son of Odin and therefore a half-brother to Thor. Grid tells Thor of Geirrod's malice and loans him her girdle of might, a pair of iron gloves and her staff, Grid's Pole. Thor soon comes to the great river called Vimur. With Loki tucked beneath the girdle of might and assisted by Grid's Pole, he makes it to the centre of the river and is about to be overwhelmed by the rising torrent when he sees that the cause of this is Geirrod's daughter, Gjalp, urinating into it, an obscenity that some critics have interpreted as also involving the secretion of menstrual blood. He hurls a large stone at her declaring, 'At its outlet a river must be stemmed.'[24]

He now manages to scramble ashore by grasping onto a rowan bush, which is thereafter to be known as 'Thor's salvation'. At Geirrod's court, Thor and Loki are given lodgings in a goat shed. Sitting on the only chair, Thor finds himself being raised up towards the rafters and in danger of being crushed but, with the help of Grid's Pole, he forces the seat back down, whereupon dreadful screaming is heard. The source of this, he discovers, is Gjalp and her sister, Greip, who were beneath the chair and now have broken backs. On entering Geirrod's hall, the giant hurls a lump of molten iron at Thor, which he catches in one of Grid's iron gloves and hurls back at his host, who is sheltering behind an iron pillar. So powerful and deadly is Thor's aim that the molten metal passes through the pillar, through Geirrod and through the exterior wall.

At some point in the latter part of the tenth century, the skaldic poet Eilif Gudrunarson composed a poem in praise of Thor known as 'Þórsdrápa' (Lay of Thor). Nineteen verses from this extremely difficult poem are copied into Snorri's edda straight after his own account of the Geirrod myth. Little is known about Eilif, except that he did service as a court poet to Earl Hakon Sigurdarson, ruler of Norway, and that, as one might expect, he was a committed worshipper of the Norse gods. Certain, arguably minor, differences exist between Snorri's account and that given by Eilif, perhaps the most notable being that it is Thor's servant Thialfi and not Loki that accompanies Thor on his journey, and that in Eilif's poem Thor has access to Mjollnir. Although there is no supporting eddic poem for this tale, Saxo Grammaticus also knew of it in Danish traditions. Saxo's *Gesta Danorum* tells of the journey of one Thorkil (given in Latin form as Thurkillus) to the kingdom of Geruth, where he and his companions come across the perforated body of an old man hunched beneath a shattered cliff and the tumour-riddled corpses of three women with broken backs. Thorkil is quick to inform his men that this is the aftermath of Thor's work: the old man has been killed by a burning ingot and the women have succumbed to Thor's thunderbolts. Nearby is a hoard of cursed treasure that results in a ghastly end for those foolish enough to plunder it.[25] Further testimony to this myth's popularity on into the Middle Ages is provided by the late thirteenth-century Icelandic tale *Þorsteins þáttr bæjarmagns* (Thorstein Mansion-Might), in which the mercurial Thorstein uses a magic marble to kill Geirrod and burn down his hall. In this version, the hero's success is credited to the patronage of the late tenth-century Norwegian Christian king Olaf Tryggvason (d. AD 1000).

THOR AND UTGARDA-LOKI

The longest space given by Snorri to one of Thor's adventures in Giantland is a tale told in 'Gylfaginning'. Gylfi is interrogating the 'gods' about the limits of Thor's might and, for once, they seem reluctant to comment. Nevertheless, the one calling himself Third, sometimes a byname for Odin, declares that he will not lie, even though the story 'does not seem to us nice to tell'.[26] Thor and Loki are travelling in Thor's chariot and decide to take their night's lodgings at a peasant farmer's house. Thor provides a meal for the household by slaughtering and cooking his own goats. The bones, Thor insists, must be tossed intact onto the goatskins, but the farmer's son, Thialfi, ignores this and, unknown to Thor, splits open one of the bones to get at the marrow. At dawn the following day, Thor raises Mjollnir aloft to perform a sacred ritual that will restore the goats to life, only to discover that one of them is lame. Fearing for his family's lives, the farmer compensates Thor with the gift of his children: his son, Thialfi, and his daughter, Roskva.

Now journeying by foot and heading for Giantland, the two gods and the children cross a great stretch of water and enter a forest. They come across what seems to them to be a large, empty, peculiar-looking building, where they decide to rest. During the night, there is a great commotion, which in the morning turns out to be a giant so large that Thor shrinks from attacking him. The giant introduces himself as one Skrymir. Readily identifying Thor, he asks what he and his companions want with his glove, for it is in the thumb of Skrymir's glove that they have spent the night. Thor agrees to have Skrymir join their company and they pool their provisions. At nightfall, they shelter beneath a tree and Thor tries unsuccessfully to untie Skrymir's knapsack containing their food. Enraged, he smashes Mjollnir onto the sleeping giant's forehead, only for Skrymir to awaken briefly and complain that a leaf must have fallen on him. With ever increasing ferocity, Thor twice more attacks the giant but again Skrymir thinks that little more than an acorn and something trifling from the branches above have fallen on him. Come the morning, Skrymir tells them that they have only a little way to go before they reach the castle of King Utgarda-Loki, and, having advised them to show all due deference to the king and his retinue, he departs.

On arriving at the castle and being unable to open the gates, they squeeze through the bars and present themselves in Utgarda-Loki's great hall, whereupon the king insists that they must perform certain feats should they wish to stay. In the first, Loki loses an eating contest against Logi, and in the second, the fleet-footed Thialfi loses three running contests against a certain Hugi, even though he successively manages to narrow the margins of defeat. Then comes the turn of Thor, who opts to demonstrate his capacity for drinking. Utgarda-Loki brings him a horn and tells him that no one has failed to drink it down in fewer than three goes. Far from being able to empty it, only on his third effort does Thor make any impression at all on the horn's contents. For the next contest, Thor must raise a large cat fully off the ground but try as he might he manages only to raise one of its paws. Thor now offers to fight anyone in single combat, but his host mocks him and brings forward his old nurse, Elli, as the only person at his court who will accept such a challenge from someone so puny. Once again, Thor fails to make any impression and the combat is abandoned. The companions are now offered lavish hospitality, after which they retire.

The following morning, Utgarda-Loki accompanies Thor and the others as far as the road outside the castle, where he obliges Thor to admit to having lost considerable face. Utgarda-Loki now tells the god that, had he known of his extraordinary strength, he would never have admitted him into his court and that his actions very nearly brought about the ruination of the kingdom. Skrymir, he admits, was none other than him. The knapsack, he explains, was cunningly tied with iron wire, and the hammer blows Thor believed had struck him had actually created three deep valleys in a table mountain. Similarly, all the contests were deceptions. Loki's challenger, Logi (Flame), was no less than a forest fire, while Thialfi's opponent, Hugi (Thought), was the king's thought. As for Thor's challenges, the horn was connected to the sea and Thor's quaffing had lowered its tides considerably; the cat was the monstrous Midgard Serpent that encircles the world; and the name of the old woman, Elli, signified exactly who she was: Old Age. Infuriated by these confessions of trickery, Thor reaches for Mjollnir but Utgarda-Loki and his castle have vanished.

The myth of Thor and Utgarda-Loki has little of the opacity that is common to unvarnished mythology; rather, in its patterning and polish, it has more of the appearance of a well-worked folk tale, and there can be little doubt that this is the case. It is also possible that the account of the laming of the goats and Thor's resurrection of them was imported from Irish hagiographic tales during the Viking Age and that similarities among Irish folk tales – such as the episodes involving the giant Skrymir and, after that, the series of contests at Utgarda-Loki's court – also indicate a Celtic provenance for this particular myth.[27] Nevertheless, there remains some cause to believe that behind the artifice there are elements of authentic sacred mythology with Scandinavian roots. When Thor returns to confront the disruptive Loki in 'Lokasenna', he is taunted by Loki who reminds him that 'in the thumb of a glove you crouched cowering, you hero' and

> strong leather straps you thought Skrymir had,
> and you couldn't get at the food,
> and you starved, unharmed but hungry.[28]

Likewise, in the verbal exchanges with Odin masquerading as the ferryman Harbard in 'Hárbarðsljóð', Thor is again reminded of his ignominy with regard to his dealings with a certain Fialar, who presumably is Skrymir:

> Thor has quite enough strength, and no guts;
> in fear and cowardice you were stuffed in a glove,
> and you didn't then seem like Thor;
> you dared in your terror neither
> to sneeze nor fart in case Fialar might hear.[29]

An even clearer analogy with, or perhaps influence on, the Skrymir element of the myth is to be found in a Russian folk tale concerning the knight-hero Ilya, whose attempts to kill the giant Svyatogor with his mace are almost identical in their effect to Thor's attempts to kill Skrymir with Mjollnir. There are also elements from folk tales recorded in the Caucasus, which tell of heroes sleeping in huge gloves, struggling with the luggage of giants and undergoing trials of strength.

While the possibility that the person of Utgarda-Loki was only later incorporated into the myth is strong, one other, somewhat puzzling, reference to him can, like that to Geirrod and his daughters, again be found in Saxo's account of the adventures of Thorkil. In the course of his wanderings, Thorkil is advised to seek out the oracular wisdom of Utgarda-Loki, but when he arrives at his squalid snake-infested lair, he finds him moribund, pitiful and bound beneath fetters. While this is certainly more analogous to the binding of Loki after he has contrived the death of Baldur than it is to Snorri's account of Thor's treatment at the hands of Utgarda-Loki, it is nevertheless provocative. In one respect, Thor's relationship with Utgarda-Loki, as described by Snorri, parallels that between Thor and Odin, particularly in 'Hárbarðsljóð', for in both cases Thor is exposed as verbally unsophisticated. Much the same, however, could be said of Thor's lack of sophistication in comparison with his frequent companion Loki, who in this myth is uncharacteristically mute and whose connivances are substituted for by those of Utgarda-Loki (Loki of the Outer Enclosures). It is also the case that Thor plays a key role in the binding of Loki (see 'Towards Ragnarok' in this chapter). The Saxo tale may, then, be a conflation of the punishment of Loki and a possible vengeance taken by Thor on Utgarda-Loki at a later point in mythological time.

Just as Utgarda-Loki can be seen as analogous to both Odin and Loki, so can his court be seen as analogous to Asgard, as, quite exceptionally in this tale, the giants are presented as being as ingenious and as culturally refined as their divine enemies.[30] At the heart of the tale, however, is an assessment of the relative strengths and weaknesses of the gods and the giants, something that, in certain ways, anticipates their confrontation at Ragnarok. Although the giants are ultimately revealed as inferior to the gods in terms of sheer might, as depicted in the person of Thor, so the limits of Thor's power are also revealed, especially when set against the magic arts. It is perhaps for this reason that Gylfi's informants are reluctant to expose the true extent of Thor's powers, for to know of this is also to know of his weaknesses. One might even consider that this tale of Thor humanizes the god more than any other. His adoption of human servants, most notably the unfailingly loyal Thialfi, underlines this perception of Thor as the one god that human mentality can comprehend and, as a consequence, trust.

THOR'S FISHING EXPEDITION: THE MIDGARD SERPENT

The Midgard Serpent, also known as Jormungand (The Mighty Snake), was one of Loki's monstrous brood along with the wolf Fenrir and the goddess Hel. According to Snorri, and as is testified in both skaldic and eddic verses, all of these were produced as a result of Loki's coupling with the giantess Angrboda, whose very name signifies 'she who brings sorrow'. When Odin perceives the great menace of these creatures, he assigns each of them places in the outer reaches, the Midgard Serpent being dispatched to the sea where it grows so large that it encircles all land. The 'gods' tell Gylfi that on Thor's return to his realm, after the debacle at Utgarda-Loki's court, he 'made up his mind to seek an opportunity for a meeting to take place between him and the Midgard Serpent'.[31] Thor's evident motivation is to restore his reputation and '[i]t is no secret, even among those who are not scholars, that Thor achieved redress for this expedition'.[32] Assuming a youthful appearance, and in such haste that he does not even bother to ready his chariot, Thor sets out alone across Midgard, until he arrives at the home of the giant Hymir, where he is given lodgings for the night.

In the morning, Hymir readies himself for a fishing trip and, despite his doubts about his guest's fortitude and strength, he demurs to Thor's insistence that he be allowed to accompany him. Told to get his own bait, Thor tears off the head of one of Hymir's oxen and they now set out to sea in a rowing boat. Thor, however, is not satisfied to fish in Hymir's usual fishing ground and, even though he is warned of the dangers posed by the Midgard Serpent further out to sea, Thor obliges the increasingly unhappy Hymir to press on farther and farther. On reaching a remote spot, Thor casts his line baited with the ox head: 'then it is true to say that Thor fooled the Midgard Serpent no less than Utgarda-Loki had made a laughing stock of Thor when he was lifting up the serpent with his hand.'[33] With the hooked serpent writhing on his line, Thor is hard-pressed, but, summoning his full strength, he forces his feet through the bottom of the boat and braces himself on the sea bed, from where he succeeds in hauling the serpent up to eye level. As the serpent hisses poison, Thor reaches for Mjollnir but in a dreadful panic the terrified Hymir takes out his knife and cuts Thor's line. Thor hurls Mjollnir after the serpent but, as Gylfi is told, whether or not he succeeded in killing it remains a matter of opinion. For his cowardice, Thor punches Hymir overboard then strides ashore.

Of all the myths recorded in the literary sources, none is more widely referenced than this one. Snorri's chief source was almost certainly the eddic lay 'Hymskviða' (Hymir's Poem), which in all likelihood was composed during the eleventh or possibly the twelfth century. In this, the context for Thor's fishing expedition is the gods' need of a large cauldron so they can brew, or, rather, force the giant Aegir to brew, sufficient ale for the winter. The god Tyr knows of just such a thing, for his father, who turns out to be Hymir, owns it. Thor and the Tyr set out in Thor's chariot and first encounter Hymir's goatherd, Egill, who secures Thor's goats and takes them to Hymir's hall. Here, they are met by Tyr's grandmother, who is appalling to look upon as she has 900 heads, and his gold-bedecked mother. The gods are advised to hide themselves behind a pillar. When the ill-tempered Hymir returns home, the women announce their presence and Hymir shatters the pillar with his gaze. He offers no paternal welcome to his son and is clearly offended by the sight of Thor, yet he seems obliged to grant his visitors hospitality for the night. During the evening meal, Thor devours two whole oxen, much to Hymir's astonishment.

The following day, Thor and Hymir go fishing and the giant lands two whales simultaneously, while Thor prepares his line with the ox-head bait. Yet unlike in Snorri's account, Thor not only succeeds in hooking the Midgard Serpent but also manages to smash Mjollnir into its head. Despite the cosmic reverberations, it remains unclear as to whether he has killed it. Returning to land, Thor carries Hymir's boat and one of the whales back to his hall. Hymir now seeks to provoke Thor by questioning his strength and challenging him to break a precious crystal goblet. Thor only manages to do this when Tyr's mother advises him to throw it at her husband's head. Hymir now offers to give them the cauldron on the proviso that one of them is able to lift it, which Thor succeeds in doing. On their way home with the cauldron, they are pursued by the rueful Hymir and a posse of giants, all of whom Thor kills. After this, one of Thor's goats goes lame, which, apparently, is the work of Loki. The poem ends by celebrating the fact that the gods can now drink their fill of ale every winter.

'Hymskviða' defies complete understanding on a number of counts and it seems likely that the poem retains elements of other, perhaps earlier, versions in which Thor's companion was not Tyr, but either Loki, whose father was definitely a giant (whereas there is no other source saying that Tyr's father was of giant descent), or even Thor's manservant Thialfi – whose father may well be the goatherd Egill, whom the gods encounter on their arrival near Hymir's hall. Interestingly, Egill, as father of Thialfi, would appear to be alluded to again at the end of the poem as the 'dweller on lava' who 'paid for it with both his children'[34] – a curious intertext with Thor's adoption of Thialfi and Roskva in Snorri's account of Thor and Utgarda-Loki and, of course, with the lame goat motif present in both the eddic verse and Snorri's edda. Yet, despite these puzzling interconnections, there are certain conceptual differences between 'Hymskviða' and Snorri's version of it as regards the status of, and attitude to, the gods, which some critics have ascribed to the relative impact of Christian thought between the times of the composition of the two accounts.[35]

Nonetheless, the popularity and centrality of the myth from pagan to Christian times can be discerned in its depiction on picture stones. The earliest of these are scenes on an eighth-century picture stone found at Ardre in Gotland showing in one frame Thor with an ox and in another with a figure in a boat. Perhaps as much as 300 years younger is the Altuna Stone in Sweden, which, like the much eroded and so not precisely datable Hørdum Stone in Denmark, shows Thor with his foot through the bottom of a boat, exactly as told by Snorri. However, a stone carving found outside Scandinavia that depicts Thor baiting his line with an ox head is of particular interest. This is the so-called Fishing Stone, now housed in St Mary's Church, Gosforth, in the old Viking settlement area of the English Lake District. While nearby the remarkably detailed Gosforth Cross indicates a Christian amelioration of pagan symbolism, the Fishing Stone is a clear indication of the resilience of pagan ideas into the Christian era.

Setting aside Snorri's rather tortuous effort in 'Skáldskaparmál' to explain the myth as a corruption of the battle between Hector and Achilles during the Trojan War, little further clarity concerning the surrounding details of the myth is achieved in turning to the numerous skaldic sources for Thor's fishing trip, all of which are pre-Christian. The earliest and most extensive of Snorri's skaldic citations describe the kernel of the fishing trip tale and are from Bragi Boddason's ninth-century 'Ragnarsdrápa' (The Death Song of Ragnar Lodbrok). In this, Bragi poeticizes the decorations on a shield given to him by one Ragnar, said – somewhat improbably in one source – to have been the legendary Viking warlord Ragnar Lodbrok. Similar to these are those citations given from Ulf Uggason's poem 'Húsdrápa' (House Celebration), composed around AD 983. This was recited at a banquet given by the wealthy Icelander Olaf the Peacock; an event that is mentioned in *Laxdæla saga* (The Saga of the People of Laxardal), composed during the latter part of the thirteenth century and replete with historically credible detail. The poem pays tribute to Olaf's splendid hall, which was lavishly decorated with woodcarvings of mythological scenes, including Thor's struggle with the Midgard Serpent. Further scattered references are made in verses by Olvir Hnufa, from the ninth century, and Eystein Valdason and Gamli Gnævadarskald, both from the tenth century. Only in Ulf's 'Húsdrápa' is it suggested that Thor killed the monster, but such is the complexity of the verse that doubts could be raised about whether this is actually what is meant. One obvious objection to Thor having killed the Midgard Serpent is prompted by the myth that tells of their mutual extinction at Ragnarok.

TOWARDS RAGNAROK

In the concluding prose section of 'Lokasenna', it is said that Loki flees from Thor and hides in a waterfall disguised as a salmon. Snorri, however, tells how the Aesir pursue Loki to a riverside hideout but that he escapes in salmon form shortly before they arrive. In the ashes of Loki's fire they see the remains of a cunningly made fishing net, the design of which they imitate. With their net stretched across the river, they slowly close in on Loki, who, realizing the danger, tries to leap the net, only to be caught by Thor. Thereafter, Loki is bound with the guts of one of his sons and a venom-dripping snake is hung over his face. Loki's wife, Sigyn, catches the venom in a bowl but when she has to leave him to empty it, Loki's convulsions are so great that earthquakes result. Loki's abusiveness towards the gods may, in itself, have been shocking enough to warrant this punishment but the greater crime had already been committed: Loki's orchestration of the death of Baldur. Thor's role in the efforts to lessen the impact of this calamity are all but non-existent; indeed, his usual repertoire of threat and violence is so wholly unsuited to the situation that he appears doltish when he loses his temper at Baldur's funeral and almost attacks the gruesome giantess Hyrrokkin, who has been summoned by the gods to help launch the funeral ship. Worse still, he peevishly kicks an unfortunate dwarf into the flames for running in front of him as he consecrates the pyre with Mjollnir. With Ragnarok now an imminent inevitability, Thor's position as the chief defender of the frontiers of Asgard and Midgard would appear to be obviated. Perhaps even more so than the other gods, he can do nothing but wait, for now the giant armies are massing and rather than him seeking his old adversaries, they will seek him.

The idea of the Old Norse apocalypse is widely referenced in the lays of the *Poetic Edda* and was quite clearly central to a pagan conception of time. As much as half of 'Völuspá' is devoted to the progress towards, and the actualities of, Ragnarok, much of which is cited in the extensive account given in 'Gylfaginning'. Following three years of destructive strife in which all the taboos of kinship will be broken, there will be the Fimbulwinter (which, says Snorri, is three years of unremitting cold and frost); the wolf Fenrir will devour the sun, while his kind will catch the moon and extinguish the stars; the giant Hrym will set sail with his armies; and the Midgard Serpent will splatter poison across sea and sky. Then Surt, wreathed in flame, will cross the Bifrost Bridge that spans Midgard and Asgard, and the bridge will collapse. So it will come about that all the enemies of the gods will converge on them, including Loki, who will lead the forces of Muspell.

Bereft of any other response, the gods take to the field with the great armies of Valhalla, led by Odin and Thor. Frey will be killed by Surt, for, as is told in another myth describing his folly, he has no sword, and Surt will originate an all-consuming conflagration. Odin will be swallowed by the wolf Fenrir but will be avenged by his son, Vidar, and Loki and Heimdall will be the death of each other. Unable to go to Odin's assistance, Thor will advance against the Midgard Serpent and will strike it dead but, stepping back nine paces, he will succumb to its poison:

> Then the glorious son of Jorth,
> Odin's son, advances to fight against the serpent,
> in his wrath the defender of earth strikes,
> all men must leave their homesteads;
> nine steps Fiorgyn's child [Thor] takes,
> with difficulty, from the serpent of whom scorn is never spoken.[36]

Although some of the gods survive to enjoy a period of renewal, a new Golden Age, during which Baldur will return from Hel, 'Völuspá' concludes by predicting that monstrosity, this time in the form of the dragon of Hel, Nidhogg, will once again bring death and destruction. Just prior to this, the seeress asserts that 'the powerful mighty one, he who rules over everything, will come from above, to the judgement-place of the gods.'[37] Although there is no consensus among critics over what this might mean, it is believed by many to be a Christian interpolation suggesting the demise of pagan beliefs.

The tales recounted above amount to only a fraction of the mythology concerning Thor that once existed. This can be deduced, at the very least, from the skaldic sources that list the names of many giants killed by Thor for which no myths have survived. In addition, in the various accounts of certain other myths, there are contradictions that make it unclear whether Thor or some other god slays a particular giant. One example is the killing of the giant Thiassi, who abducts the goddess Idun and along with her the apples of eternal youth on which the gods depend. In 'Hárbarðsljóð', Thor claims that he took vengeance on Thiassi and then cast his eyes to the sky to become stars, but in Snorri's 'Gylfaginning' it is not clear who kills the giant; however, it is explicitly stated that it is Odin who appeases Thiassi's daughter by immortalizing her father in the same way. The fact that this particular element of the myth strongly resembles Thor's story about Aurvandil's toe in Snorri's account of the Hrungnir myth suggests that mythic elements have been conflated or have migrated from one myth to another, and this once again illustrates the complexities and uncertainties that the mythographer encounters in trying to unravel the eddas.

One explanation for these problems is that those who composed on mythological subjects in the first two centuries after the conversion, attempted, much like Snorri, to relieve some of the obscurity of the early eddas by devising satisfactory solutions, but this, in the passage of time, has only contributed to the problems. As true as this most certainly is, it should also be admitted that the very nature of Norse myth is that it is not a fully coherent narrative. Unlike Judaeo-Christian mythology, there was no doctrinal authority and so no orthodoxy, and variants in the telling of it would have abounded; for example, depending on which god an adherent thought most beneficial. Equally true is the fact that myth evolves and, in due course, refines itself and becomes increasingly systematized. With the supervention of Christianity in the Old North, this process was abruptly ended. In the case of Norse myth, what we have inherited is a palimpsest through which layers of older versions of the myths are in some places tantalizingly faded, but are in others starkly and incongruously visible. So, while the mythological skies are in many places clouded, that which is illuminated, often thanks to Snorri's retrospective attempt to impose order on the myths, nevertheless permits a great deal of relatively confident commentary and analysis as to what the god Thor signified and what he meant to his worshippers.

2

Theorizing Thor

As a belief system, Norse paganism may be distinguished from certain monotheistic religions, such as Christianity or Islam, in so far as it had no evangelical mission and was in this sense unconcerned with gaining converts per se. Yet, despite this apparent open-mindedness, Norse myth was no less ideologically all encompassing and conservative in its worldview. As is the case with other mythological systems, the relationship between the myths of the eddas and the social customs of Norse society constituted a virtuous circle, as far as the myths presented, in abstracted form, the same values and, indeed, the same anxieties that generated them. Inherent in this was the framing of existential problems in such a way as to address the age-old philosophical questions: where do we come from? where are we going? how should we live? While the answers to the first two questions were presented in terms of the eschatological move from Creation to Ragnarok, the answer to the last question was in part conditioned by existing social hierarchies and the consequent expectations that were placed on individuals. It will surprise no one that Norse mythology did not tend to favour women over men, nor that this prejudice has only attracted significant critical attention since the latter part of the twentieth century.

THOR AND THE GIANTS

Thor's relationship with the giants is obviously not as straightforward as simply presenting him as their implacable and murderous enemy. Certainly his tally of giant-killings far exceeds that of any other god, but, given that his mother is named as both a goddess and a giantess, and that he may, therefore, be considered a half-giant; that he sires at least one child with a giantess and that he is not above taking help from giants (as is the case with the giantess Grid in the Geirrod myth and the giantesses at Hymir's hall), it is clear that Thor's attitude towards the giants is not indiscriminate. One way of accounting for this is to make a distinction between male and female giants. As is apparent from the eddas, there is no taboo on male gods mating with alluring giantesses, albeit that such matches are not in every case desirable; however, when male giants importune goddesses (for example, Thrym's and the Master Builder's lust for Freyja, or the giant Thiassi's abduction of the goddess Idun, one of whose functions was to guard the apples of eternal youth), then this appears to threaten the gods' very existence.[1]

Of course, while the danger posed by male giants threatens the security of all the gods, it is quite often seen as a particular threat to the goddesses. In this sense, the male giants are obnoxious sexual rivals, a retrograde and vulgar breed that, should it have its way, would degrade the gods' blood stock, limit their fertility and so terminally weaken their authority. That the same taboo does not apply the other way round is simply characteristic of the male privileges and vested interests that define patriarchies. Thor, stalwart though he is, is in many ways the quintessence of this double standard. One compelling example of what might be called Thor's misogyny can be seen in the challenge made to him by the giantess Gjalp, whose attempt to drown him in her urine and menstrual blood as he fords the great river en route to Geirrod's hall, is thwarted when the god hurls a large stone at her. Given Thor's assertion that '[a]t its outlet a river must be stemmed',[2] the stone was presumably targeted at her reproductive organs. Although it is possible to interpret this as Thor necessarily asserting his manhood in the face of 'rampant female sexuality',[3] the depiction of female power overmastered by a penetrative male act is also suggestive of deep-rooted male anxieties concerning women and the crude sexualized responses that these anxieties commonly elicit.[4] Notable, too, in this regard is Thor's fear of anything that might pose questions about his masculinity, as is the case in the comic 'Þrymskiviða' (Thrym's Poem), where he is obliged to cross-dress and so fears '[t]he Æsir will call me a pervert', the notion of a pervert being embodied in the potent concept *argr*, which also signifies unmanliness, effeminacy and cowardice.[5]

TROLL-WOMEN AND THE FEMININE IN NORSE MYTH

Yet some giants are clearly worse than others. It is repeatedly said that Thor is away thrashing or killing trolls, a mission that is evidently central to his role. While the giantess Hyrrokkin, who Thor is prevented from attacking at Baldur's funeral, in certain ways resembles trolls described elsewhere in mythological and legendary sources, there are no detailed myths specifically concerning encounters between Thor and trolls. Nevertheless, despite the fact that the distinction between the terms 'troll' and 'giant' is not always entirely clear, where trolls are specifically named in the *Poetic Edda* and *Prose Edda*, it transpires that they are exclusively female.[6] As regards the origin of monstrous females generally, 'Hyndluljóð' (The Song of Hyndla) uniquely states that Loki 'was impregnated by a wicked woman, from whom every ogress on earth is descended'.[7] Loki's maternity would account for the malevolence of the troll-women, in the same way that Loki's coupling with the giantess Angrboda accounts for the malevolence of the Midgard Serpent, the wolf Fenrir and Hel. Some insight into the mythological function of the troll-women is given in 'Völuspá' (The Seeress's Prophecy), where it is said that

> In the east lives the old one, in Ironwood,
> and breeds there Fenrir's kind.
> Out of them all comes one in particular,
> sun's snatcher in troll's shape.[8]

Snorri offers an expansion of this in 'Gylfaginning':

> A certain ogress lives east of Midgard in a forest called Ironwood. In that forest live troll-wives called Iarnvidiur [those from the Ironwood]. The ancient ogress breeds as sons many giants and all in wolf shapes, and it is from them that these wolves are descended.[9]

Although the full significance of this is not decipherable, it seems that the troll-women are progenitors of wolf-giants, that one of them will swallow the sun (as does the wolf Fenrir at Ragnarok) and that they are creatures of the wilderness. If the Norse word *gífr*, sometimes signifying 'ogress' or 'witch', can also be taken to mean 'troll-women', as seems likely, then it is apparent that the troll-women will also play their part at Ragnarok, for according to 'Völuspá', when the giant Surt advances on Asgard amid apocalyptic fires, 'the rocky cliffs crack open and the troll-women are abroad'.[10]

A headcount of the giants listed by Snorri reveals that they are much more numerous than the gods and that the male giants considerably outnumber the giantesses. Given this, Thor's determination to keep the giant population down is explicable and may partially explain the gods' rivalry with the male giants over females of both species. Nonetheless, despite the apparent numerical imbalance between gods and giants, Giantland can be understood as a structured and, in most other senses, balanced opposition to Asgard, whereby the hostilities reflect those between two different tribes in permanent competition for territory and possessions. The hostility of troll-women, however, has no such obvious motivation. It is not said that they possess or seek anything of material value, nor is any reason given for their vengefulness, such as is suggested of the giants' grievance against the gods in The Master Builder Tale. In respect of the moral values underlying the mythology, the antagonism of the troll-women is nothing less than pure wickedness. Thor, of course, shows no hesitation in killing giantesses who pose a threat to him, as is the case with Geirrod's daughters or Thrym's sister, but in the case of the troll-women, he needs no excuse.

This genocidal attitude toward a militant female tribe is, here again, indicative of deep-seated male unease rooted in a perceived threat to their authority. Some scholars have even suggested that the male chauvinism inherent in the mythology is traceable to a pre-existing matriarchy that was itself usurped by men at some point in pre-history. After this, women who either resisted or stood outside male control were mythologized as viragoes, and women generally were subject to controls and limitations by the patriarchy, particularly in respect of their sexuality. The often demonic aspect of prophetesses, whose arcane knowledge and disturbing foresight exceeds even that of Odin's, and the supreme mastery of fate ascribed to the three female Norns, could be seen to support rather than undermine this argument. Yet such speculations have been little more than just that, for finding proof of a pre-patriarchy is limited by the fact that the myths as we have them are, in themselves, inherently male constructs.[11]

THEORIZING THE GIANTS

Understanding Thor, however, requires a fuller analysis of what the giants might have meant, and this goes beyond reactionary male sexuality into questions concerning mortality and the oppositional concepts that are constituted in the human psyche. One approach suggested by structural anthropology theory, most notably in the work of Claude Lévi-Strauss (1908–2009), would be to regard the giants as abstractions of the forces of Nature which are opposed to abstractions of the forces of Culture, as represented by the gods.[12] This dichotomy is in many ways persuasive. The giants live away in the margins, in the unconquered, untamed territories, where danger inevitably lurks. With the exception of Utgarda-Loki's court, all the giants that Thor encounters live in isolated places, while the gods, like humans, are clustered in communities. To reach the otherworld of the giants, Thor must cross boundary rivers, a literal rite of passage between two states of existence: that between the nourishing safety of the social world and the isolating perils of the wild and unchartered places. This, in its most reductive form, is an opposition between life and death. Yet human beings are of both Nature *and* Culture, and in this is one of the paradoxes of existence. On the one hand, humans are untamed and seething with antisocial impulses that need to be restrained; on the other, the very conditions of human survival depend on cooperation and collective self-interest. And in the end, of course, each human life must meet its personal Ragnarok, a point at which Nature and Culture might be said to cancel each other out. Just like the gods, human beings have giant blood coursing through their veins determining their finitude.

This paradox is especially applicable to Thor, for, as noted previously, he is part god and, by immediate descent, part giant. Despite the fact that maternal lineage was not considered to be as significant as paternal lineage, and also the fact that Thor is far from unique among the gods in this mix of parents, Thor's struggle against those of his own ancestry can be interpreted as a struggle against mortality, both his own and that of all those he seeks to protect; in other words, humans and their mythologized hyperboles, the gods. Annihilating the forces that are anti-life is Thor's reason for being, so when his arch-enemy, the Midgard Serpent, finally rears against him on the battlefield at Ragnarok, it is, in more than one sense, his own death that he is combating. It is a fight that he cannot win, just as he could not win in the contest against Old Age at Utgarda-Loki's court. If, then, the giants and their monstrous allies represent all that is inimical to life – socially, politically and physically – so Thor is the essence of social security, political stability and physical health. Thor and the giants may, in one way, be opposites but, in another, they are the interrelated aspects of the human condition and the struggle to impose order on disorder – in effect, the struggle to survive.

THEORIZING THE GODS

Two gods stand in contrast to Thor: Loki and Odin. While Loki is in many ways the opposite of Thor, Odin contrasts with Thor largely in terms of jurisdiction and hierarchical positioning. But in both cases it is Thor's simplicity compared with their complexity that is most apparent. This distinction is marked not only in terms of the verbal cunning and political chicanery that characterize Loki and Odin, but also in their practice of the magical arts, something that suggests their origin in shamanic rituals, and which may also account for them having 'in bygone days' become blood brothers, as Loki claims without contradiction in 'Lokasenna' (Loki's Quarrel).[13] These magic arts were conceptualized in the Old Norse word *seiðr* and included such things as shape-shifting, spell-casting and prophecy, the former two of these practices being considered shameful as well as prospectively damaging. Although Thor can be seen to advantage himself and bring benefits to others through objects with supernatural properties, particularly Mjollnir, there is no sign anywhere of him having recourse to any other power against his foes, save that which is permitted by his prodigious strength.

THOR AND LOKI

No figure from Norse mythology is more difficult to understand than Loki. He has been variously interpreted as a god of fire or air, as a trickster god, similar to those found among the myths of the native communities of North America and Africa, and even as a symbolic deification of a spider, an association suggested by folk expressions and superstitions collected in rural Scandinavia.[14] Part of the problem with Loki is that he does not have a stable persona in the myths. As can be seen from his relationship with Thor, Loki changes over time from the god who creates problems and then ingeniously solves them, sometimes with unforeseen benefits, to the god who is openly and intransigently set on the downfall of Asgard and all associated with it. In this shift from mischief to malice, which to some extent mirrors the gradual deterioration of the world, his contrast with Thor becomes ever more marked. So it is that Loki increasingly appears to express himself in terms of his paternal and maternal descent: thus as a giant and therefore as the arch-representative of chaos and, by association, death.

As the giant within, Loki's perfidy and destructive intelligence exemplifies the vulnerability of the gods. While Thor seeks to secure the perimeters in his cease-less war against monstrosity, there would seem to be nothing he can do about the canker at the heart of Asgard. Loki, then, is everything that Thor is not. Whereas Thor is masculinity personified, Loki is sexually transgressive, a distinction that, incidentally, adds to the comedy of Thor's cross-dressing in 'Þrymskviða'. Similarly, whereas Thor is clarity of purpose personified, Loki is, for the main part, inscrutable, and whereas Thor is consistently and emphatically on the side of Culture, it is only after his proxy killing of Baldur that Loki can be fully identified as an agent of destructive Nature. In the psycho-dynamics of myth, it is tempting to view one as the alter ego of the other, whereby their pairing epitomizes the fundamental binary set of life-affirming and life-denying principles.

THOR AND ODIN

A primary distinction between Odin and Thor is given in 'Hárbarðsljóð' (Harbard's Song). This is expressed in what is, in effect, an insult delivered to Thor by Odin, who is disguised as the ferryman Harbard:

> Odin has the nobles who fall in battle
> And Thor has the breed of serfs.[15]

The inference here is that Odin is the god of the elite high-status groups, whereas Thor is the god of the common man: the farmers, the fishermen and the foot soldiers. Given that Thor was indisputably the most revered god of late pagan times, the insult does not carry any weight as regards the respective popularity of the two gods; rather, it intended to draw attention to Thor's secondary posi-tion in relation to Odin in the social hierarchy. The relative status of the gods is so important in identifying their particular functions and, therefore, meanings that it is not only definitive of the character of Norse mythology, but has also been considered as something suggestive of the origin of the entire mythological system, at least in historical and geographical terms.

THOR'S PLACE IN NORSE MYTH
THE ORIGIN OF NORSE MYTH

Since the latter decades of the eighteenth century, scholars of myth have paid increasing attention to the remarkable similarities between Graeco-Roman, Celtic, Indian, Iranian, Slavic and Norse, including early Germanic, mythology. There have been several phases to this, much of which will be relevant to discussions in later chapters concerning the post-medieval reception of Thor. In summary, scholars first noted the etymological relationship between certain words across what was subsequently called the Indo-European group of languages, which then established the discipline of comparative linguistics, for which the study of myth was central. Studies in folklore, archaeology and anthropology sought to advance understanding of the Indo-European group and it was hypothesized that there had once been a Proto-Indo-European language spoken by a European group, who during the early Bronze Age had migrated extensively east and south. By the late Bronze Age, peoples from the Mediterranean through Persia to the Indian subcontinent had fallen under their influence, both in respect of their language and their beliefs.

Exactly who these Proto-Indo-Europeans were remains a subject of much debate. One attractive, albeit much criticized, theory known as the Kurgan Hypothesis has been put forward by the archaeologist Marija Gimbutas (1921–94). This theory focuses in the first place on the burial mounds, or *kurgans*, of the early peoples of Eastern Europe and the diffusion of these mounds across the Indo-European regions. The tribes that originated the *kurgans* were technologically advanced and had developed exceptional techniques for forging metal weaponry. In addition, their domestication of horses for warlike purposes, such as pulling chariots, gave them an unassailable advantage over neighbouring tribes and so the opportunity to expand or shift their governance wherever they chose. Alongside a comparative study of myths and languages, Gimbutas concluded that the Bronze Age migrants had originated in the regions of the Black Sea, the Caucasus and the west Urals.[16]

Gimbutas's theory and more recent genetic studies have superseded the now discredited Aryan or Nordicist theory, which advanced the idea that the

Proto-Indo-Europeans were a Germanic people. This theory gained considerable currency among Western European racial supremacist groups, particularly Nazi ideologues, in the first half of the twentieth century, as did an allied notion originating in the early nineteenth century that a full understanding of Proto-Indo-European thought would provide a key to all mythologies and with it the answer to the most complex metaphysical questions. In truth, the actual identity of the Proto-Indo-Europeans may never be known for certain, despite the fact that the evidence for an ancient common racial, as well as a linguistic and what may be called ideological, identity among Indo-Europeans is now widely accepted.

The most persuasive and, without doubt, most influential argument for common origins among the Indo-Europeans has taken the form of an analysis of the various mythological systems in terms of their structure. The chief proponent of this approach has been the French philologist Georges Dumézil (1898–1986). In his Trifunctional Hypothesis, Dumézil argued that the gods of, for example, Indian/Vedic, Greek and Roman and Norse mythologies can be seen as occupying three corresponding roles or functions and that these reflect their particular culture's established social hierarchies. Designated to the first or highest stratum are the functions of rulership or sovereignty, which in turn command priestly governance and legal authority, and whose operation is frequently characterized by a mastery of magic. The Vedic Varuna, the Greek Zeus (Roman Jupiter/Jove) and the Norse Odin are gods of this function. In the middle stratum is the warrior class, whose chief concern is with the defence of the community, typically through means of extreme physical aggression. The Vedic Indra, the Greek Herakles (Roman Hercules), and the Norse Thor are gods of this function.[17] Of the third and lowest function are the fertility gods, often represented by twins accompanied by a goddess. Groupings of this function include the Vedic horseman twins, the Ashvins and the female deity Sarasvati; the Greek Dioscuri, Castor and Pollux (the Roman Gemini twins) and their sister Helen; and the Norse siblings Frey and Freyja and, in eddic myth, their father Njord (although in other, earlier Germanic traditions it is Njord's female equivalent, the goddess Nerthus). Given this basic division of functions, Dumézil is able to construct an elaborate system of correspondences in terms of form, function and detail across all the mythological systems of the Indo-European group. This theory, points out Dumézil, is not to be confused with Nature versus Culture dualisms, which purport to describe fundamental attributes of the human psyche, but is instead an analytical description, rooted in historical circumstances, of the social mores and beliefs of a geographically particular, racially linked group. The trifunctionality of Indo-European myth, therefore, is a reflection of this group's entrenched social structures and class divisions.[18]

One eddic poem that lends credence to the social class aspect of the hypothesis is 'Rígsþula' (The List of Rig), which dates from the second half of the tenth century and was composed in Denmark.[19] In this, the mysterious figure Rig, meaning 'king' in Old Irish but believed otherwise to be the god Heimdall, visits three homesteads and sires a son at each visit. In the lowly dwelling of the first, he begets the wretched slave-child Thrall; in the busy farm of the second, he begets the industrious artisan, Farmer; and in the fine hall of the third, he begets the noble Earl. Earl and his wife have a son who they name Kon the Young, which in Old Norse equates to *konungr* (king). Kon goes on to fulfill his destiny by mastering rune knowledge and magic, and thereafter conquering the country. The status quo of the tripartite structure of early Scandinavian society – slaves, farmers and aristocracy – is in this way reflected and endorsed.

THOR'S PLACE AMONG THE NORSE GODS

It is, then, the concerns, values and experiences of the middle group, the artisan class, that are articulated in the secondary positioning of Thor. Moreover, the birth of each figure from the three social classes is denoted in 'Rígsþula' by a particular colour: white for Earl, red for Farmer and black for Thrall. These colourations, observes Dumézil, are characteristic of the markers of social caste in traditional Indian and Iranian societies, where the concept of caste is synony-mous with the word for colour (*varna*). These same colours are also characteristic of the hierarchical positioning of divinities across a wide range of Indo-European mythologies.[20] Yet, while it is true that Odin is sometimes identified with the colour white in Norse myth, the evidence outside 'Rígsþula' for the slave class being associated with black is slight. Nevertheless, Thor's red beard and fiery eyes are wholly consistent with the colour denomination of the social group that he would otherwise be seen to represent in the eddas.

Early historical support for the secondary status of Thor is apparent in a Roman source from the first century AD where, in his earliest mythological incarnation, he was known as the Germanic god Donar. Contact of a usually belligerent nature between the Germanic tribes and the Roman legions had been established since the time of Julius Caesar in the first century BC, as the Romans sought expansion of their empire through Gaul, both east and west of the Rhine. Despite the co-option of many Germans into the legions, some of whom went on to achieve high rank, Roman persistence in this ambition never yielded the complete domination that they achieved in, for example, Britain and Gaul, and on more than one occasion huge German armies posed a serious threat to the empire's security. As early as the first century AD, a Roman fascination with, bordering on admiration for, the resilient and warlike Germans had developed. This was most thoroughly expressed in the last decade of that century by the Roman ethnographer Tacitus in his study of the German tribes, *Germania*. Although Tacitus's aim was as much to criticize the shortcomings of his countrymen as it was to shed light on the Germans, it offers a profound and unique insight into early Germanic customs and beliefs. It is, then, in *Germania* that we find the first mention of the relative status of the Germanic gods, whom Tacitus, in accordance with the practice known as the *interpretatio Romana*, names as the Roman equivalents: 'Above all gods they worship Mercury, and count it no sin to win his favour on certain days by human sacrifices. They appease Hercules and Mars with beasts normally allowed.'[21] Mercury, the god of commerce, whom Julius Caesar in his *Gallic Wars* also noted as the most revered of the Germanic gods, corresponds here to Odin's prototype, Wotan; Hercules, the club-wielding god renowned for his physical might, corresponds to Thor's prototype, Donar; and Mars, the imperial god of war but one-time god of fertility, probably corresponds to Tyr's prototype, Zio. As concerns the Odin and Thor figures, this is not that much different from how we find them in the eddas.

Yet in Swedish traditions, as practised a thousand years after Tacitus's account of Germanic customs, Thor's function would seem to cross the trifunctional boundaries, elevating to him to a position superior to that of Odin. Something of this can be discerned from the description of the heathen temple at Uppsala given by the German chronicler Adam of Bremen in the latter half of the eleventh century:

In this temple, entirely decked out in gold, the people worship the statues of three gods, in such wise that the mightiest of them, Thor, occupies a throne in the middle of the chamber; Wotan [Odin] and Frikko [Frey] have places on either side. The significance of these gods is as follows: Thor, they say, presides over the air, which governs the thunder and lightning, the winds and rains, fair weather and crops. The other, Wotan – that is, the Furious – carries on war and imparts to man strength against his enemies. The third is Frikko, who bestows peace and pleasure on mortals. His likeness, too, they fashion with an immense phallus. But Wotan they chisel armed, as our people are wont to represent Mars. Thor with his sceptre apparently represents Jove [or Jupiter] . . . For all their gods there are appointed priests to offer sacrifices for the people. If plague and famine threaten, a libation is poured to the idol Thor; if war, to Wotan; if marriages are to be celebrated, to Frikko.[22]

If Adam's information is broadly accurate, Thor, as Jove or Jupiter, is the supreme god who, like Jove, is a sky god with mastery over thunder and lightning; indeed, the sceptre held by Thor may well have been a misidentification of Mjollnir. In this account of the religious hierarchy, the third-level function of the fertility gods, as typically indicated in the eddas, is presented instead as the highest function, which is exemplified, at least in part, by Thor. Indicating a relatively widespread conceptualization of a divinity, such as the Thor described by Adam, are ancient Lapp ritual sacrifices. In these, conceptualizations of earth and thunder are united to encourage fertility among the livestock and to bring rain to nourish the crops. Nonetheless, argues Dumézil, strictly speaking, Thor should not be regarded as a fertility god in the same sense as Frey or Freyja; rather, his perceived assistance with food production comes about less as a result of deliberate acts aimed purely at fertilizing the earth and more as a happy by-product of his violent extra-terrestrial activities.[23]

THE COMING OF CHRISTIANITY

Even in the post-conversion era, cultural traditions regarding Thor's ranking in the Norse pantheon did not necessarily conform to that given in the eddas; indeed, like the Uppsala devotees, Christian writers also tended to see Thor as Jupiter. In their disapprobation of all pagan deities, the twelfth-century Danish historian Saxo Grammaticus, and the tenth-century English homilist and preacher Ælfric, both equated Jupiter with Thor, just as they both followed Roman tradition in equating Odin with Mercury, albeit not as a god who outranked Thor.[24] The same judgement of Thor's status is found in *Clemens saga*, one of many saints' lives translated from early Latin sources by Icelandic clerics for the edification of their countrymen during the twelfth and thirteenth centuries. In this tale of the papacy and martyrdom of St Clement of Rome in the first or second century AD, the principle of the *interpretatio Romana* is reversed, whereby the names of the Roman deities are given according to what were considered to be their Norse equivalents. Here, the translator refers to the Temple of Thor, which certainly corresponds to the Temple of Jupiter, and when Clement is rounded on by obdurate pagans, they condemn him for his blasphemy and the sorcery they claim enables his ministry, asserting that he 'dishonours our noble gods by saying Thor is not a god, our trusty patron and the strongest divinity, full of courage, and who is close at hand wherever he is worshipped'.[25]

The charges go on to include bringing nearly all the Norse gods into disrepute. Yet, not all hagiographers made the same correspondences between the Roman and Norse gods, for, depending on which Icelandic saint's life is read, Thor could be either Jupiter or Hercules, just as Odin could also be Jupiter or Hercules, as well as Mercury or Mars.[26] Nevertheless, as is commonly known, the correspondences between Norse and Roman gods did go on to achieve a kind of orthodoxy – in the days of the week. A simplified account of these equivalences would be as follows: Germanic Tuesday, or 'Tyr's/Tiw's Day' equates to 'Mars' Day' as in the French Mardi; Germanic Wednesday, or 'Odin's/Woden's Day' equates to 'Mercury's Day' as in the French Mercredi; and Germanic Thursday/ Donnerstag, or 'Thor's/Donner's Day', equates to 'Jove's/Jupiter's Day' as in the French Jeudi. This substitution of Germanic gods for Roman gods in the names of days appears to have become a convention in the Germanic territories during the third century AD.[27]

The differing estimations of the seniority of the gods and the implied differing estimations of the importance of the three divine functions are conditioned by their respective historical contexts. Trade and prosperity, which presumably included the fecundity of crops and livestock, rather than physical force and military capacities, were seemingly uppermost for the early Germanic tribes commented on by Tacitus. In later periods, however, military capacities appear to have become more associated with the protection of territories for good pasture and food production and, with these as priorities, greater significance was attached to Thor. For the common folk working the land, the seas and, in the ninth and tenth centuries, also seeking material advancement as members of Viking Age war bands, it is understandable that this would be the case. Precisely because Thor enjoyed this popularity, Christian commentators would have perceived him the most important Norse deity and so paid him particular critical attention; one unintended consequence being that, for a time at least, Thor devotees became all the more devoted. That Thor's status among the rank and file is not glorified in the eddas or in skaldic verse is mainly due to the service poets gave to the aristocracy, for whom Odin more accurately reflected their political interests and aspirations. As regards correlations between Norse and Roman deities this, too, is complicated by the fact that the relative status and attributes of a particular Roman god could also vary, depending on whether the empire was at peace or war. This may account to some extent for the varying estimations of the equivalence of one god to another in the translations of Latin texts dating back to the third and fourth centuries, such as is the case with many Icelandic sagas of saints' lives.

While the unconquered Germanic tribes east of the Rhine finally succumbed to the Christian missions during the seventh and eighth centuries, the more remote Scandinavian tribes remained insulated in the old ways until their own aggressive expansion during the Viking Age from the early ninth century onwards, when, not entirely coincidentally, Christian missions to the far north became increasingly more earnest. This led eventually to crucial conversion moments in the late tenth and very early eleventh centuries in Denmark, Norway and Iceland, when monarchs and warlords saw the advantages of conforming to the religious culture of wider Europe, while Sweden underwent a more erratic process of conversion for over a century longer. With Christianity came not only biblical scholarship, but also the classical literary culture of the Mediterranean regions. By the time Snorri Sturluson was writing his *Prose Edda* in the early thirteenth century, Graeco-Roman culture was part of the intellectual bedrock of western and northern Europe, as is clear from Snorri's euhemerized explanation for the 'error' of Norse paganism. The long history of analogies between northern and southern European pagan religious traditions is not surprising, therefore, nor perhaps is its complexity and variability. However, no such history of contact exists between the Germanic peoples and those of the Indian subcontinent. Remarkable similarities between Germano-Nordic pagan mythology and the mythologies of the East are not in any way explicable by contact stimulus during the first millennium and are, in themselves, compelling evidence for the theory of Indo-European common origins.

THOR, INDRA AND STARKAD

The myths concerning Indra, Thor's counterpart in Indian mythology, can be readily summarized where in detail they coincide with eddic myths involving Thor. Indra is a warrior god renowned for his strength, with dominion over the weather and war. His chief mission is to kill monsters, most notable among which is the great coiled dragon Vitra. He brandishes a weapon called Varja which emits lightning and thunderbolts. This weapon was forged by a shadowy figure named Tvastr, a smith of many fine artefacts for the gods. Indra's pursuit of the monstrous obliges him to ford great rivers in cruel weather. Just as Thor is the son of Odin and Jorth, or Earth, so Indra is the son of the god of the sky, or heaven, and the goddess of earth. Indra navigates the cosmos in a chariot drawn by two horses, whereas the closely related Indian god Pusan does so in a chariot drawn by goats. An ancient Sanskrit hymn to Indra in the *Rig Veda* says:

> May the strong Heaven make thee the Strong wax stronger: Strong, for thou art borne by thy two strong Bay Horses. So, fair of cheek, with mighty chariot, mighty, uphold us, strong-willed, thunder-armed, in battle.[28]

Also like Thor, Indra has a bottomless appetite, which includes his capacity to drink lakes dry, and he is a shape-changer, which, like Thor in 'Þrymskiðða', includes feigning female identity. Although, as one critic has remarked, 'there are as many differences between Thor and Indra as there are between India and Iceland',[29] the similarities that there are simply cannot be mere coincidence, and neither are these confined to details. Bearing mind the variations and mutations in mythological narratives over a long period of time, there are also major similarities between Thor and Indra at the level of their basic conception of purpose.

An important identifying feature of the Indo-European warrior god of the second function, argues Dumézil, is that he be seen to have violated social taboos and caused gross offence on three separate occasions, each of which correspond to offences against the three functions of the gods: sovereignty, defence and fertility.[30] However calamitous these sins are for the community, the broad purpose of them is to demonstrate a purging of the offending god of sin; thus to fulfill an apotropaic, or preventative, purpose. This, according to Dumézil's analysis, can readily be identified in the myths of Indra, as well in myths recounting the exploits of the Ancient Greek Herakles, but there is no correspondence in the myths directly involving Thor with such a programme of sin and expiation. Nonetheless, by association with Thor, there is almost exactly such a programme involved in the epic tales concerning the legendary warrior Starkad, whose career is chiefly recorded by Saxo in Danish traditions and in *Gautreks saga* (The Saga of King Gautrek) in later Icelandic traditions.[31]

In Saxo's account, Starkad (given in Latin as Starcatherus) is of giant descent and born with a monstrous superfluity of arms, several of which were said to have been ripped from him by Thor, seemingly to give him a slightly more human appearance and, so, an act that, although crude, could be considered as having a generous motive. The sponsorship of Thor is in this way established. Having been granted extraordinary gifts and three lives by Thor's rival, Odin, Starkad's first sin is to enact Odin's vengeance by treacherously sacrificing a certain king to the gods while he is under that same king's protection. His second sin is to exhibit a unique moment of cowardice and flee from battle, and his third sin is to accept a bribe to kill an unarmed man as he bathes. Each of these, suggests Dumézil, could be regarded in one way or another as corresponding in descending order with crimes against the three functions of the gods. Certainly, it is clear that the first crime offends the first function of sovereignty and that the second is one against the second function of heroic defence, yet it is not quite clear how the third crime corresponds to the third-level fertility function.

Gautreks Saga, which is almost certainly a refashioning of the tradition on which Saxo drew, is even more imprecise in its correspondences. Here, Starkad is presented before Thor and Odin so his fate may be judged. It quickly transpires that Thor despises Starkad for reasons of an offence given against the god by one of Starkad's ancestors. Instead, Starkad's patron is Odin. A battle of predictions ensues. Thor begins by cursing him with childlessness; Odin responds by giving him three lives, while Thor predicts criminality in each one; Odin promises the best of weapons, but Thor ensures that they will not inspire confidence; Odin guarantees victory in all battles and Thor injury in them all; Odin endows the gift of poetry to which Thor adds the curse of forgetfulness; Odin grants the admiration of the nobility and, in keeping with their respective constituencies,

Thor ensures the loathing of the common folk. In this way, Starkad's tragic destiny is determined: full of glory, crime and restlessness.

These two versions of the Starkad legend are illustrative of the complexity of analysing myth. Behind Saxo's version there may well be a story of great antiquity in which the hero and the god Thor are somehow intertwined, if not one and the same person. If this is true, at one time the Thor/Starkad narrative fitted more precisely with the sinful god seen elsewhere in Indo-European mythology. Exactly how Thor and Starkad became distinct personages – Thor in myth and Starkad as Thor's avatar in legend – is a mystery beyond understanding due to the partial nature of what has survived and the fragmentation of mythological belief and practice across the northern regions. As for the Icelandic saga, this is characteristic of the proliferation, adaptation and degradation of the myths that continued from late pagan times on into the post-mythological age. Interestingly, however, in many respects it does reflect eddic myth by establishing the highest patronage as being that which flows from Odin. In this case, something that was initially a myth attesting to the character of Thor has been subsumed by an Odinic cult, whereby Thor is presented as acting contrary to his earlier conception.

The Trifunctional Hypothesis clearly requires a great deal of qualification to take account of historical shifts in the emphasis placed on one particular function or god at any given period of time. Variations in patterns of religious observance across a wide geographical area, as well as the stimulus provided by an awareness of other mythological systems, whether for reasons of trade, warfare or, in the case of missionary Christianity, aggressive propagandizing, also add to the complexities. As is apparent, the hypothesis correlates the Norse gods with other Indo-European mythologies most convincingly when confined to what is found in the eddas; in other words, where the functions of sovereignty, defence and fertility are most fully described in myths which had reached a relatively advanced stage in their conception. The rigidity of the three social classes, for example, as is indicated in 'Rígsþula' and in the noble/serf diametric alluded to in 'Hárbarðsljóð', is no doubt the inevitable corollary of, if not the engine behind, these more sophisticated ideas about the Norse pantheon.

But, as is also apparent, the broad eddic conventions regarding a religious hierarchy did not reflect the practices of the majority. Judging from the evidence provided by place names, personal names and numerous archaeological finds, it was Thor rather than Odin who was considered the most attractive and potent of the Norse gods in virtually all of the Scandinavian regions. Nor was Thor's role confined to that of the second function, for, as the supreme god worshipped, for instance, in the Uppsala temple, he would have been associated with sovereignty, and in several different respects he was considered to be performing key fertility functions. Certainly, Dumézil and his followers do not shy away from these intricacies and, no matter how elliptical the arguments might be or how many instances of exceptions there are, it is impossible to ignore the association between Thor and his Indo-European equivalents, particularly concerning one consistent aspect of the god: his representation of, and appeal to, the ordinary folk.[32]

THOR AND HUMANITY

The identification of Thor by the common man as the god who does more than any other to promote his interests is underlined by Thor's relationship with his manservant Thialfi and Thialfi's sister, Roskva. Although the eddas have virtually nothing to say about Roskva, except that she was part of the company on Thor's journey to Utgarda-Loki's court, Thialfi's role is significant. Thor's adoption of the peasant children takes place when Thialfi transgresses the god's injunction not to split the bones of his goats during the evening meal at his father's farm. Thor's anger usually concludes with someone's death, but on this occasion he displays a tolerance and understanding of humans not shown to any other beings; indeed, no other god has such a deep association with humans, let alone has human accomplices. Thialfi shows his mettle and talent later on in the same journey when he tries but fails to outrun what turns out to be Thought, but improves his performance over three successive heats. Thialfi is Thor's brave companion in the skaldic version of the Geirrod myth, and it is likely that there was a version of the journey in which Thialfi accompanied Thor to Hymir's hall, prior to Thor's attempt to kill the Midgard Serpent. Yet, the most dramatic and helpful role played by Thialfi in service of Thor is in the duel against Hrungnir. It is Thialfi who deceives Hrungnir into thinking that Thor will arrive from beneath ground, so making the giant vulnerable to Thor's airborne attack, and it is Thialfi who demolishes the vast, if pusillanimous, clay giant Mokkurkalfi positioned beside Hrungnir. What exactly this might mean in terms of the social customs and rituals underlying the myth has given rise to much speculation.

Dumézil's examination of the Hrungnir myth notes its similarities, at least in its form, to initiation ceremonies widely attested in Indo-European mythologies and in anthropological studies. In these, the young warrior must undergo a simulated battle against a hostile force, often represented as some form of manikin. Having successfully passed the test, the warrior is then regarded as having reached a higher state of being. Yet how this might apply to Thialfi's combat against Mokkurkalfi is not entirely clear, as Thialfi is not thereafter seen to have achieved any higher state in any obvious social sense, and it is also questionable whether Thialfi could at any point be regarded as one of the warrior class. Interpreting the meaning behind the myth is no less awkward if the initiation is seen to concern Thor and is therefore a 'primary initiation'. In this case, the myth would be pitting the warrior, Thor, against the manufactured enemy, Hrungnir, who, as someone who is largely composed of stone, could be considered to signify the ritual manikin. In this eventuality, the parallel Thialfi versus Mokkurkalfi combat is a theatrical copy of a ceremonially more potent event. As the myth says this was Thor's first single combat, and as warriors undergoing initiation ceremonies are usually left with some physical sign of their ascendency (just as Thor is left with a chunk of Hrungnir's whetstone lodged in his head for all time), then the association between the myth and its possible ceremonial origins appears to be more than coincidental. But, as with Thialfi, there is no sense of Thor having reached a higher state other than the exalted one he already occupies before the duel. Lacking this crucial outcome, admits Dumézil, the Hrungnir myth may reflect a widespread initiation ceremony but it does so without any attached value.[33]

On balance, it is unlikely that Thialfi solely signifies Thor's association with the warrior class. It is more likely that Thialfi and Roskva represent the whole of humanity and thus Thor's patronage of it. Interestingly, the Hrungnir myth tells us quite a lot about Thor's family loyalties, which in turn could be seen to have bearing on his guardianship of Thialfi and Roskva. This myth is the only one in which Thor's children, Magni and Thrud, are implicated. It is Magni who comes to his father's aid, as no other can, when he is pinned to the ground by Hrungnir's dead body, and given that a kenning for Hrungnir is 'the thief of Thrud' it may be that Hrungnir has already provoked Thor's wrath. Thus, uniquely in this myth, Thor receives direct personal assistance from both his son and his manservant, and it is therefore possible to see the young males as images of each other: the human agency reflecting the divine, and vice versa. While it is less possible to see the females, Thrud and Roskva, in quite the same way, Thrud's likely role as an additional motivating force for Thor in a myth that has not survived, and Thor's evident responsibility for Roskva, also suggests a parallelism.[34]

If Thialfi and Roskva represent the whole of humanity, not just a class of it, they do so as his children, something the Hrungnir myth implies by association with Thor's actual offspring. Perhaps, therefore, two related initiations of the coming-of-age type lie buried beneath the myth, both, as might be expected, involving the young males. In one, Magni achieves adult status as the rescuer of his father from paralysis and death, as symbolized by the dead weight of the stone giant, and, in the other, Thialfi achieves adult status by deceiving Hrungnir and then toppling the clay giant, so simultaneously enacting his guardian's military ingenuity and courage. Considered in this way, the initiations of Magni and Thialfi, if this is what they are, have as much to do with gaining equality with, and respect from, the father as they do with achieving a higher state in society at large. Read as a form of family drama, measuring up to Thor *is* the higher state.

Thor's function as one who presides over – rather than one who endures – initiation rites is evident in the various uses of Mjollnir. On three occasions in the eddas, Mjollnir has a purpose other than that of a weapon. The first is in the early phase of the tale of Thor and Utgarda-Loki, when Thor uses Mjollnir to restore his goats to life in pre-dawn ritual: Thor 'took the hammer Mjollnir and raised and blessed the goatskins [and] the goats got up . . .'.[35] The second is in 'Þrymskviða', where Thor, dressed as Freyja, is sat before Thrym who declares, 'Bring in the hammer to sanctify the bride, / lay Mjollnir on the girl's lap, / consecrate us together by the hand of Var!' (Var being the god who secures pledges between men and women).[36] The third is at Baldur's funeral, during which 'Thor stood by and consecrated the pyre with Mjollnir.'[37] These acts of blessing with Mjollnir are all embodied in the Old Norse verb *vígja*, the precise meaning of which is unclear but which seems to indicate investing numinous, magical or supernatural power in something, rather than a dedication to a higher authority. The use of Mjollnir in these instances is therefore one where life is being purged of, or protected from, impurity. This can take the form of rebirth, as with the goats; endowing fecundity, as with the marriage union; or securing against evil, as with Baldur's journey to Hel. Here again, Thor is not only enacting a defensive role, but also a fertility role. In this latter capacity, Mjollnir can readily be understood as a phallic symbol; indeed, Bronze Age rock carvings found at Stora Hoglem and Hvitlycke in Sweden show a copulating couple beside whom is a large phallic figure carrying a hammer or an axe seeming to minister to them. If the interpretation is correct, this may well be a proto-Thor.[38]

Thor's role as one who both opposes and secures against harmful forces is evidenced by a number of early runic inscriptions. Monuments from the tenth and eleventh centuries bearing the invocation 'May Thor consecrate these runes', as well as others that simply depict Mjollnir, have been found across Sweden and Denmark. On the inscribed stones, the use of the verb *vígja* most probably indicates the belief that Thor's power could be invested in the monuments to shield them and their engraved sentiments from corruption, and presumably the Mjollnir pictograms were believed to be performing the same purpose. As these monuments date from late in the heathen period when Christian missions had already made significant progress in the Scandinavian regions, it is possible that Christian converts were merging ideas concerning Thor's struggles against the giants with ideas of Christ's fight against evil – in which case these monuments could indicate the accommodation of pagan concepts into traditional Christian symbolism. The conjunction of Christian and pagan images on monuments across the Viking world from this period is not uncommon, nor is the possibly deliberate ambiguity of engravings of crosses that could signify either the Christian cross or Mjollnir. With this consideration in mind, it makes it difficult to know for certain what ideological messages are actually being imparted.[39] Alternatively, and just as likely, there is the view that the monuments indicate a resurgent Thor cult that was occurring as a direct result of the perceived threat of Christianity to pagan beliefs and traditions.

The earliest inscription concerning Thor's talismanic power is found on a seventh-century buckle known as the Nordendorf fibula, which was found near Augsburg in Bavaria. Transliterated from runic script, the inscription reads *logaþore wodan wigiþonar*. While *wodan* would appear to a straightforward reference to the Germanic name for Odin, both *logaþore* and *wigiþonar* are each in their own way problematic. The first element, or indeed both elements, of *logaþore* may signify Loki or the god sometimes associated with him, Lodur, or even just 'magician', while the last element of *wigiþonar* can with more certainty be seen to signify Thor's Germanic prototype Donar. One possibility, then, is that the inscription refers to the triad of Odin, Thor and Loki, or, more precisely, refers to their early Germanic counterparts. Whatever it is that the inscription is saying about them may be embodied in *wigi-*, which is etymologically related to *vígja* and so indicates the act of consecrating. Among many suggested readings, one is 'Loki, Odin and Thor consecrate' and another 'Odin and Thor are magicians who consecrate'. Whether this is intended to invoke the gods against the influence of Christian missions in early seventh-century Germany or, conversely, a Christian protective charm against the influence of pagan deities cannot be said for certain.

As is the case with the monuments, the Nordendorf fibula provides credible supporting evidence for eddic traditions in which Thor is a god whose exercise of numinous power denotes his function as a defender and promoter of the common good. Indeed, one runic inscription found on a manuscript in Canterbury from the early eleventh century also connects Thor with acts of consecration, in this case as a healer. It translates approximately as 'Kuril of the wound-spear, go now, you have been found. May Thor consecrate you, lord of giants, Kuril of the wound-spear. Against vein-pus.' Who Kuril might be is not the least of the questions provoked by this late invocation of Thor in Anglo-Saxon England, although Thor is evidently the remedy for whatever misfortune Kuril has wrought.[40] One thing is, however, clear: belief in the power of Thor was sufficiently tenacious to maintain a grip on the imagination of those beset by problems a long time after he was eclipsed by the authority and teaching of the Christian church. He was, after all, the god who gave protection to the beleaguered.

Thor, then, is an Indo-European warrior type of god, whose function was typically secondary to that of the sovereign god. Although the evidence for Thor's Indo-European origins is convincing, there are many provisos due to the variance of religious practices, historical turbulence and the evolution of mythological narrative. For example, it was the case that in some areas and at certain times Thor was considered the supreme deity. This status is not, however, generally reflected in the *Prose Edda* or *Poetic Edda*, which, while exalting Thor's role, tend to prize the acquisition of knowledge and the exercise of intellect over strength and courage – in effect, low cunning over physical force. This would appear to reflect the aristocritization of the mythology. As the epitome of masculinity in this schematization, Thor exhibits much of the negative attitude towards women that would be expected from a patriarchy.

In the mythology, Thor acts to defend the community from all threats to its survival, typically personified as monstrous beings, but he also performs a ritual consecratory function, through which he demonstrates his power to protect life from harm. As archaeological evidence shows, this was translated by his devotees to mean threats posed by anything that might interfere with traditional customs and practices. Thor's name was therefore invoked to sanctify objects, as well as to ensure good health and good fortune. Thor has a particular regard for ordinary humans of low status and was often perceived as a sky god who could bestow fertility on the land through his dominion over the elements. Beyond the mythological narratives about Thor's exploits, everything else known about the god is hypothetical and frequently contradictory. The single abiding exception to this is Thor's patronage of humanity, for which he is unique in Norse myth. As he declares in 'Hárbarðsljóð', without his defence 'mankind would be as nothing on the earth'.[41] His common touch, his pragmatism, his single-mindedness and his reliability conferred on him a popularity unmatched by any other deity. Yet exactly what benefits the worship of Thor could bring his adherents apparently depended on geographical and historical contexts. Chapter 3 will consider how, for migrating Scandinavians during the Viking Age, this entailed a much more specific role for Thor.

3

Christ versus Thor

EARLY SETTLERS IN ICELAND

During the AD 880s, a certain Hrolf Mostur-Beard was busily running the family farm on Mostur Island off the coast of Norway's South Hordaland. He was a devout pagan and 'a friend of Thor', over whose temple he officiated. A man of large physique, who sported a strikingly long beard, his priestly devotions defined his status and he was therefore known as 'Thor-Hrolf' or Thorolf. He did not, however, share the political outlook of the ambitious Norwegian king Harald Fine-Hair, whose determination to impose taxes on his subjects was considered by Thorolf, and by many others in the western fjords, to be a gross offence against traditional laws of inheritance. So it was, that when a declared enemy of Harald's turned up on Mostur Island seeking refuge, Thorolf gave him a warm reception and, come the following spring, a fine longship. The fugitive could now flee north-west across the sea to a remote island discovered and settled some ten years earlier: Iceland. Once the king got word of Thorolf's treachery, he ordered him off his estates and demanded that he surrender himself. Thorolf held a feast and prayed to Thor for advice. Having duly received it, he readied a large ship, embarked his household and certain friends and put to sea in the wake of the man to whom he had given protection and whose fate he now shared. In pride of place among the valuables Thorolf carried with him was the dismantled temple of Thor, along with some of the earth on which Thor's pedestal had rested.

Thor gave Thorolf fair weather for the crossing and he made landfall in the south of Iceland. He then sailed west, then north along the coastline, where he sighted large inlets. Here, he cast overboard the high-seat pillars from Thor's temple with the intention of settling wherever they came to rest. The pillars drifted north around the Snaefell peninsula and then east into a deep broad bay, which Thorolf duly named Breidafjord. They finally came ashore at the place known since as Thor's Ness. Thorolf established himself at the place he called Hofsstead (Temple Farm), beside Hofsvag (Temple Creek), and set about claiming and naming the surrounding land. Then, in grand style, he built Thor's Temple.

> The high-seat pillars were placed inside the door, and nails, that were called holy nails, were driven into them. Beyond that point, the temple was a sanctuary. At the inner end there was a structure similar to the choir in churches nowadays and there was a raised platform in the middle of the floor like an altar, where a ring weighing twenty ounces and fashioned without a join was placed, and all oaths had to be sworn on this ring. It also had to be worn by the temple priest at all public gatherings. A sacrificial bowl was placed on the platform and in it a sacrificial twig – like a priest's aspergillum – which was used to sprinkle blood from the bowl. This blood, which was called sacrificial blood, was the blood of live animals offered to the gods. The gods were placed around the platform in the choir-like structure within the temple. All farmers had to pay a toll to the temple and they were obliged to support the temple *godi* [priest-chieftain] in all his campaigns, just as *thingmen* [allied farmers] are now obliged to do for their chieftain. The temple *godi* was responsible for the upkeep of the temple and ensuring it was maintained properly, as well as for holding sacrificial feasts in it.[1]

Besides this, Thorolf proclaimed that the small mountain out on his headland was also a holy place, naming it Helga Fell (Holy Fell). No one could even look upon it before washing and no violence was allowed in its precincts. Thorolf believed that he and his kin would go there after death. He held his legal assemblies on the spot where Thor's pillars – and so Thor – had come ashore. To maintain the sanctity and purity of the assembly area, a rocky outcrop in the sea named Drítsker (Shit-Skerry) was designated as the place for those needing to relieve themselves. Years later, after Thorolf's death, two men declined to use the facility at Drítsker and many were killed in the resulting fracas. Given that the assembly site had now been defiled, it was moved elsewhere on the headland. A large rock there was named Thor's Boulder and was used for human sacrifices.

The two main sources for this account of the life and religious practices of one of Iceland's earliest settlers are the early twelfth-century *Landnámabók* (The Book of Settlements), compiled originally by Ari Thorgilsson the Learned and revised several times in later centuries, and, in the latter half of the thirteenth century, *Eyrbyggja saga* (The Saga of the People of Eyri). Both sources would have relied on oral traditions, although it is clear that the author of *Eyrbyggja Saga* was deeply influenced by *Landnámabók*. As even the earliest of these sources post-date the Christian conversion of Iceland by at least 120 years, some distortion or exaggeration is perfectly possible, and questions have been posed concerning the reliability of the description of Thor's temple. Nonetheless, the arrangements inside Thorolf Mostur-Beard's temple seem modest when compared with those described in a temple that was supposed to have been built in the early tenth century by Thorgrim the Chieftain at Hof in the Kjalarnes region, north of Reykjavík. According to the often fantastical fourteenth-century *Kjalnesinga saga* (The Saga of the People of Kjalarnes),

[Thorgrim] had a large temple built in his hayfield, a hundred feet long and sixty feet wide. Everybody had to pay a temple fee. Thor was the god most honoured there. It was rounded on the inside, like a vault, and there were windows and wall-hangings everywhere. The image of Thor stood in the centre, with other gods on both sides. In front of them was an altar made with great skill and covered with iron on the top. On this was to be a fire which would never go out – they called it sacred fire. On the altar was to lie a great armband, made of silver. The temple *godi* was to wear it on his arm at all gatherings, and everyone was to swear oaths on it whenever a suit was brought. A great copper bowl was to stand on the altar, and into it was to go all the blood which came from animals or men given to Thor. They called this sacrificial blood and the sacrificial blood bowl. This blood was to be sprinkled over men and animals, and the animals that were given in sacrifice were to be used for feasting when sacrificial banquets were held. Men whom they sacrificed were to be cast into a pool which was outside by the door; they called it Blotkelda (Well of Sacrifice).[2]

The saga goes on to note that in the thirteenth century a man named Olaf Jonsson, who then owned the property where Thorgrim's house had been built, demolished the building and recovered the temple's old beams from it, which he then split and presumably reused. As a man of this name is recorded as actually having lived at Hof at that time, to some extent it increases the likelihood that a pagan temple did indeed exist there in the tenth century. A key event early in the saga's plot explains what became of the temple, which in turn could account for the original removal of the temple beams from it. The chief figure in the saga is a certain Bui, who is raised in a community of Celtic Christian immigrants. Bui, therefore, refuses to make pagan sacrifices, a refusal that so offends Thorgrim's son, Thorstein, that he has Bui outlawed on a charge of 'false religion'. Thus persecuted, Bui takes vengeance first by killing Thorstein inside the temple, then by setting the temple on fire. Despite Thorgrim's and his followers' desperate efforts to extinguish the fire, only the scorched temple beams are rescued. Although the saga does not say as much, this may be how the recovered beams went on to become incorporated into the structure of Thorgrim's house.

Interesting, too, is the temple's altar fire, which, it is said, should never be extinguished. Although this feature is not described in Thorolf's temple, the curious reference to the temple nails may also indicate a connection between Thor and fire. Thor's mastery over lightning, his fiery eyes and red beard are obvious indicators of the association of the god with fire, but the fire in one temple and the nails in another may also indicate a distant association with the ancient Lappish practice of striking flint against a nail driven into the head of a wooden representation of Thor in order to kindle fire.[3] Similarly, as late as the sixteenth century at Romove in Prussia, there were reports of a sacred grove where an oak tree housed a statue of the very Thor-like god Percuno, before which burnt a screened fire that also was never allowed to go out. The name Percuno is a late variant of the name of the ancient Lithuanian thunder god Perkunas and these names are cognate with the Latin word for oak, which may also be etymologically related to the Germanic word for thunder. It is not unlikely that the old Germanic Donar and the Anglo-Saxon Thunor (Þunor), both of whom signified thunder, were revered in a similar fashion, most probably in sacred groves of oak where lightning was known to strike.[4]

There is, too, corroboration from other medieval Icelandic sources regarding the use of a temple arm-ring for hallowing oaths, thus indicating that it was a widespread practice in the rituals associated with Thor. In one version of Landnámabók, however, it is stipulated that the arm-ring should not be less than two ounces. If this refers to the prescribed minimum weight of an arm-ring, it would be unlikely to span the circumference of an arm but it could mean that the overall worth of the arm-ring should be equal to at least two ounces of gold or silver and, therefore, that the twenty-ounce arm-ring described in Eyrbyggja Saga was a probable overall weight. Certainly, it would have had to be something of this order if a later passage in the saga is to be believed, for, in this, the turbulent and ambitious Snorri the Priest escapes injury when an adversary's sword blow almost severs the arm-ring.[5] Further evidence of the use of a ring sacred to Thor is apparent in the theft of one from a pagan temple in Ireland in 994, and, earlier in 876, it was in all likelihood upon a ring of Thor that Danish Vikings, who had been taken hostage by King Alfred of Wessex, took a sacred oath to the effect that they would quit his kingdom in return for their freedom.[6]

CHRISTIAN PERSPECTIVES

Although in certain cases the Icelandic sagas would appear to contain traces of actual pagan practices, not only of the early settlers but also, through their devotions, of ancient north European rituals, account needs to be taken of the Christian perspective of these writers. This, in the first place, would most likely have been one of revulsion at the barbarism of the pagan past but, in the second place, one of respect for the mettle and resilience of a pre-Christian ancestry and, so, a nostalgic reverence for a bygone age. One can sense an antiquarian fascination in certain remarks in *Landnámabók*, such as, 'and Thor's Boulder that was used for the killing of those who were to be sacrificed, still stands there', something that the author of *Eyrbyggja Saga* sensationalizes over 100 years later, telling his readers that 'you can still see blood on the stone'.[7] Nevertheless, that pagan temples existed in Iceland and throughout Scandinavia is widely attested from archaeological evidence (for example, the tenth-century settlement at Hofstaðir (Temple Stead) in Iceland, where a section of the great hall has been identified as a shrine, before which animal sacrifices were made). Nor is there reason to doubt that historical figures such as Thorolf Mostur-Beard were in any way exceptional in their beliefs – as *Landnámabók* makes clear, for instance, it was not uncommon for prospective settlers to establish themselves according to where their temple pillars had come ashore. Ingolf Arnarson, Iceland's first Scandinavian settler, himself a Thor devotee, had done just that.

The importance of Thor's patronage is also told of in respect of Thorolf Mostur-Beard's son, Hallstein, who was lacking the timber to fashion himself high-seat pillars and so appealed to the god by offering up sacrifices. His oblations were rewarded when a tree was washed ashore, large enough to supply pillars for every farm in the fjord.[8] Less fortunate was the prayer to Thor from one Thorhall in *Eiríks saga rauða* (Eirik the Red's Saga), when he and his otherwise Christian shipmates were stranded and starving. This coincided with the discovery of a dead beached whale. Thorhall was triumphant: 'Didn't Old Redbeard prove to be more help than your Christ? This was my payment for the poem I composed about Thor, my guardian, who's seldom disappointed me.'[9] Unfortunately, on this occasion, belief in Thor's munificence was misguided and, for reasons that were not only religious, Thorhall's shipmates ultimately rejected the god's 'payment', as all who ate the whale meat were poisoned.

The abundant medieval Icelandic literary testimony to Thor worship suggests that the common invocation to 'the almighty god' (*hinn almáttki áss*), such as that recorded in *Landnámabók* as part of the proper ritual for swearing oaths, must have been directed at Thor, at least when uttered by Icelanders or the inhabitants of the western fjords of Norway during the heathen period.[10] District assemblies in Iceland and Norway were commonly held on Thor's Day and further evidence for Thor's popularity can be gleaned from *Landnámabók*, which records 'Thor' in the personal names of almost a quarter of the 4,000 settlers named, as well as in the first element of 20 settlement place names. Saga writers who set their narratives in the pre-conversion period, as was typically the case with the authors of the Icelandic family sagas written largely in the thirteenth century, could, therefore, draw on a vast store of collective memories about pagan practices and the settlers associated with them. But, from the latter part of the ninth century, as Christian missions to Scandinavia had increasing success and the Viking expansion brought with it a widespread awareness of Christianity, saga authors were at pains to acknowledge a growing ideological conflict between pagans and Christians.

For some Icelandic settlers, as recorded in *Landnámabók*, this meant choosing the appropriate faith for the appropriate circumstance, as was the case with Helgi the Lean, who 'believed in Christ but invoked Thor when it came to voyages and difficult times'.[11] Helgi, therefore, took Thor's advice on navigating from Norway to Iceland but, once on dry land, named his home after Christ. Yet, for others who were conservatively minded or obstinate in their belief in the power of the Norse gods, Christianity was a threat. Seemingly, as never before, devotion to the gods became more entrenched, so, it would seem, stimulating a Thor cult. This was as much a matter of cultural identity as it was of religious inclination. Once Scandinavian kings converted to Christianity, which was increasingly the case during the course of the tenth century, the impetus behind the conversion process became less a matter of reasonable persuasion and more a matter of aggressive coercion. Inevitably, there were clashes and for many with a pagan point of view, Thor was their champion against Christ.

CONVERTING THE SETTLERS

In 997, the newly converted king of Norway Olaf Tryggvason (d. 1000) commissioned the Saxon missionary Thangbrand to bring the religious practices of the Icelanders in line with those that the king had proclaimed law in Norway. Thangbrand was no ordinary pious missionary, someone imbued with a passion for spreading the peaceful message of Christianity; rather, he was a homicidal bully, albeit one of some learning. Neither was his master any more enlightened, for Olaf had been a notorious Viking pirate who had ruthlessly clawed his way to the Norwegian throne and then, just as ruthlessly, imposed Christianity on his subjects. For those who resisted, dispossession and blinding were Olaf's ultimate persuaders, as he fully understood the advantages in trade that would result from being part of Christian Europe. It was, then, political and economic advantage that was, as much as anything, the inspiration behind Thangbrand's trip to Iceland.

The story of Thangbrand's mission is briefly recorded in the twelfth-century Icelandic history *Íslendingabók* (The Book of the Icelanders) but is told at greater length in two thirteenth-century sources: as an element of the saga epic *Njáls saga* (The Saga of Njal), and in *Kristni saga* (The Story of the Conversion), which recounts the events surrounding Iceland's adoption of Christianity in the year 1000. Although Thangbrand set about his mission in characteristic style, killing those who opposed or offended him (in one case by bludgeoning a man to death with his crucifix), the saga sources offer no censure of him, seeming to regard his methods as a necessary evil, a means towards a desired end. Several plots were hatched to kill Thangbrand, at least one involving sorcery, but with an increasing number of converts ready to support him, the planned assassinations all came to nought. Yet the size of the task confronting Thangbrand was amply illustrated to him when he was travelling in the western districts of the country. Here, he was visited by Steinunn, the mother of a renowned poet and something of a versifier herself. A debate on the relative merits of Christianity and paganism ensued, with Thangbrand proving the better debater of the two. Steinunn then took a different tack:

> 'Have you heard,' she said, 'that Thor challenged Christ to a duel and that Christ did not dare to fight with him?'
>
> 'What I have heard,' said Thangbrand, 'is that Thor would be mere dust and ashes if God didn't want him to live.'
>
> 'Do you know,' she said, 'who wrecked your ship?'
>
> 'What can you say about it?' he said.
>
> 'I'll tell you,' she said:

> > 'The shaping gods drove ashore
> > the ship of the keeper of bells [Thangbrand];
> > the slayer of the son of the giantess [Thor]
> > smashed Bison on the sea-gull's rest;
> > no help came from Christ
> > when the sea's horse was crushed;
> > I don't think God was guarding
> > Gylfi's reindeer [ship] at all.'

> She spoke another verse:

> > 'Thor drove Thangbrand's beast
> > of Thvinnil [ship] far from its place;
> > he shook and shattered
> > the ship and slammed it ashore;
> > never will that oak of Atal's field [ship]
> > be up for sea-faring again;
> > the storm, sent by him,
> > smashed it so hard into bits.'

> With that, Steinunn and Thangbrand parted.[12]

Steinunn was not the only one to lampoon Thangbrand and his god, one poet referring to the missionary as 'the spineless wolf of God'.[13] Feelings hardened on both sides, and Christians, too, resorted to poetic insult, most notably in the blasphemy uttered by the newly baptized Hjalti Skeggjason at the annual assembly, the Althing:

> In blaspheming the gods I am rich:
> Freyja strikes me as a bitch;
> one or the other must be:
> Odin's a dog or else she.[14]

Interestingly, however, no one appears to have dared speak so disparagingly of Thor, and Thangbrand was eventually forced to admit defeat and return to Norway to report the offensiveness of the Icelanders to King Olaf. So enraged was the king that it was only a promise made by certain prominent Icelanders to carry on the missionary work that prevented him from arranging the massacre of every Icelander he could round up.

Olaf Tryggvason's opposition to paganism in many ways comes to characterize the Christ-versus-Thor conversion scenario as presented by Icelandic authors in the Middle Ages. According to accounts of Olaf's career given in Snorri Sturluson's early thirteenth-century history of the Norwegian kings, *Heimskringla*, and in the late fourteenth-century manuscript collection known as *Flateyjarbók*, when Olaf was seeking to convert pagans in the district of Trondheim in Norway, a prominent farmer named Skeggi bamboozled the king into entering a temple of Thor to witness how they made sacrifices. The *Flateyjarbók* account describes what the king saw:

> Thor sat in the middle. He was the most highly honoured. He was huge, and all adorned with gold and silver. Thor was arranged to sit in a chariot; he was very splendid. There were goats, two of them, harnessed in front of him, very well wrought. Both car and goats ran on wheels. The rope round the horns of the goat was of twisted silver, and the whole was worked with extremely fine craftsmanship.[15]

Skeggi then cunningly invited Olaf to pull on the rope, so moving the goats along the track, but once Olaf had obliged, Skeggi informed him that he had in this way honoured Thor. Enraged at this deception, Olaf dragged Thor from his chariot and ordered his men to destroy the temple. Although the earlier account given in *Heimskringla* spares Olaf any humiliation, telling instead how Olaf simply entered the temple and set about wrecking it, both accounts report that while Olaf was busy with his demolition work, his men killed Skeggi, after which point, says Snorri, 'no-one made opposition to Christianity, so that all the people in the Trondheim District were baptized'.[16]

The lavish temple that is described in these sources may function to enhance the reputation of the king by exaggerating the power and potency of pagan adherence, although there can be no doubt that Olaf's conversionary zeal was met with considerable resistance in many areas. According to *Heimskringla*, Olaf Tryggvason was neither the first nor the last Norwegian king to have difficulties with Thor worshippers. In 936, Hakon the Good (d. 954), who had been raised as a foster son of the English king Athelstan, and was therefore imbued with the customs and practices of a Christian court, succeeded to the Norwegian throne. Although tolerant of the pagan beliefs of his subjects, he abhorred them. While visiting a powerful earl in the Trondheim district at the time of a sacrificial feast, Hakon opted to eat apart, somewhat to the dismay of his host and the celebrants. Persuaded eventually to take his rightful foremost place at the celebrations, his host duly passed Hakon a beaker of ale dedicated to Odin, whereupon Hakon made the sign of the cross over it and declined to drink. Questioned as to why the king did this, his host generously interpreted Hakon's gesture as one signifying Thor's hammer. While no one was dissatisfied with this explanation, the king's later refusal to eat horsemeat, a specifically pagan custom proscribed by the Church, provoked murmurings against him. In the end, the king was obliged to pacify his hosts by partaking of sacrificial offerings without demur. Only when he learned that his churches had been burned and his priests slaughtered did he decide to raise an army against his pagan subjects.[17]

One king arguably even more violently enthusiastic than Olaf Tryggvason about converting his subjects was Olaf Haraldsson (d. 1030), who came to the Norwegian throne in 1016 and whose Christian ardour gained him the posthumous title of Saint. On one mission to the Norwegian fjords, Olaf was confronted in open space at daybreak by a throng of farmers bearing aloft a large hollow statue of Thor wielding his hammer, borne thence from the nearby temple, where the idol was honoured by cramming meat and bread inside it. Olaf turned to his confidante, Kolbein, and told him that should he, Olaf, manage to distract the attention of the farmers, then Kolbein should strike the idol with his club. Olaf then delivered a speech disparaging Thor, 'who is blind and deaf and cannot save himself nor others and cannot budge unless he is carried, and I expect that ill will befall him soon'. At that moment, the sun rose and Olaf pointed to it declaring, 'there comes our God now with great light'.[18] On cue, Kolbein delivered the blow and, much to the horror of the assembled farmers, all manner of vermin, swollen to alarming proportions on a rich diet of meat and bread, came pouring out of the shattered idol. In this way, Olaf achieved the conversion of all present.

While Olaf Haraldsson was contending with pagans in Norway, a less successful outcome in Sweden is reported by Adam of Bremen, when the English missionary Wolfred (d. 1029) attempted to spread, or rather enforce, the word in Uppsala.

> And as by his [Wolfred's] preaching he converted many to the Christian faith, he proceeded to anathematize a popular idol named Thor which stood in the Thing [Assembly] of the pagans, and at the same time he seized a battle-axe and broke the image to pieces. And forthwith he was pierced with a thousand wounds for such daring, and his soul passed into heaven, earning a martyr's laurels. His body was mangled by the barbarians and, after being subjected to much mockery, was plunged into a swamp.[19]

Despoiling pagan temples and, in the following late twelfth-century account by Saxo Grammaticus, relieving them of their artefacts, was still a necessity for Swedish monarchs over a hundred years after Wolfred's martyrdom. During the twelfth century, Sweden was ruled somewhat controversially by the Danish earl Magnus Nilsson (d. 1134), also known as Magnus the Strong. Here, where Magnus loots the temple, the deity named by Saxo as the god Jupiter is, in effect, Thor:

> He took care to bring home certain hammers of unusual weight, which they call Jupiter's, used by the island men in their antique faith. For the men of old, desiring to comprehend the causes of thunder and lightning by means of the similitude of things, took hammers great and massy of bronze, with which they believed the crashing of the sky might be made, thinking that great and violent noise might very well be imitated by the smith's toil, as it were. But Magnus, in his zeal for Christian teaching and dislike to Paganism, determined to spoil the temple of its equipment, and Jupiter of his tokens in the place of his sanctity. And even now the Swedes consider him guilty of sacrilege and a robber of spoil belonging to a god.[20]

Of the numerous accounts, particularly in Icelandic histories, of Christian kings contending with pagan adherents of an otherwise unspecified Norse god, it is a reasonable assumption that in the majority of cases Thor was the deity in question. As regards the apparent Thor cult in Trondheim, the absence of place names bearing the god's name would appear to confirm that there, at least, it was a relatively late phenomenon of the heathen period.[21] It is equally apparent that the confrontation was not only one between Christians and pagans, but also one between the ruling orders and the common folk, and between the combined authority of the Church and the aristocracy, on the one hand, and those over whom they exercised control, on the other. Albeit in a way that was less confrontational, this distinction had been there even before the coming of Christianity, when the ruling classes had preferred Odin to the ordinary folk's Thor.

VIKING COLONIES AND CHRISTIANITY

The picture was not in all respects dissimilar in the Viking colonies or where Vikings depredations sent shockwaves through Christian communities outside Scandinavia. On these fronts, however, rather than it being the traditional mores of the common person opposing the forward-thinking policies of the ruler, it was more that of the culture of the invaded opposing the culture of the invader. In Ireland, as early as the mid ninth century, a Norwegian Viking named Thorgils – Turgeis in Irish sources – is said to have taken over the monastic centre at Armagh and rededicated it to Thor, proclaiming himself to be the high priest amid bloody rituals. Thorgils' wife, Ota, caused further outrage by invoking the god at the altar of the monastery at Clonmacnois. The many colourful legends surrounding Thorgils' deeds obscure his true history, but he appears to have attracted around him a gang of hoodlums known as the Gall-Gaedhil, or Foreign Irish, who were of mixed Celtic-Norse parentage and who renounced Christianity in favour of worshipping Thor. One despairing Irish annalist declared that '[h]owever much the Northmen proper had behaved evilly to churches, they [the Gall-Gaedhil] were worse by far, in whatever part of Ireland they used to be'.[22] In a rare show of unity, Irish warlords conspired to put an end to Thorgils in 845, most probably by drowning him in Loch Uair, although one source tells how Thorgils and his bodyguard were stabbed to death by 15 Irish warriors who had disguised themselves as alluring maidens. Not that this did anything to deter Thor-inspired Vikings from attacking the country, as it is clear from both Icelandic and Irish sources that they continued to have a disruptive effect on the Irish political and religious scene for more than 150 years. Indeed, Vikings ruling out of Dublin from the ninth to the eleventh centuries were known to the Irish as *muinter Tomair* (the tribe of Thor), and, just as in the Scandinavian regions, on the outskirts of the town was The Grove of Thor, which was eventually burnt to the ground in the year 1000 by the most famous of the old Irish kings, Brian Boru (c. 941–1014).

The imprint of Thor worship in England predates the Viking invasions and was first made by Anglo-Saxon invaders in the fifth and sixth centuries. Sites sacred to Thunor are found in charters recording locations such as Thunores hlæw (Thunor's Mound) in Thanet, and Thunres lea (Thunor's Grove) near Southampton. The god is also remembered in boundary names, for example, Thunorslege near Bexhill and Thunresfeld in Wiltshire, as well as in topographical descriptors such as Thundridge (Thunor's Ridge), and in numerous place names, for instance, Thundersley and Thurstable.[23] Of course, the Anglo-Saxons had long been converted to Christianity when the Viking invasions began, and as Christians, their view of the Scandinavian Thor equated him with the devil. In the early eleventh century, when England was suffering Viking attacks on a huge scale, the homilist Ælfric told how the devil had troubled St Martin in a number of forms, one being that of Thor/Jove, the god he noted elsewhere as the one most favoured by the Danish invaders. Similarly, Archbishop Wulfstan's near-contemporary 'Sermo Lupi' (Sermon of the Wolf) addressed to the English peoples, in part assigns the plight of the country to their sinfulness, which resulted from their failure to overcome the detestable Vikings and their false gods. This notion that Norse paganism, and in particular Thor, was a diabolical threat to Christian probity and moral decency was also apparent in the German regions, where a ninth-century Old Saxon baptismal vow insisted that new converts publicly repudiate the old gods by saying 'I renounce all the words and works of the devil, Thunaer, Woden and Saxnot, and all those demons who are their companions.'[24]

The situation in Frankia, which broadly equates to modern France, was likewise characterized by Viking reverence for their warrior deity and the anxieties this aroused amongst the French. The ruination of Christian holy places and other barbarisms were common occurrences as Vikings took full advantage of the internal disarray of the Carolingian dynasty during the ninth century. Perhaps the most notorious of the invaders in this period was the Danish Viking Hastein (or Hasting), whose long career had high points in the Loire Valley, across the Mediterranean and in Southern England. Looking back from the eleventh century, Dudo of St Quentin, in his typically lurid style, described a Thor ceremony that he links with the practices of Hastein and his fleet on setting sail:

> [T]hey used to complete their expulsions and exits by making sacrifices in honour of their god Thor. And to him they would offer no single beasts, nor herds of cattle, nor 'gifts of Father Liber, nor of Ceres' [presumably, wine and bread], but men's blood, which they deemed to be the most precious of all holocausts; because he whom a soothsaying priest would determine beforehand, they struck with one blow on the head, (as with) a pair of oxen. And then, when the head of the one chosen by lot had been struck a single blow by each man, he was laid out on the ground, and they would search for 'the tube of the heart' on the left-hand side; that is, for the aorta. And it was their custom to smear their own and their followers with the blood that drained out; and then they would quickly hoist the sails of their ships onto the winds, thinking to placate those (winds) by such a procedure, and would briskly ply the oars of their ships.[25]

Interestingly enough, Dudo appears to suggest that no such ceremony took place if the Viking army chose to depart by land rather than by sea to 'pursue the policy of falling upon other nations with deadly force'.[26]

Not until the second decade of the tenth century and the founding of the Duchy of Normandy by the Norwegian Viking warlord Rollo, known also as Göngu-Hrolf (Hrolf the Walker), did a Viking of significant enough status and influence accept Christian baptism, despite the fact that this was more a matter of political pragmatics on Rollo's part than any honest conviction. A steady process of amelioration into the manners and customs of the French aristocracy continued under the rule of Rollo's son, William Longsword, who was tireless in his efforts to re-establish a Christian infrastructure in the duchy. But William's reforms were not appreciated by all those of Norse descent, particularly not by the influx of die-hard pagan Vikings who had quit Ireland, and he was assassinated in 942. Encouraged by this turn of events, Thor worship was briefly revived in the duchy's Norse communities during the reign of William's successor, Richard the Fearless.

As regards Dudo's description of the bloody pre-embarkation Thor ceremony, it is not impossible that it is in some respects accurate, for similar horrors were also reported elsewhere. The German cleric Thietmar of Merseberg, writing in 1016, some 50 years after the conversion of Denmark, told how at Lejre in Sjaelland major cultic ceremonies had taken place every 9 years during January. At these, 99 humans and a similar number of horses, dogs and cocks were sacrificed. Little credence has been given to Thietmar's account, which has typically been regarded as a propagandizing exaggeration. Yet recent archaeological finds have forced a rethink, for a number of large halls dating back to the sixth century have now been excavated at Lejre, three in 2009 alone, along with evidence of human sacrifice and the possible discovery of a sacred burial mound. Nearby these ancient constructions is an 80 m (260 ft) long stone setting outlining a ship, which may have played a key role in the Lejre rituals. Very similar to these rituals, if on a far more modest scale, are those reported later in the eleventh century by Adam of Bremen on the practices of recidivist Swedes at Old Uppsala where Thor, Odin and Frey were honoured:

It is customary also to solemnise in Uppsala, at nine-year intervals, a general feast of all the provinces of Sweden. From attendance at this festival no one is exempted. Kings and people all and singly send their gifts to Uppsala and, what is more distressing than any kind of punishment, those who have already adopted Christianity redeem themselves through these ceremonies. The sacrifice is of this nature: of every living thing that is male, they offer nine heads, with the blood of which it is customary to placate gods of this sort. The bodies they hang in a sacred grove that adjoins the temple. Now this grove is so sacred in the eyes of the heathen that each and every tree in it is believed divine because of the death or putrefaction of the victims. Even dogs and horses hang there with men. A Christian seventy-two years old told me that he had seen their bodies suspended promiscuously. Furthermore, the incantations customarily chanted in the ritual of a sacrifice of this kind are manifold and unseemly; therefore, it is better to keep silence about them.[27]

Three large mounds dating from the fifth century are still prominent in Old Uppsala and are clearly those that were dedicated to Thor, Odin and Frey. Hundreds of smaller burial mounds surround them. As for the pagan temple, it is likely that all signs of it were erased by Christians who built their church on the same site in the twelfth century.

Grotesque though such ceremonies appear to have been, securing the patronage of Thor was quite literally regarded as a matter of life and death for his adherents. Not only do we find Thor's image or, more commonly, that of Mjollnir carved onto wood, stone and metal across the Viking world, but the need for Thor's protection is evidenced by the discovery – from Dublin to Constantinople – of dozens of Mjollnir pendants, once worn round the necks of Viking foot-soldiers, as well as hundreds of hammer rings that were once attached to the pendants.[28] Indeed, the more precarious the living conditions, the more remote and turbulent the setting, and, as a result, the less influenced existence was by the values and outlook of the traditional Scandinavian aristocracy, the more the cult of Thor appears to have flourished among Viking adventurers and their descendants. This is evidenced, for instance, in Thor-related grave goods found in the Slavic countries, where the predominantly Swedish Rus had established their centres in Novgorod and Kiev in the ninth century, and where, during the tenth and eleventh centuries, Scandinavians seeking their fortunes by whatever means available operated as large mercenary armies known as Varangians.[29] In these eastern regions, certain indigenous pagan traditions coincided with Viking beliefs and it seems that the worship of Thor merged with that of Thor's axe-wielding Slavic thunder-god counterpart Perun. As is recorded in the early twelfth-century *Russian Primary Chronicle*, Perun was the god to whom Rus rulers erected idols and whose name they invoked at times when treaties were agreed, often as the optional pagan alternative to Christ.[30]

THOR'S POWERS

Certainly, as the supreme example of warlike ferocity, Thor would have been an inspiring example for any Viking infantryman, but just as often what Thor adherents were seeking was in many ways practical assistance. Rather than the promise of eternal bliss in an afterlife, what Thor offered was security from the elements in this life. One Icelandic saga written in the early fourteenth century has the conflict between Thor and the Christians at its very heart. The hero of *Flóamanna saga* (The Saga of the People of Floi) is Thorgils' foster son Scarleg, a man for whom dreams play a significant role in his life and plans. When Christianity arrives in Iceland, Thorgils is among the first to renounce Thor in favour of Christ. Soon after, Thor appears to him in a series of dreams, threatening mishaps to Thorgils and the livestock on his farm, all of which come about. Thorgils then decides to set himself up in Greenland, but a huge red-bearded figure comes to him in a dream:

'It will go ill for you,' he said, 'unless you believe in me again; then I will watch over you.'

Thorgils said he would never want his help again and told him to go away as fast as his legs would take him: 'But my journey will go as almighty God wills it.'

Then he thought that Thor led him to a certain crag where ocean waves were dashing against the rocks.

'You will find yourself in such waves and never get out, unless you return to me.'

'No,' said Thorgils, 'Get away from me, you loathsome fiend. He will help me who redeemed us all with his blood.'[31]

Sure enough, Thorgils' voyage is beset by bad weather and the dream-Thor boasts to Thorgils that matters have gone just as he promised. When Thorgils' crew propose making a sacrifice to Thor, Thorgils forbids it and Thor again appears, at first berating him and then tempting him with promises of safe harbour. This time, when Thorgils bravely rejects the god's help, Thor seems to accept defeat, demanding only that an ox dedicated to him is returned. Thorgils duly casts the beast overboard. But misfortune and Thorgils continue to go hand in hand. After much hardship, he and his companions are shipwrecked on Greenland, where his wife is murdered, his crewmates are plagued by ghosts and a mysterious fatal illness, and his attempts at permanent settlement are foiled by hostile neighbours. Finally, he is forced to leave, and after more storm-tossed adventures, he returns to Iceland and further conflict. Despite his dreadful bad luck, much of which we can assume is a result of Thor's continued persecution of his one-time adherent, Thorgils survives to a grand old age.

Thorgils is presented in this saga as man of courage and Christian fortitude, and Thor as a petty and petulant has-been. Clearly, all this is consistent with a view of the Norse gods that had developed according to Christian lights over the three centuries since the conversion. Nonetheless, Thorgils never doubts the power of Thor, even though the god is relegated to the status of a dream figure. Thor may be yesterday's deity, but he is still a power to be reckoned with, and for those needful of calm seas, literally and metaphorically, the consequences of dismissing Thor's help are dire. As is obvious here, Thor equates to the Christian belief in the powers of Satan, and Thorgils' rejection of him codes a key message familiar to all Christians in the Middle Ages concerning the trials of human existence and the consolations in store in the afterlife. As an example to others,

Thorgils demonstrates the power of his faith by combining the often-bloody Viking honour code with the Old Testament forbearance of Job.

Thor's mastery of the seas was evidently a widely held belief, but it may be that this was just part of an even deeper belief in his control over the elements. In a detailed study of beliefs concerning Thor's power, Richard Perkins has concluded that much of it rested on Thor's perceived command over the wind.[32] Obviously, the movements of the sea are dramatically influenced by the wind, and above all else, what any sailor would wish for is a fair wind, just as any seafarer would be inclined to resort to superstitious appeals to higher powers when matters get desperate. While there is some suggestion in both mythological and legendary sources that Odin and, to a somewhat lesser degree, Frey could influence the wind, the bulk of evidence is that it was Thor who had mastery over it, a mastery that, after the conversion, was gradually transferred to Christ. Written evidence – literary and non-literary – for a belief in Thor's power over the wind include the perilous winds that beset Thorgils in *Flóamanna saga*, when the hero rejects Thor's patronage; the description of Thor in the Uppsala temple by Adam of Bremen, which states that it was believed that Thor 'presides over the air, which governs the thunder and lightning, the winds and rains, fair weather and crops' (*see* Chapter 2 for the full description); and Dudo of St Quentin's description of a Thor-inspired sacrifice in France, whereby departing Vikings sought to placate the winds. Much other medieval Icelandic literature either overtly states or otherwise implies that Thor is the author of fair and foul winds, and thus calm or raging seas – the former being granted to his adherents, the latter being inflicted on his opponents, much like Steinunn claims in her poetic invective against Christ before Thangbrand in *Njáls saga*.

Taking all this into account, Perkins goes on to present a plausible hypothesis as to exactly how Thor might have been perceived to raise the wind. During the thirteenth and fourteenth centuries, a number of sagas, typically taking the form of episodes in histories concerning the life of Olaf Tryggvason, were composed about a certain Raud (a name meaning 'red'). One group of these is known collectively as *Rognvalds þáttr ok Rauðs* (The Tale of Rognvald and Raud). In various ways, all of these describe Raud's fanatical attachment to Thor during the time that Olaf Tryggvason was forcefully seeking to impose Christianity on all those within his reach. A common element in them is Raud's attempts to confound the king by summoning Thor's power to raise a storm against the king's ship. These attempts are nonetheless confounded, as the king's protection by Christ proves mightier than Thor's magic and, depending on which variant is followed, the outcomes for Raud range from his elaborate torture and murder by the king to his eventual conversion. One variant, however, describes Raud's encouragement of Thor thus:

> And when the king got north of Naumudalr, he determined to go out to Raudsey. That morning, Raud went to his temple as was his habit. Thor was rather downcast and gave Raud no reply even though he addressed him. This seemed very strange to Raud and he tried in many ways to get Thor to talk and to find out what the matter was. Eventually Thor answered, albeit in very weary tone, that he had good reason for his mood, – 'for,' he said, 'I am put in a very difficult predicament by the intended visit to our island of those men for whom I have the greatest loathing'. Raud asked who those men might be. Thor said it was King Olaf Tryggvason and his force. Raud said: 'Sound the bristles of your beard against them and let us resist them doughtily.' Thor said that would be of little use. Even so, they went outside and Thor blew hard down into his whiskers and sounded the voice of his beard. Straightway there arose a head wind against the king so strong that it could not be withstood and he had to retire to the same harbour as he had set out from. This happened several times and the more it happened, the more the king felt spurred on to get to the island. And eventually, through the power of God, the king's good intentions prevailed over the devil who was offering him resistance.[33]

This notion that Thor could stir up the winds by blowing into his beard is otherwise unique in saga literature, and apart from being more testimony to beliefs in Thor's elemental powers, it has traditionally been regarded as something of a curiosity. Nonetheless, in his examination of the passage's related literary and linguistic associations, Perkins concludes that Thor's use of his breath and beard for wind-raising relates to an authentic tradition. Supporting this are representations of the god on several pocket-sized amulets.

Like the Mjollnir pendants, Thor amulets were thought to have had talismanic power. In the thirteenth-century *Hallfreðar saga Vandræðarskalds* (The Saga of Hallfred the Troublesome Poet), one is said to have been in the possession of the pagan backslider and court poet Hallfred, much to the displeasure of his patron, who here again is Olaf Tryggvason, and who in this case had previously honoured Hallfred by acting as his baptismal sponsor.[34] Perkins considers three amulets, perhaps similar to the one owned by Hallfred, that depict a figure that in many ways seems to illustrate the description of Thor blowing into his beard in *Rognvalds þáttr ok Rauðs*. Found in Lund in Sweden, Sjælland in Denmark and Chernigov in the Ukraine, and made respectively of ivory, amber and bronze, these figurines, each about 6 cm in height, represent a hunched male figure with pursed or parted lips clutching his long beard. These, argues Perkins, are Thor wind amulets, and to them he adds the remarkable, otherwise uncertainly identified, Eyrarland amulet found in northern Iceland, where the beard of a seated figure tapers into what appears to be a stylized Thor's hammer, such as is broadly characteristic of many Mjollnir pendants. Overall, Perkins' detailed and wide-ranging analysis of not only the Thor amulets, but also a number of other seemingly related objects suggestive of Thor the Wind Raiser is wholly convincing, including his conjecture concerning how Thor amulets might have been used during Viking sea voyages.

Just as one might expect, ideas about Thor and his powers, such as can be deduced from Icelandic literary sources, supported in a number of instances by archaeological finds, indicate that believers in the god adapted their convictions to suit their circumstances. For sea-borne adventurers of the Viking Age, Thor's patronage was critical in his mastery over the wind and thus the sea. Yet for those in the rural hinterlands, an older Thor seems to have prevailed, whereby his mastery of thunder and lightning and all manner of climatic tumult was interpreted as being beneficial to crops and to fertility generally. One further possibility, a highly speculative one at that, is that vestiges of an even older Thor is being recalled in the ritual practices and at the cultic centres described in the written sources, particularly in respect of the fire that should never be extinguished. This concerns Thor's possible association with the art of the smithy.

As is apparent, for example in Graeco-Roman mythology and in Germanic legends, smiths were typically regarded as having magical or supernatural endowments. The inextinguishable fire of the furnace, the tempering wind of the bellows and the echoing beat of the hammer, fashioning tools for survival from base elements dug from the earth, are all suggestive of attributes of Thor: fire, wind, thunder, lightning and, of course, his formidable physique. As is told in Snorri Sturluson's *Prose Edda*, Mjollnir's short haft, typical of that used by the smithy, was a result of the smithy's assistant being distracted as he blew into the furnace. And there are other tantalizing suggestions in the myths concerning

Thor and smithying, such as the molten iron hurled back at the giant Geirrod or the piece of whetstone wedged in Thor's head after the combat with Hrungnir. Certainly, in their desire to understand the source of thunder and lightning, the devotees at the Swedish temple despoiled by Magnus Nilsson had something of this association in mind, for, as discussed previously, Saxo says they thought 'that great and violent noise might very well be imitated by the smith's toil' (*see* p. 65 for full quotation). Moreover, according to a study of Lappish mythology written between 1838 and 1845, the related words *pajan* and *paja* respectively signify 'thunder' and 'smithy' and are associated with divine powers.[35] Perhaps, then, some form of proto-Thor, conceived of as a master smithy, lies behind later notions of the god's rule over specific elements. Perhaps, too, the Thor bidden by Raud of Ramsey to frustrate Olaf Tryggvason's sea crossing and the hunched figure blowing into a beard that terminates in the shape of a hammer, as depicted by the Eyrarland amulet, also recalls an antique Thor of the furnace, bellows, anvil and hone. Unprovable though it is, perhaps Thor was originally the god of technology.

Whatever extraordinary capacities Thor was regarded as having, with the coming of Christianity they were soon overpowered. Cultic sites were purged of their idolatry and Christian churches erected in their place. The pressures to conform and so benefit from economic contact with European Christendom meant that there was no place for sacrifice-greedy thunder gods. By the time the Icelanders were writing down their histories and sagas, Thor and the rest of the Norse pantheon were little more than memories of an old way, now obsolete in the religious conformity of the European Middle Ages. Thus, we see Thor cast into dreams or made an analogue for a Christian notion of evil and the misfortunes of the world. Yet, whether in the act of deploring him or of enclosing him in the customs and beliefs of a bygone age, Christian writers nevertheless had the paradoxical effect of ensuring Thor's survival. As masters of men's fates, the old gods may have diminished almost to inconsequence as time passed but in the manuscripts that recorded their trials and tribulations they lived on as potent symbols of Scandinavian identity for scholars to puzzle and argue over. So it came about, as a direct consequence of scholarly endeavours, that almost 900 years after Thorolf Mostur-Beard built his temple to Thor at Hofsstead, the eddas and sagas once more became relevant to contemporary society: artistically, historically and politically. As will be shown in Chapter 5, it was Thor, champion of the underdog and vanquisher of evil, who then caught the spirit of the time. But first it is necessary to consider just how the scene was set for his re-emergence.

4

Recovering the Past: Scholarship from the Enlightenment to National Romanticism

The curious and occasionally sensational attention given to Thor by polemicists, politicians, artists, composers and poets from the latter decades of the eighteenth century onwards cannot fully be understood without some knowledge of how Old Norse myth and legend was regarded in the centuries following the Middle Ages, those periods broadly categorized as the Renaissance and the Enlightenment. The focus of this chapter is the contexts in which ideas about the Norse pantheon developed and the theories that were put forward about the role and origins of the mythology in Scandinavian prehistory. This was a process of gradual, then increasingly rapid, recovery of the beliefs and customs of the ancient Scandinavians, played out against a background of widespread political and religious turmoil throughout Europe, during which the framework for a rebirth of Nordic culture was established.

The scholarly interest in Old Norse myths and legends that persisted in Scandinavia beyond the retrospective fascinations of medieval writers was no more a matter of nostalgia for heathendom than it had been for Snorri Sturluson. Rather, it was partly a case of patriotism and cultural pride, often defensively asserted in the face of those who considered the northern territories to be barbaric and culturally impoverished, and partly a case of continuing political rivalries between the Scandinavian countries. Given that Christian Europe regarded its cultural worth in terms of its engagement with Greek and Roman classicism, the way in which Scandinavian intellectuals perceived their own pre-Christian history perhaps inevitably gave rise to certain rather colourful arguments, rooted as they initially were in the need to reconcile biblical history with national histories. Bizarre though some these arguments may appear to us now, they laid the groundwork for what took place during the Romantic Revival, when knowledge of the Norse gods, their adherents and their detractors came to play a key role in north European history as potent symbols in the national propaganda of the Scandinavian countries and Germany.[1]

The Black Death brought economic misery across Europe during the fourteenth and early fifteenth centuries. Adding to the woes in Scandinavia were further pressures on trade as a result of the success of the German mercantile union known as the Hanseatic League, and the particularly sharp impact of a deteriorating climate in the latter half of the fourteenth century.[2] The political response of the three main Scandinavian countries was to seek union under a single monarch, with the proviso that each country would retain its distinctiveness in the operation of its national laws. The Kalmar Union of 1397, although sound in principle and prospectively advantageous, was not a comfortable arrangement, largely because Denmark and Sweden, the two main players, were distrustful of each other. In 1523, the union finally collapsed and antipathies between a Dano-Norwegian coalition and Sweden would go on to characterize political life throughout the sixteenth century, the low point being a series of wars from 1563 to 1570. Beyond this lay the religious wars of the seventeenth century and their aftermath, and during this period, Sweden and Denmark, both of which had become heartlands of Lutheranism and, so, of anti-Catholic sentiment, vied for territorial advantage.[3] Dano-Swedish relations once again turned sour during the eighteenth century and on into the nineteenth century, when Danish alliances, most notably with Russia, saw to it that a burgeoning Swedish empire across the Baltic regions was curtailed and, in due course, irrecoverably lost.

It was, then, against this background of simmering resentment between east and west Scandinavians, frequently boiling over into military conflict, that scholars endeavoured to recover and interpret the legacy of the Old North. Inevitably, claims over ownership and cultural ascendency were exaggerated and political tensions were mirrored in each country's presentations of their past, which typically entailed ethnographic insults and counter insults. Given the fact that this selfsame legacy was regarded as eccentric to the culture of wider Europe, it would take until the late seventeenth century before Scandinavian scholars would begin to have the confidence to advertise the virtues of their pre-Christian culture in its own terms, as much of it could readily be seen as running counter to prevailing Christian values and biblical 'truths'. The project of recovering the Scandinavian past was one that required considerable intricacy of argument, for, just as Norse paganism could not be allowed the status of religious authority, so no pagan god could be deemed in any way authentic.[4] The apparent contradiction between national identity and religious identity would only be mediated once historical proofs and theological rationalizations gave way to more aesthetic considerations.

For the Danes, it was Saxo Grammaticus's *Gesta Danorum* (History of the Danes) that initially provided them with an insight into the beliefs of early Danish society, a printed edition by Christiern Pedersen (c. 1480–1554) emerging in 1514 and a Danish translation completed in 1575 by Anders Sørensen Vedel (1542–1616).[5] Inevitably, it was to Iceland, a Danish colony acquired as a result of the union of Norway and Denmark in 1380, that the Danes looked for further insights, as Iceland was a storehouse of ancient manuscripts that the Icelanders alone could readily understand. Trading links between Iceland and wider Europe had done little to raise the prestige of the country, beset, as it was, by economic catastrophe. Resentful of the bad press this elicited from visitors to Iceland, an Icelandic headmaster, Arngrímur Jónsson (1568–1648), delivered a sequence of patriotic ripostes, first in 1593 with his *Brevis commentarius de Islandia* (Defence of Iceland), and then in 1609 with his *Crymogæa sive Rerum Islandicarum* ('Crymogæa' being Arngrímur's Greek neologism for Iceland). Apart from asserting that the Icelandic language, or Old Gothic as he referred to it, was the original language of the north, Arngrímur provided numerous extracts from medieval Icelandic manuscripts, so bringing Iceland's literary wealth to the attention of wider Europe.[6]

Danish scholars were particularly interested in Arngrímur's familiarity with manuscripts that concerned their own country and he was encouraged to write a history of Denmark, much of which he based on the now lost *Saga of the Skjöldungar*, a saga detailing some 20 generations of Danish kings, ranging from the conquest of the northern regions by Odin and his son Skjöld, through to the royal dynasties of the tenth century. Just as important was Arngrímur's own encouragement of the erudite Icelandic priest Magnús Ólafsson (1574–1636), who he commissioned to provide a comprehensive redaction of Snorri's *Prose Edda*. The result, published in 1608–09, was what later became known as the *Laufás Edda*. Although somewhat short of the comprehensiveness urged by Arngrímur, Magnús's alphabetically systematized edda proved to be a convenient and essential reference work for Scandinavian scholars.[7]

GOTHICISM

Influencing both Arngrímur and Magnús were the ideas underlying the nascent movement known as Gothicism, the quasi-historical roots of which were based on the expansion of the Gothic tribes from Southern Sweden in the third century, and the repeated threats they posed to Roman authority through to the sixth century. At the heart of Gothicism was the attempt to present a northern perspective on, amounting to a challenge to, the prevailing legacy of Roman culture and history. Prompted by Tacitus's often complimentary first-century account of the Germanic tribes, *Germania*; Adam of Bremen's somewhat disapproving eleventh-century descriptions of the geography and pagan peoples of the north, *Gesta Hammaburgensis Ecclesiae Pontificum* (History of the Archbishops of Hamburg-Bremen); and a sixth-century history of certain tribes assumed to be the northern Goths, *Getica*, by Jordanes,[8] Swedish scholars were not only able to glorify the heroics of their perceived ancestors but, by the early conversion of these tribes to Christianity, also to counter notions of the barbaric north. The romantic cadences of Gothicism amongst Swedish proponents were amplified by that group of fantastical Icelandic sagas known as the *fornaldarsögur* (sagas of ancient times), which are set in mainland Scandinavia before the settlement of Iceland and often involve stirring episodes in Sweden, all of which were regarded as verbatim histories.

The Gothicist assertion of the genius of the Old North found its earliest expression in Sweden in the mid sixteenth century through the writings of the brothers Johannes and Olaus Magnus (1488–1544 and 1490–1557, respectively).[9] Johannes, the last Catholic Archbishop of Uppsala, a position that would be inherited in name only by Olaus, had been in the unhappy position of trying, against all likelihood of success, to defend his faith against the encroaching tides of the Lutheran Reformation. This sense of the passing of the old and, he fervently believed, true ways of the Swedes was something that directed all of Johannes's thinking. Informed by Jordanes' *Getica* and determined to contradict Saxo's accounts of Danish humiliations of the Swedes, Johannes, however, had something more to add to his valorization of the Goths. According to his posthumously published *Historia de omnibus Gothorum Sveonumque regibus* (A History of All the Kings of the Goths and the Swedes) of 1554, the Goths were not only the most ancient of European peoples but also the inheritors of the language of God. The Goths, he argued, were originally a tribe led by the grandson of Noah, Magog son of Japheth. Magog had taken the Goths to Sweden and, if thus interpreted in strict biblical time, had avoided the chaos of languages brought about by the destruction of the Tower of Babel, a punishment wrought by God on impertinent mankind. Given this authority over all civilizations, it was the wisdom, fortitude, nobility and all-round decency of the Goths, insisted Johannes, that had inspired the rise of civilized, rational values from the Ancient Greeks through to the birth of Christ, and it was these very same virtues that had later enabled them to conquer the contemptible Romans. Thereafter, it was by comparison with the morally dubious and militarily inadequate Danes that the Goths-cum-Swedes were best able to define their divinely inspired uniqueness. For Johannes, the surviving evidence of the *ur*-language of the Goths is Gothic script; in other words, runes – a Swedish phenomenon.

Equally influential, indeed for many decades more so, was the work of Olaus Magnus. After Johannes's death, Olaus went to some lengths to ensure that Johannes's *Historia* achieved publication, for he entirely subscribed to his brother's theological reasoning and shared his anti-Danish sentiments, all of which he instilled in his *Historia de gentibus septentrionalibus* (A Description of the Northern Peoples) of 1555. Olaus's stated purpose was to offer

[a] history of the Nordic people's different manners and camps, [that is] also about the wonderful differences in customs, holy practices, superstitions, bodily exercises, government and food keeping; further on war, buildings and wonderful aids; further on metals and different kinds of animals, that live in these neighbourhoods.[10]

Yet, behind the colourful accounts of sea monsters, which, in 1539, Olaus had marked out on his remarkable *Carta Marina* (Map of the Sea),[11] and descriptions of arctic nights, dramatic landscapes and an indomitable people, lies the deeper purpose of reminding the Swedes of their origins and preparing them to rid themselves of the 'misery of misfortune' that had come about through the Reformation.[12] Much of his work is therefore devoted to a study of the art of warfare as traditionally practised by the Swedes, whose enemies were reminded 'how unwise it is to join battle with the elements themselves'.[13] Unlike Johannes's relatively neglected *Historia*, Olaus's patriotic battle cry to the future encouraged translations into English, Italian, German and Dutch.

Compared to such extremes of chauvinism in Sweden, Danish translations and editions of Saxo must have appeared relatively anodyne. Yet, with the assistance of the Icelanders, a shift of emphasis on manuscript sources would do just as much for the Danes. The key figure in the early to mid seventeenth century was Ole Worm (1588–1655), a medical scientist and personal physician to King Christian IV of Denmark. It was through Worm's influence that the work of Icelandic scholars, such as Magnús Ólafsson, came to prominence and that the Norwegian scholar Peder Clausson Friis (1545–1614) gained posthumous publication of his translation of Snorri's history of the Norwegian kings, *Heimskringla*.[14] At the heart of Worm's thinking was the belief that runes were the key source of knowledge about the origins, not only of the Danes, but also of language itself. According to Worm, all Scandinavian literature was originally written in runes, a communication system that he believed was invented by the Danes and derived from Hebraic script; thus, a more sober conclusion than that made by Johannes Magnus if, nonetheless, an equally erroneous one. Worm's extensive publications, replete with runic and Latin translations of Old Norse poetry, include his treatise of 1636, *RUNIR seu Danica literatura antiquissima . . . eller Literatura runica* (Runes or the Most Ancient Danish Literature). For Worm, those who first carved these runes – that is to say, the Danes – were a people of exceptional character and vocation. Epitomizing, indeed, defining, the image of the fanatical and fearless Danish warrior was the heroic poem 'Krákumál' – widely known as 'The Death Song of Ragnar Lodbrok' – which had been brought to Worm's attention by Magnús Ólafsson and which duly found a place in *RUNIR* as both a runic transcription and a Latin translation. In this, the dying Ragnar recalls his lifelong prowess in battle, relishes the coming of Odin's valkyries to take him to Valhalla – where he will drink ale from the skulls of his fallen enemies – and famously concludes with the declaration, 'Laughing shall I die'. It would take centuries before the arresting idea of the 'human skull-cup' would be correctly understood to mean merely horn.

Worm's ideas had some strange consequences; for example, when they caught the attention of the Englishman and Worm's fellow antiquarian Walter Charleton (1619–1707), once a physician to the executed English king Charles I. In 1663, enamoured of Worm's arguments, Charleton concluded that the English stone circle Stonehenge was once a site where the ancient Danes had crowned their kings.[15] As Stonehenge was also believed to have been an overnight refuge for the beleaguered Charles II after his defeat by Oliver Cromwell at the Battle of

Worcester in 1651, once the English monarchy was restored in 1660, it became associated with the assertion of Charles II's historic entitlement to rule. The poet John Dryden was moved to celebrate the 'proof' of Charles' legitimacy in a prefatory verse for a presentation copy of Charleton's study to be given to the king.[16] Yet, not all considered Worm's claims to be so significant and, early in the eighteenth century, the English poet and satirist Alexander Pope in his attack on what he regarded as feeble scholarship, 'The Dunciad', disparaged Worm in particular and Gothicism generally, judging that, 'To future ages may thy dullness last, / As thou preserve the dullness of the past!'[17]

Inspired in part by Worm's ideas and in part by the Icelanders' discovery and eventual delivery to Denmark of those manuscripts that became collectively known as the *Codex Regius* (King's Book) or *Poetic Edda*, Latin translations of Old Norse poetry and prose continued apace in both Sweden and Denmark. Most notable among publications in Denmark was the landmark study by Bishop Peder Resen (1625–88), *Edda Islandorum* of 1665, a Danish and Latin translation of Snorri's *Prose Edda* that also included translations of the eddic poems 'Völuspá' (The Seeress's Prophecy) and 'Hávamál' (The Sayings of the High One). One significant aspect of Resen's study of the eddas was his determination to reveal their metaphysical depth. Thus, rather than subjecting them to the classicist interpretations that Enlightenment scholars typically employed to convey a flavour of contemporary respectability and, indeed, readability, Resen attempted to show that beyond the technical complexities in the articulations of Norse mythology lie 'certain higher, spiritual truths, to be apprehended intuitively but not completely translatable into ordinary language'.[18] This, in itself, was a new and telling departure that in due course would come to characterize analytical discourse on the mysterious 'otherness' of the eddas.

Yet, national rivalries were rarely far from the scene of scholarly investigation. In the later decades of the seventeenth century, political antipathies were reflected in the work of two of the most celebrated scholars of the time: the Danish Thomas Bartholin the Younger (1659–90), and the Swedish Olof Rudbeck (1630–1702). Between Rudbeck and Bartholin there may also have been a personal score to settle, for Bartholin's father, who, like Rudbeck, was a medical scientist by profession, had bitterly contested with his Swedish counterpart over which of them had the right to claim priority over the discovery of the human lymphatic system, a controversy that remained unresolved in their lifetimes. Precisely to what extent this rivalry had bearing on Rudbeck's and Bartholin the Younger's studies of Scandinavian antiquity is difficult to assess, but it is unlikely to have done anything to endear them to each other's nations. Given this, and the fact that Sweden was enjoying political and territorial ascendency over Denmark after the Thirty Years War earlier in the century, it is perhaps no coincidence that the theses of Bartholin and Rudbeck marked a new height in competing claims over the respective roles of their ancestors in Scandinavian prehistory.

Olof Rudbeck began his four-volume *Atlantica* (Atland eller Manheim) in 1679 and continued working on it until his death in 1702. Taking his general direction from Johannes and Olaus Magnus almost 150 years earlier, Rudbeck employs the methodological apparatus of empirical enquiry to prove that Sweden is the cradle of civilization named by Plato as Atlantis, 'the womb of mankind', and that the Swedish language lies in direct descent from the language of Adam, and is thus a precursor to the Hebraic language that Ole Worm argued to be the basis of runes. In a vast, rambling and increasingly digressive argument, Rudbeck links etymology and mythology in an extreme form of the principles of euhemerization employed by Snorri in the *Prose Edda* but goes much further in claiming that Greek and Roman mythology had its origin in Atlantian Sweden. Rudbeck's use of word and concept associations allowed him almost endless flexibility of interpretation, so that when, for example, Plato refers to elephants in his description of Atlantis, Rudbeck can argue that he is actually signifying Swedish wolves.[19] In effect, the eddas were viewed by Rudbeck as an allegorical code that he was convinced he had cracked. Although Rudbeck's procedure attracted criticism inside and ridicule outside Sweden, it influenced writers on Norse mythology for generations to come.

Thomas Bartholin the Younger was Rudbeck's junior by some 30 years but was precociously scholarly, having become professor designate at the age of 18 and Denmark's royal antiquary at the age of 25. In his short life (he died aged 31), he probably did more than any of his predecessors to draw attention to the literary legacy of the Scandinavians. As was the case with *Atlantica*, Bartholin's study was fully embedded in eddic and saga lore, citing extensively from some 90 eddic poems or Icelandic sagas. Ultimately, however, it was more concerned with highlighting admirable Viking machismo than with fabulous theories – so, more muscular than metaphysical – but it was nonetheless just as influential; indeed, more so in the longer term. Following on from Ole Worm, Bartholin

obviated discussion of the relative merits of east and west Scandinavians by simply referring to all Scandinavians as Danes. His revealingly titled *Antiquitatum
Danicarum de Causis Contemptae a Danis adhuc Gentilibus Mortis* (Danish
Antiquities Concerning the Reasons for the Danes' Disdain for Death) of 1689,
adduces widespread evidence of the stoicism of the early Danes, their adventur-
ous spirit, their talent for versifying, and, with Ragnar Lodbrok's death-song
yet again exemplary, their joyful post-mortem transportation to Valhalla.[20] In
support of the Danes' enthusiasm for a lusty afterlife, Bartholin calls to witness
the first-century writings of the Roman poet Lucan, despite the fact that Lucan
considered this belief among Scandinavians and Celts to be an absurdity.[21]
Nevertheless, that the examples set by the gods were reflected in the habits of the
people can be noted, for instance, in how the Danes enjoyed drinking bouts just
as much as Thor, who 'led the way' in this regard.[22]

As for Rudbeck's 'Atlantis' theories, Bartholin gives no quarter, noting the
author's ignorance and poor scholarship, and accusing him of 'having no more
purpose in all of the heap of his work than to attack the history of the Danes',
by which method, '[he] attempts to do away with us altogether'. Concerning
Rudbeck's support for his theories as derived from the literature of Graeco-Roman
classicism, Bartholin despairs: 'Oh, wretched condition of the History of the
Northern Lands, if, indeed, upon the testimony of the Greek poets it shall stand
or fall!'[23]

In this, of course, Bartholin is conveniently ignoring his own tendency to do
likewise when it suits him. Yet what Bartholin was ultimately set on validating
was the manly virtue of the Noble Heathen, that individual who, through no fault
of his own, had not benefitted from the revealed faith of Christianity, but who,
nonetheless, lived according to the principles of a Natural or Primitive Religion,
a precursor to Christian conversion. This rehabilitation of the pagan, mooted in
the works of Worm and his Icelandic informants, marked another significant step
toward Romanticist interpretations of Norse myth and legend that would come
to dominate enthusiasm for the Old North.

Just as Worm's grand theories had been heavily dependent on the scrupulous
scholarship of Magnús Ólafsson, so Bartholin's were dependent on that of
another Icelander, Árni Magnússon (1663–1730), four years Bartholin's junior.
As assistant to Bartholin, Árni transcribed and translated thousands of pages of
Icelandic manuscripts, many of which he had himself collected together from

across Iceland, in places ranging from monastic libraries to humble farmsteads. Apart from his assistance to Bartholin, Árni's diligence and expertise proved invaluable to his countryman Þormóðr Torfason (1636–1719), perhaps better known as Torfaeus, who had been appointed Royal Historian of Norway in 1682. Among many another influential studies, Torfaeus went on to compile a history of Norway and to provide Latin translations of saga literature concerning episodes in the Faeroes, the Orkneys, Greenland and Vínland (this latter believed then, as now, to have been a Viking settlement on the north-east coast of the United States). In a life dedicated to securing and preserving the old literature, Árni's efforts did not attract the same attention as Bartholin's, but despite much of his manuscript collection being lost in the massive destruction of the Copenhagen fire of 1728, his endeavours have meant that he will be remembered as one of the most important scholars of the Enlightenment period. Somewhat pithily he summed up well the pitfalls and principles that so often underlie scholarship: 'And that is the way of the world, that some men put errors into circulation and others afterwards try to eradicate those same errors. And so both sorts of men have something to do.'[24] Árni might well have been describing his own corrective influence over the reception history of Old Norse-Icelandic literature. His name is enshrined in the titles of the national manuscript libraries of both Iceland and Denmark.[25]

Rudbeckian Gothicism fell into disrepute in Scandinavia during the eighteenth century, giving way to less-nationalist and, by this time, better-informed studies, such as those made by Ludvig Holberg (1684–1754) in Denmark and Olof Dalin (1708–63) in Sweden.[26] Although euhemerist interpretations of Norse myths remained axiomatic, the structure of the myths was now being favourably studied in comparison with other mythological systems, such as Greek, Roman and Iranian, while their contents were being increasingly lauded as uniquely and majestically northern, a dramatic contrast to sun-dappled Arcadia. Moreover, the supply of new translations and editions of Icelandic sagas was virtually inexhaustible and some of these tales of courage, individualism and tragic love would in future years capture the imagination of literary artists and the reading public across Europe.[27] Nevertheless, during the first half of the eighteenth century, studies of northern myth and legend were still, for the main part, an almost wholly Scandinavian pre-occupation. Strong interest was aroused amongst a handful of intellectuals in England, most notable among whom was

George Hickes (1642–1715), whose *Linguarum vett. septentrionalium thesaurus grammatico-criticus et archæologicus* (Treasury of the Old Northern Languages) of 1703-5 included the very first translation of Norse poetry into English.[28] Yet, lacking the stimulus of national rivalries and insecurities over the Scandinavian past, English interest was largely antiquarian and/or linguistic.[29] And there can be no doubt that it was national rivalries and the need to establish a clear line of cultural identity that had done most to provoke scholarly investigation, no matter how tendentious, up until the mid eighteenth century. From 1750, however, these pressures inside Scandinavia suddenly began have a wider European significance.[30]

Renaissance and Enlightenment scholars had accepted as incontrovertible the ranking of the gods and their particular roles and relationships as in the eddas; thus, if any god attracted more attention than any other it was Odin, the conqueror of the north. Considerations of Thor were mainly as Odin's son and, as it were, his strong right arm. What changed this, what allowed and inspired a freer interpretation of the significance of the gods was the shift in sensibility – democratizing and humanist – that was taking place in philosophical and political discourse and, as a consequence, in artistic expression across Europe. The free Viking spirit that had emerged from eddas and sagas was in perfect time with the dawning of a new age of liberty, equality and fraternity.

CHANGING THE PERCEPTION OF SCANDINAVIA

The determination of the Scandinavians to contradict the view of Scandinavia as a cultural backwater remained as strong as ever in the eighteenth century. For King Frederick V of Denmark (r. 1746–66), one remedy was to commission a new history of the country, one that could take advantage of the latest scholarship. Yet, it was not to a Dane that he turned to execute the task but to the respected young Swiss writer and pedagogue Paul Henri Mallet (1730–1807), a man of respectable aristocratic descent and Protestant persuasion. Appointed professor of French in Copenhagen in 1752, the first fruits of Mallet's research, written in French, appeared in print in 1755 as *Introduction à l'histoire de Dannemarc, où l'on traite de la religion, des loix, des mœurs et des usages des anciens Danois*, then in 1756 he expanded on his studies of Norse myth in *Monumens de la mythologie et de la poésie des Celtes, et particulièrement des anciens Scandinave*. These studies were much in the traditions of the classically trained scholar who is chiefly concerned with the technicalities and intricacies of the poetry; however, in 1763, Mallet reconsidered his material and reordered his approach and published his six volume edition *Histoire de Dannemarc*.[31] It is from these latter volumes that the romance of the Old North can be properly dated, the enthusiasm for which spread beyond both the confines of Scandinavia and the provinces of scholarship.

Mallet's *Histoire* offers extensive citations from all known early histories, from Tacitus to Saxo, and is openly indebted to Danish and Icelandic scholarly traditions, most notably the translations and commentaries of Arngrímur Jónsson, Torfaeus, Resen, Worm and Bartholin. But Mallet is not appreciative of all previous efforts to record Scandinavian history, particularly Swedish ones of the Gothicist persuasion, such as Rudbeck's Atlantis theory. All those who had advanced the notion of the historical primacy of Swedish Goths are politely dismissed amongst other 'pretended guides'.[32] Mallet's study ranges across legal, military and religious practices among the ancient Danes and offers a French translation of 'Gylfaginning' (The Deluding of Gylfi) derived from Peder Resen's edition of the *Prose Edda*, as well as commentaries on those mythological and heroic verses that had, over time, become canonical in studies of Old Norse poetry.[33] One glaring error of judgement, one that he had inherited from other studies and one that his translators, such the Englishman Bishop Thomas Percy (1729–1811), would be at pains to put right, was his assumption that the languages and beliefs of the Nordic peoples and the Celts were of the same origin.

As for the origins of the mythology, Mallet rejects the *Prose Edda*'s Prologue as 'useless and ridiculous', raises doubts about whether Snorri actually wrote it and declines to bother translating 'this absurd piece'.[34] Nevertheless, Mallet does not abandon the euhemerist approach, and instead of having Greek warriors settling and conquering in the north after the Trojan War, he confidently informs his reader that Odin was in fact the ruler over a region known as Scythia that lay between the Black Sea and the Caspian. Odin had been forced to flee north during the first century BC, when the Roman legions of Pompey had routed the armies of the dominant ruler in the region, Mithridates VI, to whom Odin had allied himself. Having conquered Denmark and set his son Skjöld to rule over it, he passed on to Sweden, where he subjugated (and deluded) a certain King Gylfi. After his death, Odin and his inner circle became revered as gods across the northern regions.

While it is clear that Mallet is drawing heavily on the histories of Arngrímur Jónsson and Torfaeus, what characterizes and enlivens this second edition of his *Histoire* are the emerging principles of pre-Romanticism. These were chiefly derived from two sources, both of which impacted on Mallet between publishing his first and second editions. On the one hand, there was Edmund Burke's study of the concept of the sublime published in 1756, which analyses a type of beauty that is unlike the emotional gentility of Greek and Roman classicism and is instead composed of a stimulating, even terrifying, grandeur, untamed and untameable;[35] on the other, there were Jean-Jacques Rousseau's revolutionary theories, first aired in 1755, concerning 'natural man' or the 'noble savage' living at one with Nature.[36] Indeed, the cold climate of this Scandinavian Nature, had, in 1748, been remarked on by the political philosopher Montesquieu as something that conditioned the courage and energy of the denizens of the far north, an opinion that Mallet pursues with some relish.[37] By the same token, says Mallet, the vigorous, freedom-loving ancient Danes set great store on family values and accorded their women the highest honour, one consequence of this being the origin of chivalric romance, a view that proved attractive to many in northern Europe and absurd to just as many in its south. Nonetheless, for the first time, eddic poetry had a modern theoretical underpinning that distinguished it in type from classical poetry, yet rivalled that poetry in quality, while the ancient Scandinavians could be perceived as having lived in a manner that championed freedom as a natural right, a condition that should be emulated rather than thought primitive and vulgar. In short, Mallet's *Histoire* went a great distance towards fulfilling his brief of repudiating the slur that Scandinavia was a cultural wasteland resting on a barbarous history, establishing instead the literary genius and superior moral character of the Danes and their ancestors.

Yet, Mallet is quite clear that to accept wholesale the veracity of all that was recorded in the ancient manuscripts would be to commit an error, one perpetrated by many previous historians; nevertheless,

[t]he most credulous writer, he that has the greatest passion for the marvellous, while he falsifies the history of his contemporaries, paints their manner of life and modes of thinking without perceiving it. His simplicity, his ignorance, are at once pledges to the artless truth of his drawing, and a warning to distrust that of his relations. This is doubtless the best, if not the only use, we can make of those old reliques of poetry, which have

escaped the shipwreck of time. The authors of those fragments, erected into historians by succeeding ages, have caused ancient history to degenerate into a mere tissue of fables. To avoid this mistake, let us consider them only on the footing of poets, for in effect they were nothing else; let us principally attend to and copy those strokes, which, without their intending it, point out to us the notions, and mark the character of the ages in which they lived. These are the most certain truths we can find in their works, for they could not help delivering them, whether they would or not.[38]

Mallet was therefore providing a history that distinguished between culture, what the ancients thought, and real history, what they actually did. As the truth about a society can be found as much in its ideas as it can in its deeds, then no extravagant explanations were required to justify or demystify its cultural products: sacred, profane or plain foolish. With this distinction in mind, Mallet's readers can approach an understanding of Old Norse mythology as a set of beliefs, irrespective of its truth value or their own beliefs; as Mallet says of the eddic poets: 'We must consult them in person and hear them (as it were) in the coverts of their dark umbrageous forests, chant forth those sacred and mysterious hymns, in which they comprehended the whole system of their religion and morality.'[39] Read purely 'on the footing of poets', the truth value or otherwise of the mythology is irrelevant. What matters is the sophistication and artistry of its vision.

As regards Mallet's study of Thor, he is identified as the 'third principal deity . . . the most valiant of the sons of Odin', who is analogous to the Roman Jupiter and the Welsh Taranis, both known for their mastery over thunder, although Mallet admits that he cannot discover that this attribute was ever credited to Thor in the mythology.[40] Mallet also notes that most reverence was given to Thor in Norway and Iceland, whereas for the Danes it was Odin and for the Swedes Frey, and that in the myths Thor's chief antagonists were monsters, giants and Loki – this last observation being one that would become significant for later champions of Thor. In his remarks on the fables of the *Prose Edda*, Mallet repeatedly identifies Thor as 'the divinity most favourable to mankind', but is perhaps most influential in conveying the meaning of the god in what he has to say following his translation of the Thor and Utgarda-Loki episodes. In this, Mallet sees the twin principles of Good and Evil described 'in allegorical manner' – an interpretative method over which Mallet advises caution.[41] Surprised that Thor should be 'liable to illusions, snares and trials', Mallet nevertheless dismisses the suggestion that Thor's feats are an imitation of those of Hercules, 'the analogy being so small', and suggests that for the origin of the fable one should look to the original homeland of Odin, that is to say, Scythia. So, although Mallet gives little space to discussing Thor, his perception that it was this divinity who alone acted as the protector of mankind and could be understood as the positive aspect of a Good-versus-Evil dualism would become the basis for all future analysis of, and enthusiasm for, the god.

The reception of Mallet's *Histoire* across northern and western Europe, although at first variable and in some quarters downright hostile, was in the long run extraordinary in its effect. The general view of its impact on the English scene has long been that '[a]ll subsequent Norse study and all the revival of the Norse element in English literature may be traced back to Mallet's book'.[42] This is certainly true of Bishop Percy, who in 1770 mediated Mallet's work to an English speaking readership in his critically revised translation of Mallet's 1763 edition of his *Histoire*, and whose interest in the world of the eddas had been stimulated by Mallet's earlier editions of 1755 and 1756. So much is apparent in Percy's notes and commentaries to his *Five Pieces of Runic Poetry* of 1763 and in his influential edition of indigenous English balladry *Reliques of Ancient English Poetry* of 1765.[43] Yet, although having read Mallet in the late 1750s, the renowned English poet Thomas Gray (1716–71) wrote two fairly free translations of eddic poems in 1761, which were recorded in the studies of Torfaeus and Bartholin, and was clearly musing on old northern skies some time before Mallet's first publications. Along with illustrative material by the German painter Henry Fuseli and the poet and artist William Blake, Gray's odes did much to encourage others to ponder or imitate the new mode of the 'Gothick'.[44] The combined effect of all this can be seen in references to the Norse pantheon or plans to base future creations around certain gods by poets such as Wordsworth, Southey, Coleridge (who, incidentally, contemplated writing a poem about Thor) and Byron. In France, too, where, as in Britain, knowledge of the European Viking Age was slight, Mallet's *Histoire* aroused considerable interest, although, as we shall see in Chapter 5, it would be among German intellectuals that the Nordic legacy would prove most controversial.[45] Nevertheless, all this may not have amounted to quite as much had it not been for the strange story of an ancient Celtic bard, one Ossian.[46]

THE SIGNIFICANCE OF OSSIAN

In 1760, the 24-year-old Scot James Macpherson (1736–96) published his *Fragments of Ancient Poetry Collected in the Highlands of Scotland, and Translated from the Gaelic or Erse Language.* Two years later came *Fingal*, followed in 1763 by *Temora*, both of which were full-length verse epics concerning the lives, times, beliefs and tribulations of the Highland tribes as told by the blind bard Ossian, a figure who appears in Irish myth and legend as Oisín, son of Finn. Their setting and original composition of what became collectively known as *The Poems of Ossian* were said to be the early Dark Ages, at which time, so Ossian recounts, the chief enemies of the Celts were barbarous, sea-borne Scandinavians, who had settled the Orkney Islands and were worshippers of the brutal god Loda (who Macpherson equates to Odin). What is more, Macpherson said he had the manuscripts to prove it. All told, Macpherson's Ossianic poetry was a sensation, attracting a reading public across Europe, eventually prompting translations into 26 languages and exciting intense debate among the critics.[47] On the one hand, there were those such as Hugh Blair (1718–1800), a professor of rhetoric and belles-lettres at the University of Edinburgh, who wrote a preface for *Fragments* and published his *Critical Dissertation on the Poems of Ossian* in 1763; on the other, there were those who had considerable doubts about Macpherson's sincerity, such as Dr Samuel Johnson (1709–84), who judged the Scot to be 'a mountebank, a liar, and a fraud'.[48] Macpherson's failure to produce the manuscripts did nothing to pacify his accusers.

Yet, it matters little whether Macpherson's translations were authentic – although, of course, they were not – for they sparked what one recent critic has called 'a frenzied enthusiasm for "antique poetry"', which, as a contemporary of Macpherson put it, offered 'genuine delineations of life in its simplest stages'.[49] Wreathed in supernatural shadows and oracular dreams, set amid craggy mountains and misty glens, describing a people of fortitude, good manners and fundamental decency, and delivered in a verse form well suited to the tastes of the periwigged and powdered of the literary salons across late eighteenth-century Europe, Macpherson's 'recoveries' both captured and constructed the mood of the moment. Most remained deaf to those who cried foul. Literary tourism became the fashion, either to prove or disprove Macpherson's claims and, in the course of time, Napoleon, Beethoven, Mendelssohn, Goethe, Schiller, Hazlitt, Balzac, Wordsworth, Burns and Tolstoy were among the many who regarded Ossian as the northern equivalent of Homer.[50] The boost this gave to Mallet's *Histoire* cannot be underestimated.

Ossianic poetry was the first literary creation in the English language to pay any significant attention to the ancient Scandinavians, albeit that the attention it did pay was far from flattering and that Macpherson's grasp of Old Norse mythology was at best superficial.[51] Certainly, Macpherson claims familiarity with Mallet's *Histoire* of 1755, citing it on several occasions, but either what Mallet had to say did not suit his purposes, he did not understand what was being said or he was getting his information piecemeal from Hugh Blair's *Dissertation*, which he read in 1762, a year before its and *Temora*'s publication. Whatever the case, Macpherson grossly distorts those bits of Mallet he opts to reference. It has also been noted that ideas expressed in 'The Death Song of Ragnar Lodbrok' play an increasingly large role in Macpherson's descriptions of the Scandinavians and this is definitely a text that he sourced from Blair, who translated it directly from Ole Worm's *RUNIR* and thought it 'like passing from a savage desart [sic], into a fertile and cultivated country' when compared with reading the poetry of Ossian.[52] This pretty much sums up what Macpherson, via Blair, thought of both the Scandinavian heritage and the ancient Scandinavians.

It is, therefore, not a little ironic that Macpherson's prejudicial and unsympathetic plundering of Mallet's history of the ancient Danes was done to lend authenticity to a forgery, and that in so doing the Ossian phenomenon became the single most important factor in Mallet's work gaining the substantial audience that it did. Indeed, were it not for Macpherson's *Fragments of Ancient Poetry* of 1760, it is quite possible that Thomas Gray would not have been so keen to pen his Norse odes, nor Bishop Percy so devoted to recovering English ballads and to getting Mallet's *Histoire* better known. One further irony is that Ossianic poetry did more for the cause of Scottish nationalism than any other work of literature, coming as it did just 15 years after the virtual annihilation of the rebellious Jacobites at Culloden. Thanks in part to Macpherson, something similar was about to happen back in Scandinavia, where, although romanticized by the likes of Mallet, the primary material was, at least, both old and authentic. The consequences there, however, would be rather more dramatic, for in this case it was not a blind bard or a beleaguered tribal chieftain that would be the focus of attention, but a hammer-wielding thunder god with a penchant for violence. Moreover, this time it would not be Thor as Satan, but Thor as Saviour.

5

Thor in Denmark: From Klopstock to Grundtvig

THE IMPACT OF OSSIAN IN DENMARK

In 1751, just one year before the appointment of Paul Henri Mallet to a chair at the University of Copenhagen, Germany's most celebrated and in some ways most controversial poet, Friedrich Gottlieb Klopstock (1724–1803), at that time only 27 years old, also took up residence in the Danish capital. Like Mallet, Klopstock had been encouraged to come to Denmark by King Frederick V, who was a great admirer of Klopstock's verse, particularly his as yet incomplete Miltonic epic *Der Messias* (The Messiah).[1] But it was not just the promise of a royal pension that attracted Klopstock and kept him in self-imposed exile for 19 years, but also, equally, if not more so, his strong feelings about the then ruler of Prussia, Frederick the Great (r. 1740–86). Klopstock was passionate about German culture and was disappointed, to say the least, that his enthusiasm was not shared by the enlightened absolutist King of Prussia, whose own tastes leaned toward the classical manners of French poetry and Latinate culture generally, even to the point of disdaining the German language. While Klopstock fully appreciated and admired Frederick the Great's military brilliance and statesmanship, something he regarded as a model of German heroism, his Francophilia was regarded by the poet as little short of a betrayal of the German people. Klopstock's move to Copenhagen was as much a political statement as it was an opportunity to fulfil his poetic mission. As the prestige language of the social elite in Denmark was German, Klopstock was not particularly inconvenienced by his relocation; indeed, to the contrary, Copenhagen offered precisely the milieu that suited him, including a king who, unlike Frederick the Great, appreciated his work, and a place where he could hold court amid the Copenhagen Circle and enjoy the esteem that was his due.[2]

Throughout the 1750s, Klopstock showed little interest in anything other than the pietistic fervour that inspired his composition of *Der Messias*. Even so, despite Mallet's publications of 1755 and 1756 going unmentioned and seemingly unnoticed by Klopstock, the poet's fierce views on German culture, including its folk traditions, meant that he was inherently, if unknowingly, disposed towards a form of ideological northernism.[3] In the 1760s, this predisposition became manifest through two influences. In the first place, it was the craze for Ossian that came to Klopstock's attention through partial translations into German in 1762 and 1764, which led to a full translation in 1768 composed by the Bavarian Jesuit Michael Denis (1729–1800) using the classical hexameter verse form, a contextually odd tribute to the master of that poetic style, Klopstock himself.[4] In the second place, it was the arrival in Copenhagen in 1765 of the German-speaking Heinrich Wilhelm von Gerstenberg (1737–1823), a Danish cavalry officer who certainly had taken a great deal of notice of the revitalization of interest in ancient Scandinavian literature, even before that which was stimulated by Mallet.[5]

Klopstock was convinced that James Macpherson had shown the way forward in the recovery of a bardic past, and was one of those who felt Ossian's poetry to be as good as Homer's and in some respects better.[6] He even went so far as to pay the ancient Celt the highest possible tribute when he declared that surely Ossian was German, a compliment that was at the same time an appropriation. From the late 1760s, Klopstock's correspondence is full of praise for Macpherson's discovery, admiring its rhythms, its moods and, of course, its authenticity, although he was rather disappointed that Macpherson failed to supply him personally with the 'original melodies' that Macpherson claimed would have accompanied the Gaelic verse.[7] Klopstock nonetheless defined a new mission for himself: he would liberate the voice of a uniquely German poetic diction. Urging him on was Gerstenberg, who regarded Mallet's work as legitimizing his fervent belief in the necessity of a folk literature, a *volkslied*. In 1766, Gerstenberg published 'Gedicht eines Skalden' (Poem of a Skald), an imaginative and sentimentalized reformulation of the eddic poem 'Völuspá' (The Seeress's Prophecy) in which a hero of the Old North, one Thorlaug, awakes from his grave to proclaim the splendour of the Norse gods. It was at this point that Klopstock took heed: 'Some of our friends in Copenhagen,' wrote Klopstock to Gerstenberg, 'or rather those of them who have been interested enough, know that I first took up an interest in the mythology of our ancestors after you had written *Skalden*'.[8] Germany's greatest poet of the

Romantic era, Johann Wolfgang von Goethe (1749–1832), later described this coincidence of antique Celtic and Scandinavian influences as the point at which '[e]verything converged in Klopstock to create such an epoch'.[9]

Klopstock was far from alone among German intellectuals in seeing Ossianic poetry as a revelation.[10] The philosopher and passionate advocate of *volkspoesie* (folk poetry) Johann Gottfried von Herder (1744–1803) similarly saw it as 'songs of the people, songs of an uncultivated, sense-perceptive people'.[11] When Gerstenberg expressed mild doubts about their origin, Herder responded by dismissing them as trifling compared with the lessons that Germans could learn from Macpherson's master class, although he was initially highly critical of Denis's use of sophisticated hexameters in translating such powerful folk art and equally critical of Gerstenberg's approval of them. The Ossianic lesson, thought Herder, was one that Klopstock had been the first to absorb fully and so had 'bestowed on our language a delicacy, fullness and melody undreamt of before his time'.[12] Dazzled by Ossian and inspired by the prospect before them, Klopstock and Herder paid no heed to the growing scepticism over the authenticity of Macpherson's finds that was being expressed in England, nor, at first, would they heed the corrective scholarship that distinguished the Celts from the Scandinavians.[13] The heady brew of Ossian, the eddas and howling bards was a matter of patriotism, not one for nitpicking doubts.

Fully Ossianized and furnished with a fresh store of northern symbols from Mallet, Klopstock led the way in the asserting the vernacular genius of German literary art. From the mid 1760s, his poetic themes are the glory of Mother Nature, the sacred mysteries of the celestial bodies and the immortality of friendship and romantic love, all typically highly abstracted from such topics as skating on frozen lakes, boating trips, the simple beauty of rural toil and the apotheosis of God's Creation in the German landscape. It was during this period that Klopstock and Gerstenberg became set on recovering what Macpherson might have overlooked. Surely, they eventually concluded, such 'Germanic' material was still in abundance in the remoter regions of the north, for example, in the Scottish Isles and Iceland? All that was required was the right poet to uncover and reframe it. One Danish poet seemed to fit the bill exactly: Johannes Ewald (1743–81).

Hitherto, Ewald's literary career had not been distinguished by an interest in Nordic myth and legend, but Ewald had other attributes that Klopstock and

Gerstenberg could admire. First, he was fiercely patriotic, a war veteran and the darling of the common folk in Denmark; second, his poetic talent had remarkable range; third, he was one of the few Danes who admired Klopstock's poetry. Yet, ideally placed as Ewald must have seemed to be to advance the type of field research started by Macpherson, Klopstock and Gerstenberg had not reckoned on his chronic alcoholism. With plans at an advanced stage, Ewald's health took a turn for the worse and, with no understudies waiting in the wings, the project was abandoned. Nevertheless, all was not lost, as personal contact with Klopstock inspired Ewald to turn his not-inconsiderable gifts towards the romance of the Old North in a more sedentary manner.

In 1778, the Royal Theatre in Copenhagen premiered a three-act operatic poem, a *singspiel*, which was not only the first Danish tragedy, but also the first public airing of a drama taking as its subject matter Danish antiquity. This was Ewald's *Balders Død* (The Death of Balder), a work that he had been revising for the stage since 1773. *Balders Død* marked a new direction for Danish literary culture and, in this sense, the beginning of a redefinition of what it meant to be Danish. Such a new departure, however, required careful staging to carry its audience and the first attempt to produce the play in 1777 failed on precisely this count, mainly because Ewald's challenge to the familiar diet of French-inspired farce and Italian-inspired melodrama needed a good deal more visual power. The success of its revival the following year was largely due to the recognition that such a big topic required a big production, and this time the *mise en scène*, supplied by the respected theatrical painter Peter Cramer (1726–82) and the eminent artist Nicolai Abildgaard (1743–1809), provided the necessary epic trappings of the Gothic sublime and supernatural wonder, albeit juxtaposed alongside neoclassical costumery.[14] In this, too, *Balders Død* was precocious. However, what is significant for the way in which the Norse gods would be perceived in the future is the role Ewald gave to Thor and, as Thor's antithesis, to Lok (Loki).

THOR IN EWALD'S *BALDERS DØD*

Ewald's source material for *Balders Død* was Saxo Grammaticus's *Gesta Danorum* (History of the Danes), a work that, under Klopstock's and Gerstenberg's direction, Ewald had mined earlier in the decade for his brilliant, but unstageable, *Rolf Krage*, a verse drama centred on the heroic tragedy of the legendary Danish king.[15]

Taking inspiration from Shakespeare, significantly *Macbeth* and *Othello*, *Balders Død*'s main theme is the prophecy of the death of the most beloved of the Norse gods, Balder (Baldur).[16] This prophecy will come to pass as a consequence of Balder's unrequited love for the Norwegian princess Nanna, and will be caused by a spear forged from Surtur's branch (a kenning for mistletoe), triggering thereafter the destruction of the gods by the giants. Rivalling Balder for Nanna's affections is Hother, the valiant Danish king, and although Nanna wishes to placate both suitors, she is certain that her destiny can only lie with the mortal and not with the god. Thor, perceiving the danger, tries repeatedly to bring the inconsolable Balder to his senses, but his efforts are undermined by the malign Lok. Although much provoked by Hother, Balder refuses to kill him, preferring instead to hold on to the possibility of winning Nanna. This, however, only leaves Hother in a state of suicidal shame, for he has failed to fulfil his oath that one of them should die and, worse still, he has now been granted his life by his rival to whom he is now indebted and so can no longer harm. But neither the pleading of Nanna, nor the wise counsel of Thor, can prevent the scheming Lok from ensuring the prophecy is fulfilled. Armed by Lok with the fatal spear, Hother encounters Balder, and in the confusion that follows, Balder accidentally falls on the spear and dies. It is not just Lok that is the villain of the piece, but also blind passion, as Thor laments, while standing over the body of the slain Balder:

> Gods of battle stern and gory,
> Weep ye over the hero slain!
> Balder, thou the Aser's glory!
> Love, base love, has proved thy bane.[17]

Enthused by the dramatic potential of the literature of Scandinavian antiquity, Ewald would seem to have coded a number of political messages into his drama, and it is Thor, the voice of reason, who can be seen to be articulating them. The drama rests on a perceived conflict between myth and history, personified respectively as Balder and Hother, a conflict that the treacherous Lok wishes to encourage to its ultimate tragic conclusion. Similarly, in the course of this conflict, Denmark and Norway, personified as Hother and Nanna, are denied each other through pride and folly. Passionate possessiveness and self-interest prevail, obscuring the wider perspectives that only Thor and Lok perceive. They are, in this respect, the opposing forces of political harmony and disharmony, an allegorization that strongly resembles the Good-versus-Evil dichotomy that was suggested by Mallet in his analysis of Snorri's account of the Thor and Utgarda-Loki episodes. The outcome in *Balders Død*, however, is not a vindication of Good but one of mutual damage and disunity. In effect, Ewald's depiction of the Scandinavian past functions as a metaphor for the Scandinavian present, divided by ancient rivalries, oblivious of its shared destiny and on course for disaster. Yet, in Ewald's example of the conciliatory Thor, there is the possibility that such divisiveness could be set-aside in the recognition of common values and common cause. What Ewald was arguing, therefore, was the case for pan-Scandinavianism, and his symbolization of Thor as the prospective saviour of the Scandinavian peoples is one that would become, in one fashion or another, the stock-in-trade among National Romanticists.[18]

Although Ewald wrote two more dramas based on old Scandinavian subjects, *Frode* and *Helgo*, neither made it into the public arena, for after numerous mishaps leading to his complete invalidity, he died just three year after the opening of *Balders Død*, oblivious to how profound and long-lasting the impact of his excursion into the Old North would turn out to be. By the turn of the century, Saxo-inspired productions were exploring the possibilities opened by Ewald, including Vicenzo Galeotti's *Lagertha*, the first ballet ever to be set in the Viking Age (1801).[19] If still somewhat tenuous in its grip on the public imagination, Scandinavian Romanticism, rooted in a pride in the derring-do of Gothic heroes and charged by the dramatic emotional colourations of the mythico-legendary past, had arrived on the Danish cultural scene.

KLOPSTOCK AND THE RISE OF GERMAN NATIONALISM

Klopstock, meanwhile, had returned to Germany in 1770, still with his pension and honorary Danish titles, and it was there that he completed *Der Messias* in 1773. His conversion to the cause of what he regarded as Germanic antiquity, including all things Scandinavian and, it would seem, Celtic, remained undiminished. Yet, the hymnal, *naturpoesie* spirit that Klopstock had derived from Macpherson was one thing, but Klopstock's mysticism, his *Gefühlsschwarmerei*, was quite another, and even had a political edge. Ossianic poetry, whatever its merits, was, after all, an assertion of the Celtic role in the history of Britain, and in that, a claim staked by a marginal people. Klopstock and others saw a similar situation among the Germanic peoples: united culturally and linguistically but politically divided and, so, weakened. Was there, then, a figure in German history comparable to Ossian's tribal hero Fingal, who could speak just for the Germans? The answer to this was simple and had been known since the early sixteenth century. It was the first century AD Arminius of the Cherusci. As a model for the kind of reinvention that Thor would soon receive, Klopstock's 35-year span of interest in the life of Arminius is worth consideration, not least for the underlying strains of incipient German nationalism, wherein, at one point, Klopstock sees both the legendary Arminius and the mythological Thor as key symbols for German national revival.[20]

The full story of the ancient German tribal hero Arminius had first surfaced in full with the printing of Tacitus's *Annales* in 1515.[21] Tacitus recounts how, in AD 9, Arminius, leader of the Cherusci, had united the German tribes and vanquished the Roman legions of Varus in the Teutoberg Forest, so halting Roman expansion beyond the Rhine. The significance of the Arminius story to German patriots can be glimpsed in the way in which his name was creatively etymologized: de-Latinized as Hermann and then etymologized not only as 'Army man' but also as cognate with Germani. 'Arminius', according to these arguments, meant both warrior and the very name of the old Germanic peoples, the Hermanns.[22] The Arminius story had not only been studied, but also artistically dramatized, almost from the moment of its discovery. But it was with Klopstock that the Arminius story became central to the politics of German unification, which Klopstock envisaged taking shape in the first place with his own project for a German Republic of Letters.[23]

Klopstock had first touched on the Arminius legend in 1752 in his ode 'Hermann and Thusnelda'. In this, Thusnelda, the hero's bride, celebrates the homecoming of the blood-stained conqueror, exclaiming 'Hermann, Hermann immortal is found!' and regretting that Emperor Augustus himself had not been leading the legions and the whole Roman Empire put to ruin.[24] It is a romantic cameo, patriotically charged but lacking the contemporary political messages of his later formulations of Arminius. It would not be until the height of his Ossian-inspired phase that Klopstock would return to the subject. First, in 1767, came his ode 'Hermann', in which Klopstock dramatizes the 'leader of the most bold' and 'liberator of his fatherland' but, by analogy, vilifies those selfish princes whose resentment of Hermann's prowess led eventually to his murder, for '. . . in his blood lies the soul of he who embraced / The noble thought of Fatherland.'[25] Then, in 1769, interrupting his Hermann sequence, came Klopstock's cryptic and bombastic poem 'Wir und Sie' (Us and Them), seemingly an attack on British naval authority and a lamentation over the apparent feebleness of 'the fatherland' when it came to defying it. Here, Klopstock begins and ends by invoking the spirit of Thor in what would appear to be a criticism of the Prussian aristocracy's contempt for traditional German culture: 'What has your fatherland done to you, Thor? / I despise it. Does your heart not burn at the sound of its name?' The eleven stanzas enclosed in this frame amount to a polemic aimed at an unnamed opposition. As both the composer George Frideric Handel (1685–1759) and the baroque painter Godfrey Kneller (1646–1753) are mentioned in the poem as examples of what 'we' can accomplish, and as both were Germans who became naturalized as English, it seems likely that the castigated 'them' of the poem are the English, in the sense of the Anglo-Saxons, rather than the broader assignation of the British. It is not only the English theft of German talent that enrages Klopstock, but also English accomplishments in the sciences and, worse still, English naval prowess, against which the Germans can offer no immediate rival:

> They are victorious in the dark battle,
> Where ship lays itself thundering against ship!
> We conquered once like them!

On all counts, claims Klopstock, a reinvigorated Germany could outstrip anyone, and he longs for a revival of the spirit of Hermann:

> When our princes are Hermanns,
> Our armies are Cheruscans!
> Cheruscans, cold and keen!

Were such a revitalization possible, then none could stand against the Germans, particularly, it would seem, the English:

> Oh, if we could only see them in that battle
> Which we alone understand, just once close up
> With bright steel.[26]

Of course, all this can simply be dismissed as an obscure rant, and what specifically it was that excited Klopstock's resentment of the English is hard to pinpoint. Certainly, he was disdainful of post-Miltonic English poetry and he may well have believed that the British, as Prussian allies, had not been as helpful as they might have been during the Seven Years War (1754 and 1756–63), from which Britain emerged as the most powerful colonial nation with an unassailable navy. However, his resentment of Frederick the Great's neglect of German cultural traditions remained explicit. Klopstock's invocation of Thor as the god of a lost – or, rather, neglected – spirit of German courage and creativity is a marker of how mythological personages were becoming a rallying point for nationalist causes, whose targets were not only foreign powers, but also domestic rulers who failed to recognize the rich treasures of their own heritage.

In the same year as Klopstock wrote 'Wir und Sie', he composed the first of three *bardiets* about Hermann, dramatic poems for the stage. 'Hermanns Schlacht' (Hermann's Battle) locates the defeat of Varus as the paramount event in German history, contrasting the haughty and unjust tyranny of Rome with the innate decency and just cause of the Germans. The theme here is militant German unity, which is metaphoricized as 'the storm . . . from the north', as one bard says, and poignantly illustrated by the selfless sacrifice of the leader of a druid tribe, a certain Werdomar, a name that Klopstock had long ago adopted as his cognomen.[27] The two following *bardiets* did not appear until the 1780s, over ten years after Klopstock's return to Germany. Although it is clear that he had been working on them for much of the 1770s, doubts about Ossian's pedigree troubled him throughout the 1780s, and by the 1790s he regretfully drew a veil over the whole affair. Nevertheless, 'Hermann und die Fürsten' (Hermann and the Princes) of 1784 and 'Hermanns Tod' (The Death of Hermann) of 1787, remain very much in the style and spirit of Ossian.[28]

Unlike 'Hermanns Schlacht' these latter *bardiets* are tragedies that explore the antithesis of the initial theme of German unity – German discord. In the first, set on the eve of another battle, seven years after the defeat of Varus, Hermann is portrayed as isolated and resented by the quarrelsome princes. Desertion, treachery and lust for power lead inevitably to near destruction, and though the gods love Hermann for his patriotism, he is unable to unite the tribes under his leadership. Yet, although ruination is almost upon him, he continues to proclaim the ideal of German unity and independence in the face of bitter realities. In the

final and longest *bardiet*, civil war rages. Hermann is besieged by his own countrymen and is doomed to die with all he loves. Albeit closely following Tacitus in
the description of Arminius's demise, Klopstock's aim is to set forward a critique
of a factionalized, visionless Germany, while at the same time idealizing the 'death
before defeat' spirit deep in the German soul.[29]

'Hermanns Tod' was to be Klopstock's last dalliance with both Arminius and
the time when 'Fingal fought and Ossian sung'.[30] Yet Arminius, the gods of the
Old North and Ossian – irrespective, in this last case, of Macpherson's discredit
– continued to be held up as symbols of German national pride and models for
national unity on into, and well beyond, the wars waged by Napoleon, who was
also so enamoured of the Scot that he carried a copy of *The Poems of Ossian* into
battle. When Goethe gave praise to Klopstock's verse, he meant the forging of a
uniquely German poetic voice, free from imitation. But there was more to it than
this. Those medievalized patriotic yearnings that fuelled burgeoning romantic
sensibilities were rapidly transformed into National Romanticism and, thereafter,
into a more belligerent nationalism.[31] From Klopstockian notions of cultural
and linguistic autonomy to ideas of a political hegemony incorporating those
regions identified as historically German; from seemingly abstract claims about
a German *kulturnation* to concrete claims about German soil, was no great step.
Klopstock's ideology typically employed the rhetoric of a transcendent purity
of origin and being, and this too soon hardened into notions of racial superiority and a discipline of cultural productivity that disapproved of anything that
might appear to adulterate the purity of the project's means and ends. Just how
Klopstock's patriotism was being seen by a new generation of literary enthusiasts
is a fair indication of the way things were moving.

On 12 September 1772, a group of student poets, a bardic brotherhood from
the University of Göttingen in Lower Saxony, gathered together at midnight in
a leafy glade. Bedecked with oak sprigs and amid declarations to the moon and
the stars, they joined hands, swore eternal friendship and set about cavorting
round an old oak tree. They then consecrated the ground to German poetry
and announced themselves to be Der Hainbund (The Covenant of the Grove).[32]
Motivating them was the poetry of Klopstock; indeed, their very name was
derived from Klopstock's bardic ode 'Der Hugel und Der Hain' (The Hill and
the Grove), in which one bard declares to two others that 'The stream on the
hill murmurs of Zeus, / Of Wodin the stream in the grove.'[33] As Der Hainbund

rightly understood, Klopstock was asserting that the time was due for the long neglected genius of German poetry to take its place alongside that of Ancient Greece. On 2 July 1773, they met again. It was Klopstock's 49th birthday. This time the gathering celebrated by building a bonfire and stoking it with books that fell short of Klopstock's ideals. It was the work of a one-time devotee and imitator of Klopstock, Christoph Martin Wieland (1733–1813), that did most to fuel the fire, for, in recent years, Wieland had turned his back on Klopstockian bardic enthusiasms in favour of neoclassical dramas in the French style. For Der Hainbund, Wieland was an apostate. The ritualization of their devotion to Klopstock and their dutiful distaste for Wieland, was, as Joep Leerssen amusingly puts it in a slightly different context, a distinction between 'the frugal, virtuous sons of the [German] soil and the ooh-la-la culture of frivolous France'.[34] In the coming decades, it was to become central to the definition of German identity, whereby anything that was deemed to be out of step would be consigned to the ashes of history.

Thus far, we can see a build up of proto-nationalist tensions and pressures in which figures from antiquity, whether historically real or mythico-legendary, were becoming idealized versions of national character and, so, of the cultural and historical legitimacy of an actual or would-be nation's identity. In the figure of Klopstock, one can perceive that this tendency has a kind of desperate, even belligerent, acquisitiveness; whereas with his protégé Ewald, this same tendency looks towards a more united future. As regards ideas about Thor in the late eighteenth century, it is already apparent that there are two interpretations of him. On the one hand, from Ewald, Thor is a redemptive figure; on the other, from Klopstock, he is the neglected spirit of German power and authority. To put it simply, one interpretation emphasizes Thor as protector, the other emphasizes him as aggressor. During the nineteenth century, this difference in emphasis would, in certain cases, become a polarization and along with this sharpening divide would come less abstract interpretations of national culture extending beyond symbolism into matters of territorial ownership. Meanwhile, in Denmark, the step change towards a more nationalistic outlook came with the poet Adam Oehlenschläger (1779–1850) and, for him, there was no finer image of Scandinavian character than Thor.

THOR AND DANISH NATIONAL ROMANTICISM

Klopstock and Oehlenschläger could never have met, although Oehlenschläger's mother reported to her son that Klopstock's personality was too 'exaggerated in style' for her taste.[35] Not that this diminished Oehlenschläger's admiration for the man and the service he had done to Danish letters in giving direction to Ewald.[36] Perhaps not surprisingly, the pan-Germanic literary nationalism espoused by Klopstock, Gerstenberg and succeeding generations of German intellectuals had not taken root in Scandinavia. Romantic sensibilities and the Napoleonic wars sharpened and localized nationalist movements, so that separate Scandinavian nations eagerly looked forward to reclaiming their national identities, purifying their languages of the contamination that had resulted from the political domination of neighbours, and asserting their right to independence. For the kingdom of Denmark, this meant that Norway slipped away from its control. The Danish monarchy was further undermined when, during the Napoleonic wars, its membership of the Armed Neutrality of the North brought the country into conflict with Britain in 1801 and 1807, when, in this last instance, Copenhagen was bombarded by the British Royal Navy. Forced to seek protection from France, Denmark was harnessed to Napoleon's fate, which led, eventually, to bankruptcy and a further weakening of monarchic absolutism. Among the educated, a new liberalism opposed to state authoritarianism and fired with enthusiasm for a specifically Scandinavian cultural identity was gaining ground. It was in this political climate that Oehlenschläger began to hone his considerable poetic talent.

If Ewald had set the stage for Oehlenschläger, it was German-inspired Romanticism that directed the performance. In 1802, the philosopher and scientist Henrik Steffens (1773–1845) returned to Copenhagen after four years in Germany, where he had studied under Friedrich von Schelling (1775–1854) at the University of Jena, the leading figure in German Romantic philosophy; and, in his subsequent two-year stay at the University of Freiburg, Steffens had been profoundly influenced by Friedrich Werner (1768–1823), a disciple of Rousseau.[37] During the course of 1802, Steffens gave nine lectures at Copenhagen's Valkendorffs Kollegium. Attending them all was Oehlenschläger, and it is reported that Steffens personally instilled in him the key principles of German Romanticism in a single conversation lasting 16 hours.[38] A deep reverence for the sublimity of nature and passionate nationalism combined in

Oehlenschläger as they had in no other, and in his long-held enthusiasm for Nordic myth and history he found the perfect arena in which to articulate his ideas. For Oehlenschläger this was a specifically Scandinavian, at times specifically Danish, enterprise and it was to Anders Sørensen Vedel's late sixteenth-century translations of Saxo Grammaticus that he turned, where he could study, absorb and revive native Danish expressions long since fallen into disuse.[39]

Oehlenschläger's first collection of poetry was composed in a state of ecstasy during the same year that he attended Steffens' lectures. Among the collection was the epoch-making 'Guldhornene' (The Golden Horns), published in *Digte* (1803), considered to be the manifesto of Danish National Romanticism. The subject of the poem is two elaborately decorated fifth-century golden drinking horns discovered in 1639 and 1734 in southern Jutland, which had been stolen from the royal cabinet in Copenhagen in the same year that Steffens had converted Oehlenschläger to the causes of Romantic idealism.[40] In 'Guldhornene', Oehlenschläger sees the loss of the horns as analogous with the disseverance of the Danes from their ancient history; a betrayal of national identity, he implies, that had received its greatest disavowal from rationalist intellectuals. Yet, the horns also symbolize the chance to recover and embrace a lost nobility of national character. As the gods proclaim in the poem, this achievement would not be for ordinary folk but,

> For the chosen few
> Who understand our gift,
> Who are unfettered by earthly chains
> But whose souls rise
> To the summit of eternity,
> Who can sense the High Place
> In Nature's eye.[41]

Over the course of the next 20 years, Oehlenschläger produced a vast store of poetry and drama on mythological and legendary subjects, including the northern tragedies *Hakon Jarl* (Earl Hakon, 1807), *Baldur hin Gode* (Balder the Good, 1808), a prose version of the eddic poem 'Völundarkviða' (The Lay of Volund), the cycle of verse-romances *Helge* (1814) and several paeans to Saxo, the 'Spirit of Antiquity'. Oehlenschläger's emphasis on the primacy and sacrality of Nature led him inevitably to the conflict at the heart of Norse mythology: the enmity between gods and giants. In 1819, now professor of aesthetics in Copenhagen, he published his longest verse epic *Nordens Guder: et episk digte* (Gods of the North: An Epic Poem). All of Oehlenschläger's previous musings on Norse myth, including his largely comic, eddic-inspired 'Thors Reise til Jotunheim' (Thor's Journey to the Land of the Giants, 1806), can be regarded as a rehearsal for this magnum opus. Oehlenschläger gave Thor the leading role.

In the brief introduction to *Nordens Guder*, Oehlenschläger explains that, 'The gods and the giants represent the two conflicting powers of nature: the creative embellishing power; and the defacing destructive one'.[42] Loke (Loki) represents 'the variable spirit of the age', which vacillates between both gods and giants and, as such, is a duality of the god Asa Loke and the giant Utgard Loke. As Oehlenschläger's nineteenth-century English translator William E. Frye observes, Loke equates to moral degeneracy, both spiritual and physical.[43] Central to the conflict in Nature is the arch-enemy of the giants, Thor, whom Oehlenschläger presents as the power that controls or leavens those forces of Nature that might harm the virtuous and innocent. In the father and son relationship between Odin and Thor is an expression of a moral and physical ideal, the antithesis of Loke and the giants.

Nordens Guder ranges freely, although not without considerable scholarly insight, across eddic myth. Framing the narrative is the loss to the giants of Thor's hammer and its eventual recovery. Loss and recovery are, indeed, central to all that intervenes, with Thor acting as the agent of recovery and Loke as the agent of loss. The theft of Sif's hair, the enfeebling abduction of Iduna, the deadly threat posed when Freyja is demanded by the giants as the price for Thor's hammer, are all potential catastrophes encouraged by the mendacious Loke, and all averted by Thor. Only when the rash Tyr loses his hand while binding the wolf Fenrir and, at the same time, Frey forfeits his sword in his love for the giantess Gerda, does Thor stray from the paths of virtue and momentarily becomes that self-same force against which he is set in opposition. Perceiving that, 'In this way the influence of the giants on the gods is apparent', he wildly and unjustly vents his anger against mankind, but even here he recovers his reason, repents, and compensates his victims with eternal bliss. Thor's role, then, is that of defender and healer. Like 'the chosen few' of 'Guldhornene', Thor is the hope of the future, and it is to Thor that a seeress reveals herself at the close of the drama, prophesying the ultimate doom of the gods but, thereafter, in what is clearly a Christian-inspired revelation, 'with the assurance of a better life to come, together with complete innocence and joy'. It is tempting to regard Oehlenschläger's depiction of Thor as a dramatic metaphor for the role he had defined for himself: the guardian and champion of Scandinavian historical integrity, charged with the recovery of Danish pride.[44] In 1829, in Lund, Sweden, Oehlenschläger was crowned with laurels and celebrated as 'The Nordic king of singers and heir apparent of the world of poetry' by Bishop Esaias Tegnér (1782–1846), the celebrated poet-translator of the Norse romance *Frithiofs saga* (1825), and acknowledged as the greatest Swedish poet of the Romantic Age.[45] Relations between Sweden and Denmark, at least in terms of the accord between artists, had clearly come some distance since the fierce scholarly debates of the Enlightenment period.

THOR IN SWEDEN

Taking a lead from what Ewald, Klopstock and Oehlenschläger had set in motion in Copenhagen, something similar was at work among the Swedes, whose own history of investigations into their origins in Scandinavian pre-history continued to play a significant role in ideas about Swedish cultural identity. Olof Rudbeck's 'Atlantica' theory may have long ago lost credibility in scholarly circles, but in the late eighteenth and early nineteenth centuries, his attempts to place Gothic Sweden at the centre of world civilization were recalled with admiration by Swedish artists and patriotic thinkers. Also, as in Denmark, many Swedes were equally keen to achieve a break from prevailing tastes for French art and literature, and it was the Ossian phenomenon that provided both the model and the incentive.[46] Again, like the Danes, certain Swedish literary artists saw their own cultural redeemer in the image of Thor.

The earliest pronouncements on Swedish antiquity and its relevance to modern Swedish literary endeavours were made in 1787 by Thomas Thorild (1759–1808), who penned his prophetic poem 'Harmen' (Indignation). Perhaps owing more to Thorild's knowledge of the classics than to that of the eddas, and certainly strongly influenced in his conception of Thor by the Christian mysticism of Emanuel Swedenborg (1688–1772), the Thor of 'Harmen' is a champion of a faith free of the oppressive doctrines of religious leaders. In response, he is condemned as a dangerous heretic:

> Burn!
> Burn him! Cry
> The holy men, the tyrants and learned men:
> And fire flames against the cloud in the sky.[47]

It took two decades before Thorild's ideas had significant impact, but from the end of the first decade of the nineteenth century, the Nordic Revival in Sweden was apace, due largely to the efforts of two interrelated schools of thought. On the one hand were the Gothicists, whose enthusiasms were promulgated through their publication *Iduna*. For the Gothicists, northern antiquity required no reference to any other mythological system or cultural tradition. On the other were the Fosforists, who, in their relatively short-lived journal *Fosforos*, sought to elevate the status of northern antiquity by determinedly equating it to other mythological systems, notably Greek, Hindu and Judaeo-Christian. The originator of the Fosforist movement, a young poet who was later to become a professor of philosophy and then aesthetics at the University of Uppsala, was Daniel Amadeus Atterbom (1790–1855), a devotee of the works of Rudbeck.

Obsessed with the poetical and literary store of Scandinavian antiquity since childhood, Atterbom was set on giving this subject matter the highest possible place in the literary canon and the endeavours of his contemporaries, and so to 'seize the Swedish heart with Swedish songs', a resolve that did not at first win unanimous approval.[48] In the 'Prolog' to the launch of *Fosforos* in 1810, Atterbom proclaimed a poetic rallying cry to his countrymen, referring to them as the 'sons of Thor'.[49] The following year, inspired by the romantic cadences of Adam Oehlenschläger's early verse, he published 'Skaldarmål' (Speech of the Poet), a tribute to Scandinavian myth and legend, a repudiation of the declining standards of modernity, and a plea for a national Swedish poetry based on indigenous Scandinavian models. Along with it, Atterbom presented his copious notes on his mythological sources, which, in themselves, were more influential in Swedish intellectual circles than the verses which they annotated. Atterbom's theories attracted both praise and criticism in equal measure in correspondence from Gothicist luminaries such as Lars Hammarskjöld (1785–1827) and Esaias Tegnér.

Thor, explained Atterbom, is the greatest of the Norse gods, a personification of the sun, a 'symbol of the masculine principle of the Deity, light, or reason, which fertilizes the nature element or the original imagination, unites the form and content and thereby becomes the origin of the real creation.[50] In essence, claimed Atterbom, Thor is the Nordic corollary of Vishnu and Christ. Despite later acknowledging certain errors in his 'lost fantasy of the north', what really mattered for Atterbom was an 'appeal to the genius of Sweden' and a desire to see the political revitalization of the Scandinavia states, a precondition of which was a recovery of the age of mythology.[51] Irrespective of early criticism and, in 1820, a satirical debunking by J. M. Stjernstolpe of Atterbom's theories in his 'Mytologierna eller gudatvisten' (The Mythologies, or the Dispute of the Gods), which sees the Norse gods humbled by those of Ancient Greece,[52] Atterbom's campaign eventually succeeded in promoting the notion of a Swedish national poetry. Some 30 years on from the publication of 'Skaldarmål', Atterbom was still refining his Thor-inspired 'hero-religion' according to the principles of what he declared to be 'nature philosophy'. Defending his Thor-centred hyperboreism, Atterbom explains that Thor

> represented the supporting and mediating power, whose glory we imagine most beautiful in the form of the element of light ... The meaning is not that Thor had his seat in the sun, but that the sun in certain *Beziehungen* [connections/relations] was an image of his majesty ...[53]

Atterbom's theories, although evidently influential, grew increasingly complex and were, for some, rather too complex; for example, his Fosforist colleague Wilhelm Fredrik Palmblad (1733–1852) somewhat cuttingly remarked that Atterbom's schematization would not be completed unless 'God deigns to prolong his life by eighty years'.[54] Nonetheless, Atterbom's Thor, like Oehlenschläger's, is at one and the same time, a transcendent figure and a champion of the ordinary folk; that is to say, specifically and, in many ways, exclusively the folk of true Scandinavian stock. This proprietary view of Thor among Scandinavian mythographers was one that could readily be translated from the language of aesthetic mysticism into that of a political ideology. Back in Copenhagen, which remained the centre of the Nordic renaissance, one commentator was doing just that.

THOR AND DANISH NATIONALISM

Theologian, historian, poet, educator, Lutheran minister, and politician, the exceptionally prolific N. F. S. Grundtvig (1783–1872) was at the forefront of

reformist liberalism in Denmark. Like Oehlenschläger, Grundtvig attended
Henrik Steffens' lectures in 1802, like Oehlenschläger he was inspired by them,
and like Oehlenschläger he saw Old Norse mythology as the key literature on
which to expound his ideas. Yet not even Oehlenschläger could rival the zeal and
absolute conviction with which Grundtvig approached his campaign to revivify
Danish culture and learning through an understanding of northern mythology:
Grundtvig regarded the eddas as not only a neglected heritage, but also as a
symbolic expression of the 'truth' of the northern soul. If Oehlenschläger was
the guardian of the old religion, Grundtvig was its evangelist, and he saw no
contradiction between this vocation and his undeniably profound Christian faith;
rather, he regarded the two as mutually stimulating or, even more than this for
the dulled northern psyche, mutually essential.

Among his formidable output of translations and commentaries, the summa-
tion of Grundtvig's thinking on northern mythology was his *Nordens Mythologi
eller Sindbilled-Sprog, historisk-poetisk udviklet og oplyst* (The Mythology or
Symbolic Language of the North, an historical and poetic exposition and explanation), published in 1832 as a considerably revised and enhanced presentation
of his thoughts on the subject in 1808.[55] In the introduction, Grundtvig sets out
his ideas for establishing a characteristic national literature for Denmark and the
North generally, including the English, whom he felt had a long road to travel
before they could benefit from their northernness. The chief problem, argues
Grundtvig, is 'Rome', meaning everything associated with Latin learning: art,
literature and religion. If Klopstock had been set on elevating the German bards
to the heights of the Greek poets, Grundtvig's intention was to downgrade the
classicism of Ancient Rome to the point of complete irrelevance. In effect, he
wished it driven from the North. By contrast, inherent in Greek mythology, says
Grundtvig, is a philosophy as admirable as that of the North, not that he thought
that the two should be confused. Latinate culture was to Grundtvig the greatest
inhibition holding back the northern peoples, who, once buoyed by a pride in
their own ancient history and educated with knowledge of their own mythology,
would be freed from the shackles of foreign cultural oppression.

The myths of the eddas are not just used to frame Grundtvig's argument –
peppered as it is with references to Old Norse mythological personages and
events – they *are* his argument, for what he perceives in northern myth is the
symbology of a contemporary battle against all that is deleterious to the probity

and power of the North, all that is alien to it. The central mythic expression of this battle is the diametric opposition of gods and giants, and, more subtly, the opposition between Thor and Loke. In the person of Thor is the liberating force of Nature, with man at one with his world and able to explore his own unique potential. In the person of Loke, and his complex double-dealing between gods and giants, is debilitating Culture, imprisoning mankind in convention, rationalism, regulation and restraint. Unlike Oehlenschläger's 'chosen few', Grundtvig believed that the reclamation of Thor was something that was for everyone, the people, *folktet*. However, Grundtvig's famous dictum 'Freedom for Loke as well as for Thor' suggests a more complex attitude to Loke than simply desiring the obliteration of all that he represented. The opinions of Loke, debilitating though they might be, were, for Grundtvig, defensible as a democratic right to free speech, and *this* the liberating spirit of Thor would not deny, no matter what the provocation.[56]

A schematization of Grundtvig's mythico-political manifesto would be as follows: on the side of Thor are Nature, life, popular and primarily oral folk 'literature', spirituality, tolerance, and the North; on the side of Loke are Culture (meaning Latinate culture), death, the written literature of the privileged few in the establishment, materialism, censorship, and 'Rome'.[57] With the triumph of Thor over Loke will come the triumph of youth over age, the renaissance of the North. And it was to the young that Grundtvig felt that this message should be most forcefully delivered. To this end, it was his aim that the teaching of Old Norse myth should play a central role in a Danish national curriculum to be delivered in Folk High Schools across the country, the first of which was founded in a Danish-speaking area of Slesvig in 1844. The fact that Grundtvig's plan for a Norse-based, Thor-inspired, curriculum in the High Schools did not eventually succeed, being regarded as somewhat eccentric by his critics, does not detract from the huge influence that it had on the consciousness of the rural communities, so long sidelined and ignored in national politics, nor did it obscure the potency of Grundtvig's nationalism.[58] In 1832, Frederick VI of Denmark was becoming increasingly discomfited by the populism generated by the overthrow of the absolute monarchy of King Louis Philippe in France two years earlier, the so-called July Revolution. Unsettled even further by Grundtvig's campaign against Loke, Danish absolutism would not long survive and in 1848 the constitution was reformed and what remained of absolutism abolished. Yet

Grundtvig's targets were not merely the agencies of oppression in his homeland and the pernicious influence of 'Rome', there was an ever more worrying target just to the south: Prussia and the wider Germany. On these peoples the spirit of 'Rome' was heavily, perhaps indelibly, imprinted and what was more they posed the most obvious and direct threat to the Danish fatherland.

German militarism looked increasingly ominous to the Danes as the century progressed, particularly in respect of the agitation to break free from Danish authority in the duchies of Slesvig and Holstein, where the German language pre-dominated, and where separatist movements were encouraged by the Prussians. In 1838, Grundtvig lectured in Copenhagen on 'Teutonism', reminding his audience of the repressive measures taken by the Prussian government against reformists in German universities in the years 1815–20, declaring that he lacked historical impartiality and admitting that, 'I have a reputation for being almost as bitter an enemy of the Germans as of the Romans', although making it clear that his quarrel was not with the German people themselves. Even so, a Prussian annexation of the duchies, thought Grundtvig, could well be the thin end of the wedge, for he feared that Denmark might be 'swallowed up whole' should the disparate German states achieve political unification and therefore be able to combine themselves into one 'monstrous German war-machine'.[59] As well as worrying that a united Germany might menace Danish sovereignty, Grundtvig suggested that Danish cultural identity could also find itself subordinated: 'Denmark is no more the tail of Germany than the Norse spirit is a sprite serving the Imperial German reason'.[60] As Grundtvig and his contemporaries knew very well, German intellectuals did not always distinguish fully between German and Germanic. It is to the arguments behind this reasoning and its consequences that we turn next.

6

Thor in Germany: From Grimm to Himmler

In the National Museum of Stockholm there is an early eleventh-century, granite baptismal font, about two feet high and two feet eight inches in diameter. Engraved around the font's barrel are eight rectangular scenes, seven of which are quite clearly Christian inspirations: the Fall, Baptism, Confirmation, Heavenly Mysteries, Paradise, the Vine and the Crucifixion. The sixth in the sequence is, however, anomalous: a depiction of Thor. Bearded and bearing scars on his forehead – perhaps as a result of his confrontation with the giant Hrungnir – Thor brandishes Mjollnir in one hand, and in the other, an oar – most likely an allusion to his attempt to bait the Midgard Serpent. As a collocation of Christian and Norse religious imagery set together on wood or stone, the font is typical of many similar remnants of Viking Age hybridized beliefs found across Europe. Nevertheless, in the latter decades of the nineteenth century, this particular engraving carried a much larger significance for at least one expert in Scandinavian antiquity, the expatriate English runologist, philologist and, from 1855, professor at the University of Copenhagen George Stephens (1813–95).

Stephens' attention had been drawn to the font by Rev. Claes Johan Ljungström whose colleague, Rev. M. Florell, had rescued it from the ruins of the old church at Ottrava in Vástergotland and taken it to the nearby new church at Dimbo. It was from there that Ljungström sent Stephens a detailed drawing of the carvings. Stephens considered the Thor carving to be wholly exceptional and published *Thunor the Thunderer, carved on a Scandinavian font of about the year 1000. The first yet found God-figure of our Scando-Gothic forefathers* in state of some excitement in 1878.[1] Setting aside, for now, who Stephens might have meant by 'our Scando-Gothic forefathers', one would have to say that Stephens' commentary is somewhat bizarre. It begins, unannounced, with a 13-page medieval sermon that Stephens imagines would have accompanied the original unveiling of the font, wherein the imagined preacher declares about the Thor panel, 'Children, whenever you see your Thur [Thor], resolve to be no less daring and dauntless against foul wight and false wanderer and fierce waylayer than he.'[2] Having thereafter apologized to his reader for 'this unexpected little homily, to some perhaps a mere rhapsody',[3] Stephens delivers a learned analysis of Thor motifs on monuments and rune carvings across Scandinavia and England. Then, again without warning or conjunction, Stephens turns briefly to the failure of English and, seemingly more worryingly, German scholars to recognize the presence of Thunor in line 177 of *Beowulf*.[4] That said, he concludes with 'The Moral of the Whole', effectively a rant against all things modern and a paean to the still present spirit of the morally impeccable and unfailingly protective Thunor:

THUNOR, speaking alway of STRENGTH, WORK, DUTY, TRUTH, HONOR
BRIGHT. *He* is Truly the 'Land-áss', the Land-Ans, the Guardian Genie of
the Fatherland, the 'Ótti Jötna', the dread of every Bug and Ogre; the 'Bani tröll-
quenna', the relentless slayer of Troll and Hag and Witch-quean, whether tripping
winsome in guise of Light-angel fair, or stiffly striding with scowling fire-red
balls and matted snake-hair, her crooked fingers grasping the torch and dagger of
destruction and despair.

God help that Heart, that Home, that Land, that Age where

NO THUNOR IS![5]

While all this is certainly oddly conceived, Stephens' outpouring was wholly consistent with the pronouncements of N. F. S. Grundtvig – like Grundtvig, Stephens believed that the ownership of Norse mythology was at stake; part of which entailed establishing the true character and – in a symbolic sense – the loyalty of Thor. As Stephens well knew, the prize for winning possession of the mythological past was not just gaining the high ground of philological discourse, and so laying claim to the linguistic and cultural heritage of the north European peoples, but also, once and for all, to underwrite the commonality of the territories on which these peoples were traditionally settled. In short, what Stephens saw in the Thor font was a racial, moral and political ideology that united the northern peoples, among whom he included the English, and from which he excluded the Germans. The Thor font spoke for pan-Scandinavianism and against pan-Germanicism, and when Stephens rails against the 'crooked fingers' of trolls, he is signalling, among other things, German ambitions to arrogate the heritage of the Old North and political ascendancy over its inheritors along with it. Thus, when Stephens refers to 'our Scando-Gothic forefathers', it is quite clear whom he does *not* mean.

Yet by 1878, as Stephens also surely knew, the spoils had already gone beyond the reach of his Scandinavian Thor and lay largely in the possession of a German Thor. The political marker of this was the second Slesvig-Holstein war of 1864, which finally obliged the Danes to cede the duchies to their southern neighbour, a humiliation partly justified by Denmark's enemies on both contemporary and ancient linguistic grounds, just as Grundtvig had feared back in 1838. Indeed, by the time Stephens was expostulating about German 'trolls', the Slesvig-Holstein affair was widely regarded by Danish patriots as the thin end of the wedge. As Andrew Wawn points out in his study of Stephens' career, the failure of the English to come to the aid of the Danes, 'their "nearest kin" and "cousins" of Thunor', was regarded by Stephens as unforgiveable.[6]

Stephens' Germanophobia was rarely below the surface of his voluminous output as a philologist. In 1852 he declared that German linguistic theories were 'an insult to our nationality and scholarship' and feared 'the wholesale annexation, the theft bodily, by Germany in modern times ... of the whole mythic store of Scandinavia and England',[7] a view he underlined five years later in his translation *The Scandinavian Question: Practical Reflections by Arnliot Gellina. Translated from the Swedish Original by an English Scandinavian* (1857). In all this, Stephens' target was quite expressly the philological theories of Jacob Grimm (1785–1863), whose unifying principles of comparative linguistics were profoundly at odds with Stephens' own somewhat eccentric and often contradictory belief in linguistic diversity and multiplicity.

THE POLITICS OF LANGUAGE

Jacob Grimm and his brother Wilhelm (1786–1859) are probably best remembered for their collection of folktales, gleaned, claimed the brothers, from the rural communities of Germany and revised and supplemented from 1812 to 1857 as *Kinder- und Hausmärchen* (Children's and Household Tales). Read by most people since as diversions in the nursery, the Grimm brothers' actual intention was to grant to the German people, the *Volk*, something tantamount to a national epic comprising traditional lore, *sagen* and *lieder*. It was an undertaking that had been urged since the late eighteenth century, most notably by the *kulturnation* enthusiasm and *Volkslieder* garnering of Herder. This in turn was given a more explicit political and chauvinist direction by Johann Gottlieb Fichte (1762–1814) in his *Reden an die deutsche Nation* (Addresses to the German People) of 1808, which advocated individual subordination to the 'higher purpose' of the German nation, a social duty founded in an all-consuming 'love of the fatherland'.[8] In the first decade of the nineteenth century, the decade of the ascendancy of Napoleon and, as a consequence, a period of great damage to German pride, defining what it was to be German was an undertaking that, perhaps inevitably, gathered increased urgency.

Yet, establishing the uniqueness of an indigenous German culture was, for the Grimms, a concern that went beyond both traditional folktale and national boundaries – actual or proposed – and into an investigation of the essence and influence of the German language and, thus inevitably, into the realms of myth. In Wilhelm Grimm's edition of traditional Danish folk literature, *Altdänische Heldenlieder, Balladen und Märchen* (Old Danish Heroic Lays, Ballads, and Folktales) of 1811, he was already espousing the essential 'Germanness' of this Scandinavian material, a proposition to which Jacob Grimm gave far-reaching significance in his compendious *Deutsche Mythologie* (German Mythology) of 1835 and one that was axiomatic in his *Deutsche Grammatik* (German Grammar) of 1819.[9] In these works lay certain ideas that, as Stephens knew very well some decades later, would soon surface in crude form as the intellectual bulwark for an aggressive German nationalism. 'So much evil may flow from one rash assumption!' was Stephens' assessment of the Grimms' pan-Germanic theories.[10] Stephens was surely referring to Jacob Grimm's definition of 1846 in which he sees language, nation and ethnicity as all being aspects of the same thing: 'Let me begin with a question, What is a people? – and reply with the equally simple answer: A people is the sum total of persons speaking the same language.'[11] As Grundtvig, Stephens and others in Scandinavia already knew, Grimm's notion of the 'same language' also included any language that could be perceived as having a debt to the German language.

The politics of Jacob Grimm can appear contradictory when considered from a modern vantage point. On the one hand were his views on German domestic policy, for as a liberal and a democrat, Grimm's career was characterized by his belief in the necessity of constitutional reform, a cause that brought him into conflict with the authorities, costing him his professorship at Göttingen in 1837.[12] On the other were Grimm's patriotic ideas concerning German foreign relations and policies; for instance, his views concerning German entitlement to the duchies of Slesvig and Holstein at the expense of Denmark, which were made abundantly clear to the Frankfurt National Assembly of 1848 when he asserted that 'other nations would not tolerate even a sod to be taken off the dwelling place of their renowned ancestors'.[13] Such aggressive political statements were entirely consistent with the intellectual arguments Grimm set out in his astonishingly ambitious philological projects, which, taken together, had profound implications for Old Norse mythology and its relationship to a wider Germanic identity. In the introduction to *Deutsche Mythologie*, Grimm declared his intention:

> I have undertaken to collect and set forth all that can now be known of German heathen-ism, and that exclusively of the complete system of Norse mythology. By such limitation I hope to gain clearness and space, and to sharpen our vision for a criticism of the Old German faith, so far as it stands opposed to the Norse, or aloof from it; so that we need only concern ourselves with the latter, where in substance or tendency it coincides with that of inland Germany.[14]

The qualifying expression 'so far as it stands opposed to the Norse, or aloof from it' is telling, for behind it lies what Tom Shippey has called Grimm's 'buried theses'.[15] Grimm is not signifying that the hunt for the Old German faith is a separate undertaking from the steady accumulation of knowledge about Old Norse mythology; on the contrary, he is signifying a process of investigation that implicitly incorporates Old Norse mythology into a Germanic heritage in which the Old German faith played a central, indeed formative, role.

The broad argument underlying Grimm's introductory remarks is, first, that mythology and language are of equal importance in the effort to prove that Scandinavia is an inextricable part of a Germanic past; and second, that the Scandinavian languages are fundamentally Germanic dialects. Behind these dialects lie the primary language and religion of the Germanic territories, and it was this that Grimm was determined to reveal, thus allowing the inference that Old Norse mythology was a derivation of it. Given the ancient migrations northward from Germany to Scandinavia, Germany would be the place where the *ur*-gods of the *ur*-religion would be discovered in the remnants of a primitive Germanic language. In the absence of a coherent body of inland German mythology, this language would need to be reconstructed from whatever was available: place names and naming practices generally, Christian religious commentary from the first millennium and the Middle Ages, ancient inscriptions and – in the degradation of myth – folk tale and folk language.[16]

The linguistic element of this argument, as set out in Grimm's *Deutsche Grammatik*, was one that ran contrary to the views of his Danish counterpart Rasmus Rask (1787–1832), who rejected Grimmean linguistic theories and resented the German appropriation of his own theories. While Rask acknowledged the relationship among a wide range of northern tongues, he argued that the Scandinavian languages were far too divergent from the German to be included in Grimm's Germanic dialect group and, therefore, that the Scandinavians are a distinct 'people'. Causing Rask particular irritation was Grimm's generic use of the term 'Deutsche' (as in *Deutsche Grammatik* and *Deutsche Mythologie*), a usage, which Rask ascribed – perhaps ironically – to Grimm's 'great patriotism'.[17] As Rask doubtless perceived, the scale of Grimm's philological project, coupled with his declaration 'I was wishful to exalt my native land', was vulnerable to distortion and abuse from politicians seeking to legitimize belligerence through German linguistic nationalism.[18] Given the growing tensions between Denmark and Germany, it is not difficult to comprehend why some Danes suspected that political and cultural expansionism were hand in glove in the German psyche.

DONAR

While Jacob Grimm's study of Thor is only a fraction of the overall scheme of his work in *Deutsche Mythologie*, it is nonetheless a fascinating insight into his method, for Grimm was not really studying the Norse god Thor at all, but what he considered to be his earlier incarnation, Donar. In his chapter devoted to 'Donar, Thunar (Thorr)', Grimm sifts through the evidence and finds the ancient god hidden in the names of rivers and mountains and, in the south and east of Germany, in close proximity to the sites dedicated to the Roman god Jupiter, with whom he shared a number of tumultuous characteristics. Thunder, lightning and the hurling of wedge-shaped stones from mountaintops are all phenomena or actions associated with Donar and can be discerned in onomatopoeia and expressions in folk dialects. Further proving that 'this myth of the thundergod is the joint possession of Scandinavia and the rest of Teutondom' is the god's hammer, Mjollnir, which, as Grimm notes, the Thor of the eddas hurls at giant skulls amidst a fury of thunder and lightning.[19] Yet *hamar* in various languages of the north can itself signify both 'thunder' and 'rock/stones', as can *donner*, as such indicating the god's origin as a personification of natural catastrophes, and partly explaining the later demonization of Donar in post-mythological Lower Germany, where the words for 'hammer' and 'devil' became interchangeable.[20] Furthermore, compounds associating Donar with goats give additional credence to his existence and the derivation from him of Norse mythological tales about Thor's goat-drawn chariot.[21] The notion of Thor as a saviour – the interpretation placed on the god by Scandinavian commentators since the late eighteenth century – says Grimm, happened as a consequence of the stimuli of Judaeo-Christian myth finding its way north and thereafter 'at an early stage' insinuating itself into the pagan worldview. One example of this would be Thor's struggle with the Midgard Serpent, which, thinks Grimm, derives both from the myth of Leviathan and the sacrifice of Christ on the cross; moreover, some proof of this is surely apparent in the similarity between Thor's hammer and the sign of the cross.[22]

But Grimm was no Atterbom or Grundtvig:

> Against the error which has so frequently done damage to the study of the Norse and Greek mythologies, I mean the mania of foisting metaphysical and astrological solutions on but half-distinguished historical data, I am sufficiently guarded by the incompleteness and loose connexion of all that has been preserved.[23]

The Norse Thor may have gathered kindly and protective features to mitigate his violent reputation, but his German archetype Donar lacked such attractions, and Grimm does not distort his findings in the interest of Romantic colourations. While it is to the heaven of 'the elegant, stately Wuotan [Old Norse Odin]' that heroes go, it is the common folk who go to Donar's, and in him there is 'something plebeian, boorish and uncouth', an assessment which is consistent with the human social classes posthumously assigned to the keeping of either Odin or Thor in the eddic lay 'Hárbarðsljóð' (Harbard's Song).[24] That said, Grimm is quite sure that Donar was one of the greatest, perhaps the oldest, of the Germanic gods. What Donar lacked in intellect and sophistication, he made up for in sturdiness and strength, the very attributes admired by those lower down the social order. For Grimm, the Norse Thor is only interesting when shown to be carrying forward information that proves his origin in inland Germany. Whether or not Grimm intended it and whether or not it is convincing, Grimm's presentation of Donar and the rest of the heathen pantheon had far greater implications for the future of German nationalism than Grundtvig's and Oehlenschläger's presentation of a tolerant, democratic Thor did for the future prestige of Denmark. Under the terms of the argument, as Rask clearly saw, Thor owed his existence to Donar, just as the Scandinavian languages and Scandinavian mythology owed theirs to a lost German blueprint.

JACOB GRIMM'S LEGACY

Jacob Grimm worked in isolation from the Romanticist movement that swept Europe in the first half of the nineteenth century, and its tendency towards over-wrought nostalgia would have held little interest for him. Grimm was first and foremost a scholar, and the depth and extent of his life's work has meant that he was, almost certainly, the most influential thinker on North European languages and early medieval culture in the nineteenth century. Much of his work remains relevant to scholarly research to this day. Some measure of the importance of Grimm's investigations can be gleaned from an anecdote told by the Icelandic lexicographer Guðbrandur Vigfússon (1827–89), who as a young scholar visited Grimm at his home in Berlin in 1859.[25]

Despite having called on Grimm unannounced, Guðbrandur was ushered into a book-lined study, a meticulously well-ordered and wholesome room. Grimm was, of course, familiar with the younger man's work, remarking of Guðbrandur's *Um tímatal í Íslendínga sögum* (On the Dating of the Icelandic Sagas) (1855) that '[y]ou have done a fine thing', and enquiring what he was doing now. Guðbrandur was pleased to report that he and his fellow countryman Jón Sigurðsson (1811–79) had just finished editing an extensive range of *Biskupa sögur* (Bishop's sagas) and that he had the manuscript with him. Encouraged by Grimm's praise, he handed it over. As Guðbrandur stood aside watching his host read, he was alarmed to observe that 'something in it displeased him'. 'I see that there are some differences between you Icelanders and the Norwegians', commented Grimm. The source of Grimm's displeasure, as Guðbrandur quickly realized, lay in the edition's orthography. Unlike the Norwegians, such as Peter Andreas Munch (1810–63) and Carl Rikard Unger (1817–97), who had adopted a Grimmean method when it came to spelling, Guðbrandur had followed the practices of Rask, 'as if there had never been a Grimm'. Specifically, Guðbrandur had failed to distinguish between the vowel sounds /œ/ and /æ/, 'a point on which Grimm insisted'. Somewhat dismayed, Guðbrandur rather clumsily dismissed the matter as 'trifling'. Grimm apparently did not think so, as a few minutes later he raised the matter again only to be met with the same flustered response from his visitor. Grimm 'good-naturedly let the subject drop' and after a glass of wine the interview came to an end. Grimm duly returned to the last great but uncompleted labour of the industrious philological careers of himself and his brother, the *Deutsches Wörterbuch* (German Dictionary).[26]

In 1885, when Guðbrandur was recalling with pleasure his one and only meeting with Jacob Grimm, he would almost certainly have reflected on his own burdensome and time-consuming lexicographic task, that of completing Richard Cleasby's *Icelandic–English Dictionary*, which was eventually published in 1874.[27] If Grimm's mild rebuke had any lasting effect on him, it may be discerned in the orthographic policies of this work, as here the vowel sounds /œ/ and /æ/ 'are treated as one letter' and the older form /œ/ is 'not noticed in this dictionary except now and then for etymological purposes'. While this might well have been a policy that would have pleased and displeased both Rask and Grimm in equal measure, at the very least one can surmise that Guðbrandur had come to regard matters of orthography as very important indeed and not in the least 'trifling'. In effect, what Guðbrandur and every other scholar working in the field of northern antiquity had sooner or later come to understand (and in many cases taken inspiration from) was that underlying the philological niceties that expressed, say, a preference for one orthographic system over another, was the far headier matter of 'ownership' – ownership of the language, ownership of the cultural heritage cradled within that language and, in the broader politics of Europe from at least the mid nineteenth century, ownership of the land on which that language was spoken. Agonizing over a vowel sound may seem like a pedantic matter but, at the time, it was also a one of national identity and, following on from this, security.

THOR AS FRIEND AND HERO

Irrespective of Jacob Grimm's sober attention to detail, the medievalism of the bardic revival urged on by Klopstock and Gerstenberg in the 1760s eventually took firm hold in Germany, provoking there an outpouring of national senti-ment, as it had done previously in Denmark.[28] For the poet Ludwig Uhland (1787–1862), extreme patriotism was frequently articulated in the construction of an idealized medieval past, suffused with chivalric nobility, fraternity and romantic yearning.[29] Uhland was democratic in outlook and the leading advo-cate for the rights of Swabians in south-west Germany, but, like Jacob Grimm, Uhland found his political views incompatible with his position as a professor of German literature at the University of Tübingen, and he regretfully resigned in 1833 to enter politics full time. During this period, lasting little more than five years, Uhland maintained his interest in the northern medieval past and focused his energies on analysing the meaning behind the names given in Old Norse mythological poetry, which he published in 1836 as *Der Mythus von Thor nach Nordischen Quellen* (The Myth of Thor from Nordic Sources).

Uhland's study of Thor pays no regard to Grimm's Donar and is firmly rooted in eddic mythology. As a consequence, much like Thor's Scandinavian interpreters, Uhland reveals an altogether more palatable god, whose stone throwing suggests not a violent demeanour but, when considered symbolically, can be seen as an expression of Thor as a munificent fertility god, a point that Grimm alludes to in passing. Similarly, when Thor's hammer splinters the skull of the giant Hrungnir, it signifies 'the conversion of hard and stony ground to cultivable soil'. Thor therefore stands in opposition to malevolent nature as represented by the giants, and when the worker cultivating the field – personified in myth as Thor's assistant Thialfi – regards the mountain (the stone giant) being assaulted by thunder and lightning (thus, Thor), then, as Thialfi, he 'feels that he does not work alone, that there is a mighty god there to help him, and while he does the lowly toil, the god will carry out the great work and has already prepared the hardest part'. Thor as the cultivator is additionally indicated in the tales of Groa and Aurvandil in Snorri's 'Skáldskaparmál' (The Language of Poetry). It is Groa who tries to remove the shard of the giant's whetstone from Thor's skull and, as her name indicates, this signifies 'healing', which in agricultural terms means 'growth and greening' and 'the herald of the harvest to come'. Aurvandil, whom Thor carries from the north, represents Thor's winter role as the one who 'preserves the germinating plant-life over the winter', and when Aurvandil's toe is frozen and falls off as Thor wades the icy stream, it signifies that the seed has been planted too early.[30]

Uhland sees in the accumulated myths of Thor more than his restricted role as 'the thunderer'. In his year-round importance as the god who nurtures the crop, Thor is all-embracing and his true significance is as 'lord and protector of the earth and its inhabitants', for 'the meaning of each single myth has led up to this'. In contrast to Odin, who 'brings about poetic and warlike inspiration' and whose 'appearance always reveals a dark and gruesome background', Thor 'works good-naturedly and cheers one's hearty labour'. He is 'the most human, the most popular, the friendliest of the Aesir, the "beloved friend" of his worshippers' and the poems about him have 'a seasoning of careless mirth'. Thor has 'the most marked personality of all the Nordic divinities', and in his concern 'with the entire people', even the thralls, he represents 'the democratic element'. As for the reverence in which he was held, 'a people that can recognise in the peal of thunder the nearness of a friend shows sound sense'.[31]

Uhland's ideas about Thor exceed even those of Grundtvig's in ascribing to the god qualities that reflect nineteenth-century social and political idealism. Yet, while there is nothing explicit in Uhland's extravagant analysis of the god that makes a case for a specifically German Thor, not far from its surface one can discern the shades of Uhland's patriotic and democratic colours; in this all-embracing deity there is surely suggestion of a pan-Germanic Thor, who not only favours national, but also racial, equality among the Germanic peoples and, by implication, unity. In this, and perhaps only in this, Uhland occupies the same ground as Jacob Grimm. While Uhland's approach to Norse mythology may not have appealed to philologists such as Grimm or to commentators in Scandinavia, it did win particular praise from the hugely influential English historian and proponent of the 'Great Man' theory of history, Thomas Carlyle (1795–1881), who also regarded Thor as essentially a fertility or sun god. In 1841, Carlyle recounted many of the eddic tales involving Thor in the first of his lectures on the subject of heroes, 'Hero as Divinity. Odin. Paganism: Scandinavian Mythology'. Dissatisfied with Grimm's etymologically-based scepticism regarding euhemerist theories of the origin of the gods, Carlyle affirms his belief that, for example, Odin was once '[a] Teacher, and Captain of soul and body; a Hero of worth immeasurable' but laments that '[i]t is all gone now, that old Norse work, – Thor the Thunder-god changed into Jack the Giant-killer', adding that 'Thor is vanished, the whole Norse world has vanished and will not return ever again'.[32] Carlyle's nostalgia for the passing of the Norse gods was, in effect, part of his much wider critique of what he saw as the deleterious and deadening influences on civilization that constrained the emergence of a new breed of heroes. Anti-Semitic, anti-Christian, anti-democratic and deeply pro-German, Carlyle's views on heroes and the heroic gained widespread popularity in the latter decades of the nineteenth century and were a significant influence on the poet Matthew Arnold during his Norse myth-inspired period.[33] But Carlyle's ideas proved contemporaneous and lost credibility and respect in the twentieth century, except, that is, in Nazi Germany, where he was read with enthusiasm by, among others, Adolf Hitler (1889–1945). This was not the kind of future for Germany that Ludwig Uhland would have wanted, nor, one suspects, would Carlyle have wanted.

THE IMPACT OF NATIONALISM

Looking back over investigations into northern mythology from Mallet to Uhland, it is apparent that nationalism in its various forms – romantic, linguistic, racial and cultural – underlay the imaginative and scholarly efforts of poets and philologists to delineate the attributes of Thor. For Klopstock, Thor epitomized the criminal neglect of German national culture; for Ewald, pan-Scandinavian unity; for Oehlenschläger and Atterbom, the recovery of national pride; for Grundtvig, the liberation of *folktet* and the cleansing of Danish culture; for Uhland, Christian democratic utopianism. Only Jacob Grimm declined to see 'the thunderer' in contemporary terms, yet, somewhat ironically, his analysis of Donar-Thor was at least as politically charged as any campaign-driven configurations of the gods of the Old North. In both Denmark and Germany, the revivification of northern antiquity was typically framed in such a way as to criticize the policies of monarchs and governmental authorities, implicitly and explicitly. Klopstock, to a certain extent, and Grundtvig, Grimm and Uhland, to a large extent, were prepared to take the consequences of their dissidence rather than remain silent. Yet, the generation of national pride often provokes a disdain for other nations that can be harnessed to more aggressive causes. Grundtvig saw as much in the German threat to Slesvig-Holstein, as did Rask in Grimm's 'great patriotism'.

What is also apparent is that National Romanticism took the analysis and recovery of Old Norse myth and legend out of the exclusive preserve of scholars, most often supported by national governments to assert a particular nation's primacy in the origin of northern society and culture, and into the realms of a bourgeois public, typically as a result of the dramatizations of literary artists. In Scandinavia and Britain, the production of serious-minded creative works based on northern antiquity declined in the second half of the nineteenth century, giving way to social realism and more modern tastes but leaving in its wake a bourgeois populism bordering on what might be called 'Viking kitsch'.[34] There were exceptions, such as the English cultural polymath William Morris (1834–96), whose translations of, and poetic extemporizations on, Icelandic sagas, guided by the Cambridge-based Icelander Eiríkr Magnússon (1833–1913), drew a wide audience but whose influence on a new generation of literary artists was relatively short lived.[35] Scholars and linguists continued to devote themselves to their studies of the Scandinavian legacy, and in Iceland, for example, such research lent credibility to the movement for national independence. Only in Germany did Old Norse myth and legend remain at the heart of cultural life, where it gathered around itself ever more virulent claims about the ancient genius, superiority and territorial rights of the German peoples. And it was in Germany that the Scandinavian legacy, which, largely thanks to Jacob Grimm, was widely understood to be a Germanic or even German legacy, that a gestalt was about occur that would forever enshrine the Norse gods in the top rank of European art. It would prove to be a mixed blessing.

In 1864, when Prussian forces were crossing the Dannevirke in south Jutland to lay claim to the disputed duchies, an impecunious composer by the name of Richard Wagner (1813–83) was escaping his creditors in Vienna and fleeing to the protection of King Ludvig II in Munich, where he was to resume work on his operatic tetralogy *Der Ring des Nibelungen* (The Ring of the Nibelung), better known as the *Ring* cycle. Twelve years later, in 1876, while George Stephens was beginning his study of the Thor panel at Dimbo, Wagner was at Bayreuth presiding over what was one of the defining moments for European culture in the latter half of the nineteenth century. It is a fair indication of the extent to which pan-Germanicism had, by this time, become a doctrine central to German cultural assertions that Wagner largely based the *Ring* on the medieval Icelandic *Völsunga saga* (The Saga of the Volsungs) and its related eddic sources, rather than on the parallel, courtly and non-mythological Middle-High German epic poem *Das Nibelungenlied*.[36]

In addition, Wagner had carefully studied both the *Poetic Edda* and the *Prose Edda*, and had drawn further inspiration from the fantastical thirteenth-century Icelandic saga *Þiðreks saga af Bern* (The Saga of Thidrek of Bern), which improvises on the lives of numerous legendary heroes of Germanic antiquity, including the hero of *Völsunga saga* and *Das Nibelungenlied*, known respectively as Sigurðr Fáfnisbani (Sigurd the Dragon Slayer) and Siegfried (the name used by Wagner). Assisting Wagner to develop both a coherent narrative and distinctive characters out of all this material were the studies of the Grimm brothers – to some extent Wilhelm's *Die deutsche Heldensage* (The German Heroic Saga), but more extensively Jacob's *Deutsche Mythologie*, as well as the studies and German translations of the Norse material by the scholars Franz Joseph Mone (1796–1871) and Karl Simrock (1802–76).[37] Wagner, however, was not constrained by tradition or strict authenticity and allowed himself imaginative free reign over the material such as no one had ever before envisioned. Nor was he so emphatically 'northern' in his art that he sought only northern models for the *Ring*, as it is clear that Greek tragedy supplied the structural template, Aeschylus's *Oresteia* being his chief guide.[38]

Wagner's grand scheme in the *Ring* spans the whole of the Norse mythological sequence, concluding with his version of the doom of the gods, which nonetheless hints at a purging leading to a glorious regeneration, the model for which was the eddic 'Völuspá' (The Seeress's Prophecy). It is within this that Wagner frames the Volsung legend and, so, the tragic tale of the love between Wotan's outcast Valkyrie, Brünnhilde (Old Norse Brynhild), and his expression of the ultimate human hero, Siegfried, a figure who, like Arminius of the Cherusci, had come to symbolize the heroic spirit of the ancient Germans. It is quite expressly delivered as a German national epic, a grandiloquent celebration of German genius, destiny and racial superiority, and a challenge to the ruinous forces of modernity and industrial capitalism. With its soaring metaphysics framed within the awe-inspiring world of the sublime, it was a creation that sought to unify all the arts into a single expression of Germany's exalted place in world history; past, present and future. It was Wagner's *Gesamtkunstwerk*, his total art work.[39]

WAGNER'S THOR

Thor's role in Wagner's version of Norse myth and legend cannot be said to be a starring one, a marker of this being his demotion from son of Wotan (Old Norse

Odin), as in the mythology, to that of his brother-in-law. What is interesting, however, about Wagner's Thor – Donner, as he calls him – is that he owes more to Jacob Grimm's Donar than, for example, to Uhland's saviour god.[40] Grimm's description of the Germanic proto-Thor as 'plebeian, boorish and uncouth' may not exactly fit Donner's character in *Das Rhinegold* (The Rheingold), the first and only part of the *Ring* in which the god figures, but, with one notable exception, Donner's main contribution is belligerent hotheadedness, his first recourse being to hammer-wielding and threats, rather than to diplomacy and cunning, as is the case with the legalistic Wotan and the conniving Loge (Old Norse Loki).

The drama of *Das Rhinegold* centres on two simultaneous crises. First, the theft from the Rhinemaidens, the guardians of the Rhinegold treasure hoard, of the ring of power by the loathsome dwarf Alberich and, second, the demand of the giants for their contractually agreed payment of the fertility goddess Freia (Old Norse Freyja) in return for building the gods an impregnable fortress, an obvious allusion to the Master Builder Tale, as told in Snorri Sturluson's 'Gylfaginning' (The Deluding of Gylfi). The former threatens the supremacy of the gods, the latter their immortality. While Donner's bluster and bombast is of no avail, Loge's plan to steal the ring from Alberich, and then use it to redeem Freia from the giants, proves effective, albeit with dire future consequences, as the ring is now cursed. Irrespective, Wotan and the gods are now at liberty to take possession of their mountaintop fortress, Valhalla, but are unable to ascend through the thick mists that envelop it and, by implication, their futures. It is at this point that Donner shows a more constructive mien, summoning thunder and lightning to clear the heavens and causing a rainbow bridge to form a pathway for the gods to cross to their new home.[41] Wagner's Donner is, thus, both an instinctively violent aggressor and a triumphant liberator. It is not difficult to see how the unsophisticated Donner equates, in large part, to German militarism: a blunt instrument with the power to rescue and secure.

VÖLKISCH

Those two conceptions of Thor that emerged throughout the nineteenth century were both met in *Das Rhinegold*: on the one hand, Uhland's radiant champion, and, on the other, Jacob Grimm's no-nonsense warrior Donar, a hero of subaltern rank. Both these formulations – the hieratic and the demotic, the redeemer and the warrior – in many respects symbolized the aspirations of a Germany keen to establish its cultural credentials as equal to, if not greater than, nations such as France and Britain. Those late eighteenth-century resentments espoused by Klopstock were undiminished. Yet, these were no longer the politically disunited German peoples that Klopstock wished to see as one. Bismarck's new Germany, founded in 1871, was set to become the single most powerful military force in mainland Europe. The 'monstrous German war-machine' that Grundtvig had dreaded had become a reality. In this heady and excited atmosphere, all the disparate elements of German nationalism were to combine as an ideology. After Wagner's epic reworking of Old Northern myth and legend, spotted with prejudice and elitism, and composed in tribute to the glory of the German *Volk* and their history, whatever previous analyses of the gods of Nordic antiquity there had been soon became fodder for the appetites of German national self-assertion. So it happened that an increasingly powerful Germany, a politically enfeebled Scandinavia, a theory of linguistic purity, and a proposition regarding Germanic origins that hinted at supremacism were gradually articulated under a single heading: *völkisch*.

The basic meaning of the term *völkisch* is 'of the folk' or 'folkish', particularly in a populist sense; however, as a concept, its embrace reaches beyond this into precepts about race and notions of a collective biological and even linguistic identity, with, of course, negative and pejorative perceptions of those excluded from this club. In Germany, *völkisch* ideas or, rather, ideals, had been simmering throughout the nineteenth century, but in its latter decades they became formalized, if not in terms of a logical programme of beliefs, then certainly in terms of propagandizing populism. From the 1880s, there emerged an increasing number of *völkisch* magazines celebrating German *kultur*. Among the titles were *Heimdall*, named after the guardian god of the Norse pantheon, and thereafter, as the century turned, *Odin* and the Thor-inspired *Hammer*, for, post-Wagner, the incorporation of the myths and legends of the Old North into German *kultur* was a mere given.[42]

As discussed at the outset of this chapter, the revival of interest in folk culture is traceable to the late eighteenth century, in particular to the powerful arguments set forward by Herder. One consequence of this was that, for much of the nineteenth century, the notion of indigenous, traditional culture and its centrality to ideas of national identity was a widely shared belief in Northern

Europe. The harvesting of folk tales by the Grimms prompted similar projects in the Scandinavian countries. In Norway, Peter Christen Asbjørnsen and Jørgen Moe published *Norske Folke-Eventyr* (Norwegian Folk Tales) (1841–42 and 1852), in which remnants of Norse myth still survived in perilous encounters with trolls and other monstrous beings in tales such as 'The Three Billy Goats Gruff' and 'Tatterhood', which, as George Webbe Dasent noted in his English translation of 1859, retain echoes of the troll-slayer supreme, Thor.[43] Similarly, in Iceland, Jón Árnason recovered a rich store of troll-infested folk material of mythological descent, which he published in raw form in 1862–64.[44] This antiquarianism played its part in promoting national causes, which in Iceland meant seeking independence from Denmark, and in Norway independence from Sweden. Yet compared to the hypernationalism that was taking hold in Germany, national campaigning in the Scandinavian countries remained relatively sober, if nonetheless persistent.[45] For here, in the most general terms, obsessions with Nordic antiquity had largely returned to the study and the library and were, in any case, already deeply embedded in aesthetic and populist expressions of cultural distinctiveness.[46] For the Germans, however, it was as if a whole new cultural identity needed to be established, and at the extreme fringes of the *völkisch* movement some very strange ideas and beliefs rooted in Norse mythology were being generated. As a consequence of these conceptions of the Nordic/Germanic past, there emerged the least palatable and, in many respects, most deranged interpretations of Thor's significance.

RACE THEORY

German racial supremacist theories, broadly encapsulated within the concept of Aryanism, rejected Christianity and despised its religious parent Judaism on the grounds that Abrahamic thinking had vitiated the spirit of the old Germanic tribes, many of whom had fled north into the Scandinavian regions where they remained free to practise paganism, or so the theory went. Given a more formal socio-philosophical treatment by the French aristocrat Joseph Arthur, Compte de Gobineau (1816–82), race theory became central to the doctrines of a German intellectual elite, in large part due to the promulgation of 'Gobinism' by Wagner's son-in-law, the Englishman Houston Stewart Chamberlain (1855–1927).[47] For some, a new religious metaphysic became oriented around Germanic paganism, which became known as Ariosophy, a system of mystical ideas modelled on the principles of Theosophy expounded and popularized by the Russian spiritualist Madame (Helena Petrovna) Blavatsky (1831–91). Founding and formalizing this movement was the Austrian Guido von List (1848–1919), who further spiced the mix with his belief in the magical powers of runes, which, once mastered could endow one with the insight and power of Odin, Thor and Loki – hence the 'New Age' religion of Wotanism. Influential societies were formed, such as the Thule Society and the Edda Society, which espoused both eugenics and runic occultism, and there was even a popular form of transcendental outdoor exercising known as runic gymnastics, invented by another fanatic, Friedrich Bernhard Marby (1882–1966), as well as an unusual form of meditation involving rune yodelling. All of this *völkisch*-inspired mumbo jumbo might have turned out to be nothing more than a distastefully eccentric footnote to European history, except that much of it fed straight into the ideology of the Nazis, whose moment in history was about to dawn.[48]

As is widely acknowledged, the catastrophe of World War I did nothing to dampen the ardour for *völkisch* ideals in Germany; instead, it opened up the way for the biological community to fulfil its destiny and adopt a strong leader, a 'hero' in the Carlyle mould, capable, not only of rebuilding the nation, but also of uniting all the German peoples and purging the collective of impurities of blood, decadence, deviation of thought and imperfections of physique.[49] Thus the *völkisch* concept became legitimized in its most extreme form, not just as a social, racial and political ideal, but as an 'enduring link between the German's racial lineage and their land (*Blut und Boden*).[50] If Wagner had been the chief architect behind a German temple of 'higher truths', and Guido von List and his circle had appointed themselves as the high priests, the Armanenschaft, then there was one rising star of the National Socialist party who was sure which god should be enshrined at the altarpiece: Heinrich Himmler (1900–45), and his candidate was Thor.

HIMMLER'S THOR

Himmler was raised in upper-middle-class privilege in Munich. His father was a classicist with an equal passion for the literature of northern antiquity, which he frequently read to his young son. By the age of ten, young Heinrich had memorized long passages from the eddas, the Icelandic sagas and *Das Nibelungenlied*. For father and son recreation, they would wander the Bavarian countryside and visit sites of archaeological interest and search the surrounds for coins, rusted weaponry and rune stones. All this and Himmler's youthful and precocious readings of German military history appear to have seamlessly combined in his psyche. Denied a career in the German army after university by the sanctions imposed at Versailles, Himmler soon found an outlet for his military enthusiasms as a member of the anti-communist Freikorps and, through this, in the political ambitions of Adolf Hitler, under whose influence he became a member of the National Socialist movement. By 1925, he was deputy-Reichsführer of the Waffen Schutzstaffel, the elite Nazi SS.[51]

Throughout his career, *völkisch* ideology was central to Himmler's philosophy, because, as Hitler says in *Mein Kampf*, 'To the same degree as the basic ideas of the National Socialist movement are folkish [*völkisch*], then folkish [*völkisch*] ideas are National Socialist.'[52] Nevertheless, Himmler's ideas were somewhat beyond 'basic' and were not entirely in tune with those of the Führer, for, despite being a Catholic, he is known to have had strong links with Ariosophists and runic occultism. Although Hitler may not have shared Himmler's interest in *völkisch* metaphysicality (except, that is, where it espoused Aryan racial supremacy), it was not wholly disreputable, being underpinned by scholarly research into 'Germanicness' (Germanentum) by leading scholars, such as the Berlin-based philologist and translator of Old Icelandic literature Andreas Heusler (1865–1940). Heusler's formulations of the principles of Germanicness soon became standard in the rhetoric of Nazi propagandists, as in, for example, the assertion that 'German Germanicness is a metaphysical form of character, derived from a Nordic essence, which reveals itself in a creative power based on a heroic attitude . . .'[53] In 1935, Himmler and his associates formalized study of the Aryan past through a Berlin-based think tank of scholars known as the Ahnenerbe. It was from this group that archeological excavations and the gathering of ancient artefacts and manuscripts were launched on a global scale, with the intention of proving that the Nordic peoples, now a synonym for the Germanic peoples, had once ruled the world. Even Olof Rudbeck's seventeenth-century Atlantis fantasies concerning the origin of the Goths, long since discredited, were revived and remodelled to suit Aryan claims.[54]

In 1933, the intoxicating brew of pseudo-scientific mysticism enjoyed by

Himmler brought him into contact with a retired Austrian colonel and one-time psychiatric patient, Karl-Maria Wiligut (1866–1946), a dedicated Ariosophist. Wiligut's view of Ariosophy, however, was as a devotee of the aristocratic and, allegedly, ancient faith of the Irminists, whose prophet was Baldur-Chrestos. Wiligut firmly believed that this Germanic messiah had been crucified by Wotanists some 12,000 years before. For Wiligut, contemporary Wotanism, like that practised by Friedrich Bernhard Marby, constituted a dangerous schism and when the opportunity finally arose in 1936, Wiligut denounced Marby for 'bringing the Holy Arian heritage into disrepute', so precipitating Marby's arrest and imprisonment by the Nazi authorities. As Heather O'Donoghue remarks, the distinction between what was acceptable and what was not 'is not a self-evident one to modern commentators'.[55]

Among many other extraordinary claims (such as having a memory of the world when it had three suns and was inhabited by giants and dwarves, some 200,000 years before Christ), Wiligut declared his direct descent from Thor, one consequence of this being that he was a savant. With this realization, Wiligut changed his name to Weisthor (Wise Thor). Himmler's first task for Wiligut was to have him research an appropriate insignia for the Waffen Schutzstaffel. He settled on two 'S' runes followed by a curious runic symbol of his own design. This was meant to signify his own lineage as Weisthor and, given the double lightning bolt-like appearance of the 'SS' element, was a likely allusion to Thor's cosmic powers. Beyond this, Wiligut was granted permission to preside over SS officer weddings, which entailed rune-symbol ritualizations, along with other pseudo-pagan paraphernalia.[56] Yet his main service to Himmler was to divine the exact spot where the ultimate confrontation between East and West would one day take place. Satisfied with Wiligut's pronouncements, Himmler called together his chief of staff and declared: 'We know, we have learned now where the battle will be – in Westphalia and, more precisely still, near the old road of German heroes that leads from Paderborn via Soest in a westerly direction.'[57] In effect, this would be right on the edge of the Teutoberg Forest, where Arminius of the Cherusci had routed the Roman legions in AD 9. For ultra-nationalists like Himmler, it could scarcely have been elsewhere and he chose the seventeenth-century castle of Wewelsburg as the place where he would establish an SS Vatican City, except the ideology at Wewelsburg would be pre-Christian. No expense was spared.

Leading officials of the Ahnenerbe did not share Himmler's high regard for Wiligut, the Rasputin of Himmler, as he became known,[58] and in 1939 Himmler was forced to accept that Wiligut was mentally unstable and dismiss him. Not that this detracted from Himmler's belief in the historical reality of Thor. Frustrated that Hitler did not share his enthusiasms for the early Germanic tribes, Himmler gave him a cast of an ancient swastika for his birthday, a symbol of Thor's power.[59] Yet whether or not Hitler could apprehend the crucial significance of Germanic antiquity, Himmler had the intellectual energies of the Ahnenerbe at his disposal, and in 1940 he set out the objectives:

> Have the following researched: Find all places in the northern Germanic Aryan cultural world where an understanding of the lightning bolt, the thunderbolt, Thor's hammer, or the thrown hammer exists, in addition to all the sculptures of the god depicted with a small hand axe emitting lightning. Please collect all of the pictorial, sculptural, written and mythological evidence of this. I am convinced that this is not based on natural thunder and lightning, but rather that it is an early, highly developed form of war weapon of our forefathers, which was only, of course, possessed by the Aesir, the gods, and that it implies an unheard of knowledge of electricity.[60]

By November 1944, with the war all but lost, an increasingly desperate Himmler was working hard on a plan to build his secret weapon, a gigantic Mjollnir that would emit electrical charges and render the Allies' communication systems, radar and tank ignitions unworkable.[61] All that was required was to bring the earth's atmosphere under control; a task, Himmler was shocked to discover, beyond the reach of current technology. Six months later, having betrayed Hitler in his failed attempt to broker a deal with the advancing enemy and now under interrogation by the British, he bit down on a cyanide capsule. The *völkisch* dream of a Thousand Year Reich had lasted 12 years.

From Romantic symbol to national saviour to a god of war (this last, ironically, his chief function in the eddas), Thor's journey through the nineteenth and the first half of the twentieth centuries was, to say the least, a highly controversial one. George Stephens could never have imagined the extent to which his Thunor could be prised from the grip of his beloved Scando-Gothic forefathers. Had he been able to, he might well have taken comfort from a comment made by Euripides about a different pantheon: 'Those whom the gods would destroy, they first make mad.'

After the fall of Nazi Germany, everything associated with the study of Old Norse mythology in Europe came to be regarded with deep suspicion, as did the cradles of high culture in which ideas about racial supremacism had been nurtured. None of this is surprising considering the Aryan hysteria that gripped Germany and led Europe to near ruin. What is surprising, almost to the point of being incomprehensible, is that the country even N. F. S. Grundtvig conceded 'deserves much credit for freedom and enlightenment in modern Europe' should, in the century following, have so comprehensively lost its way.[62] Back in 1936, Carl G. Jung (1875–1961), the founder of analytical psychology, had written his essay 'Wotan', describing the god as 'the truest expression and unsurpassed personification of a fundamental quality that is particularly characteristic of the Germans' – not that he was convinced that this was in all respects a constructive characteristic, as it may lead to 'perdition'.[63] A year later, with Wotan's spirit rampant, he declared that Hitler 'is a medium, German policy is not made; it is revealed through Hitler. He is the mouthpiece of the Gods of old . . .'[64] In 1946, in his essay 'After the Catastrophe', he was more conventional in his judgement of the apparent intermediacy of the Nazi leadership, remarking that '[e]ven a saint would have to pray unceasingly for the souls of Hitler and Himmler', and, in deep anguish, spoke of 'moral downfall', 'the contaminating touch of evil', 'expiation', 'political psychopaths' and 'collective guilt'.[65] Jung's sense of being an observer of tumultuous and unprecedented forces, over which he personally had no control, was one common across Europe, and in this respect, 'collective guilt' was something that many other European nations deserved to share.

But the popular fascination with the gods of the Old North did not die with the Third Reich, it merely migrated away from the dangerous pretensions of high culture into the often sardonic company of the mass-culture merchants. It is there that we will find Thor in the latter half of the twentieth century and on into this one – or at least where we will find versions of him. This takes us away from the jealous tensions of Europe and across to a melting pot of cultural traditions, to a land where novelty can be both iconoclastic and part of a new mythology at the same time: the United States.

7

Thor in America: From Longfellow to Lee

In 1962, the comic-book superhero The Mighty Thor, brainchild of Marvel Comics editor Stan Lee (Stan Lieber, b. 1922), arrived on the scene in the United States. Like most other Americans, Lee would have been quite aware of a native constituency of Scandinavian descent and their interest in anything associated with Nordic culture. He could therefore suppose a reasonable response to his version of Thor from a 'Scandinavian' demographic that was in the region of 15 million in the mid twentieth century, as well as millions more with descent from other countries in northern and western Europe. In the early 1960s, Lee had something of a Midas touch when it came to judging consumer appetites for superheroes, and would become a leading figure in the resurgence of the comic-book market after its years of decline in the 1950s. As a result of Lee's enterprise, The Mighty Thor has had a continuous presence in US culture, and in many other countries where US culture is consumed, for almost 50 years. Given the production of the spin-off movie *Thor* (dir. Kenneth Branagh, 2011), there is little sign of his popularity waning. That Marvel Comics have produced over 600 issues of *The Mighty Thor*, exceeding in volume any other single body of work associated with the thunder god, including the eddas, is in itself a phenomenon.

The launch of *The Mighty Thor* was, in one sense, quite banal, in as much as it was simply just one among many speculative storylines proposed by Lee.[1] In this respect, the highly selective construction of Thor the superhero was chiefly motivated by profit, a unique circumstance in Thor's history up until that point. Yet, the particular character of the comic-book Thor – the way he reflects aspects of a wider cultural and, indeed, socio-political psyche – is, to quote that most famous of Danes, 'the abstract and brief chronicles of the time'. It was no less the case in previous discussions of the views of north European poets, dramatists, philologists, polemicists and politicians. There were, then, three main contextual influences informing the creation of The Mighty Thor: first, most probably indirectly, the reception history of America's supposed original discovery by Viking explorers; second, obviously directly, the development of the superhero formula; and third, significant for both previous contexts, the rise of mass entertainment media.

AMERICA'S VIKING FOUNDATION MYTH

The settlement of Greenland and the later exploration of an area believed to be on the north-east coast of the United States, led, in the first place, by Leif Eiriksson around AD 1000 are recounted in two thirteenth-century Icelandic sagas: *Grænlendinga saga* (The Saga of the Greenlanders) and *Eiríks saga rauða* (Eirik the Red's Saga). Known collectively as the Vínland sagas, they had become increasingly widely known to European audiences since the early eighteenth-century Latin paraphrases of them by the Icelandic scholar Torfaeus (Þormóður Torfason).[2] Thereafter, in the latter half of the eighteenth century, Paul Henri Mallet's *Histoire de Dannemarc* and Thomas Percy's English translation of Mallet's study, *Northern Antiquities*, brought these tales of the westward expeditions of Viking explorers to a much wider reading public. Among influential Americans who first showed an interest in medieval Scandinavia were Benjamin Franklin (1706–90), who thought the brief account he had been given of the Vínland voyages had a 'great Appearance of Authenticity', and Thomas Jefferson (1743–1826), who advocated the teaching of Old Icelandic.[3]

During the course of the nineteenth century, this saga material took on a new significance for hundreds of thousands of Scandinavians seeking a fresh start in North America, a high concentration of whom settled in the New England states. A form of foundation myth began to emerge, according to which any artefact or monument that might be considered of early medieval Scandinavian origin was, in time, regarded by some enthusiasts as proof that there had at one time been a Viking diaspora stretching west as far as Minnesota. In fact, it would not be until the 1960s that a settlement site discovered at L'Anse aux Meadows in Newfoundland, Canada, would be verified as the only actual evidence of a Viking presence in North America, albeit a relatively short-lived one.[4] This mythologizing of the discovery of America by a Germanic people had implications for the better-established history of Christopher Columbus's (1451–1506) discovery voyage, which took place almost 500 years after Leif Eiriksson was said to have sailed to Vínland. As the nineteenth century progressed, those of Anglo-Saxon, German and Scandinavian descent became less comfortable with the idea of Columbus as the founding father for two main reasons: first, Columbus was a Catholic, although the fact that Christianized Vikings, such as Leif Eiriksson, could only ever have been Catholic tended to be excused; and second, according to the Gobineau-style race theories cherished by some Anglo-Nordic Americans, Columbus's Italian origin meant that he belonged to a lower caste of Europeans.[5]

Bolstering the Viking foundation myth was the work of the Danish antiquarian Carl Christian Rafn (1795–1864), who, in 1837, published an account of all the Viking voyages to America entitled *Antiquitates Americanae*. With translations and notes in Danish and Latin, and 'An Abstract of the Historical Evidence Contained within this Work' in English, it attracted considerable attention in the United States and northern Europe, for it included commentary on every possible artefact, every 'runic' inscription, that Rafn believed to be of Viking origin in the eastern United States.[6] *Antiquitates Americanae* has been described as the 'CD Rom disc of nineteenth-century Vínland scholarship, praised for its production values, but mocked for lending unwonted encouragement to a new breed of cult archaeologists in North America.[7] Among Rafn's supposed archaeological evidence is the so-called Viking Tower of Newport, Rhode Island, a circular stone structure resting on eight open archways. This, Rafn believed, was the baptistery of a church built by Norse settlers in the twelfth century, a view eagerly accepted by those keen to confirm links with the Scandinavian ancestral homeland, but one regarded dubiously by Newport locals, who thought it to be a folly built on top of an old windmill by the seventeenth-century provincial governor Benedict Arnold. As it turned out, the locals were right.

Nevertheless, the myth of the Viking Tower persisted and this, alongside the discovery in 1832 of a brass-clad skeleton at Fall River, Massachusetts – probably the remains of a high-status Native American – inspired Henry Wadsworth Longfellow (1807–82), the most celebrated poet of the day, to write his melodramatic ballad 'The Skeleton in Armor' (1841). Longfellow imagines a ghastly Viking cadaver 'in rude armor dressed', who appears to his fearful narrator and, much in the manner of Coleridge's Ancient Mariner, recounts his life back in Norway, his love for a Norwegian princess, and their elopement to the New World, where

> Built I the lofty tower,
> Which, to this very hour,
> Stands looking seaward.

The haunter ends his tale with the tragic death of his loved one, his own miserable suicide and his ascent to 'native stars', a combination of the Christian heaven and the Norse Valhalla, where 'from flowing bowl / Drinks deep the warrior's soul'.[8]

Longfellow took a keen lifelong interest in medieval Scandinavia and had studied Old Norse under Rafn in Stockholm in 1835. Although he did not achieve a scholar's mastery of Old Norse, he was capable of reading it and derived much stimulation from the Icelandic eddas and sagas. He also drew inspiration from the Finnish myths and legends compiled and reformulated by Elias Lönnroth (1802–84) as *The Kalevala* in 1835, and it was from this that Longfellow borrowed both the verse form and the atmosphere for his celebrated Native American romance *The Song of Hiawatha* (1855). In some ways, Longfellow belonged in a north European literary tradition, as his extensive library testifies. The year 1835 was a formative one for Longfellow and, following his studies in Stockholm, he journeyed on to Copenhagen, where he set about familiarizing himself with the works of Johannes Ewald, Adam Oehlenschläger and N. F. S. Grundtvig.[9]

A sizeable number of Longfellow's poems were prompted by his reading of Samuel Laing's (1780–1868) 1844 translation of Snorri Sturluson's *Heimskringla*, which subsequently inspired him to write a sequence of poetic dramatizations based on episodes from the life of the late tenth-century Norwegian missionary king Olaf Tryggvason. Among the better known of Longfellow's poems from this Nordic phase is 'The Challenge of Thor' (1863). Although it would be an exaggeration to say that Longfellow had a particular obsession with Thor, the Thor-versus-Christ themes inherent in medieval Icelandic accounts of the conversion of the north found their way into his 'Tegnér's Drapa' of 1847, a verse tribute to the Swedish poet Esaias Tegnér who had died the previous year. In 'Tegnér's Drapa', Thor is a vanquished god, who

> Shall rule the earth no more,
> No more, with threats,
> Challenge the meek Christ.[10]

Yet, 16 years later, in 'The Challenge of Thor', Longfellow deliberately leaves the religious conflict unresolved in anticipation of Olaf's missionary triumph over Thor worshippers, such as is celebrated in his poem 'Raud the Strong'.[11] In Longfellow's depiction of Thor's confrontation with Christ, Thor announces himself as 'the War God', boasts of his weaponry, declares Jove to be his brother and concludes:

> Force rules the world still,
> Has ruled it, shall rule it;
> Meekness is weakness,
> Strength is triumphant,
> Over the whole earth
> Still is it Thor's Day!
>
> Thou art a God too,
> O Galilean!
> And thus singled-handed
> Unto the combat,
> Gauntlet or Gospel,
> Here I defy thee![12]

Taken by itself, 'The Challenge of Thor' could also be read as a compound metaphor for the mixed feelings of US-Scandinavian immigrants, whereby, on the one hand, the redemptive image of Christ correlates with the immigrant's hopes for a better future in the US, while on the other, the ancient claims of Thor correlate with their nostalgic yearnings for the homeland. Certainly, Longfellow's own Christian faith presented him with some difficulties when he first set about reading the eddas, and his early efforts to write a poem entitled 'The Fishing of Thor' were abandoned, as he found it difficult to reconcile his own beliefs with the mythology of paganism.[13] Like much of Longfellow's poetry, 'The Challenge of Thor' entered into the repertoire of both US and European high culture, being set to music by, among others, the eminent Icelandic composer Sveinbjörn Sveinbjörnsson (1847–1927) and the Danish-born American composer Carl Reinhold Busch (1862–1943). Longfellow's poems about Olaf Tryggvason, including 'The Challenge of Thor', reached a large audience in Britain through

Edward Elgar's (1857–1934) choral work *Scenes from the Saga of King Olaf* (first performed in 1896). Elgar establishes two contrasting musical leitmotifs which he states as signifying 'the gauntlet [Thor] and the gospel [Olaf]'.[14]

Similar poetic responses to the Viking legacy were offered by the Quaker and prominent campaigner for the abolition of slavery John Greenleaf Whittier (1807–92) and the essayist, satirist and diplomat James Russell Lowell (1819–91). Whittier's collections *Narrative and Legendary Poems* and *The Tent on the Beach* include a number poetic tributes to the Viking past, such as his musings on a stone carving of uncertain provenance entitled 'The Norsemen' (1841), perhaps 'A fragment of Valhalla's Thor, / The stormy Viking's god of War . . ', as well as extemporizations on Scandinavian folk tales involving the sinister threats of trolls and dwarves.[15] Appearing to be better informed than either Longfellow or Whittier, and catching somewhat more of the spirit of the Vínland sagas (despite a rather loose modelling on these sources), was Lowell's 'A Voyage to Vinland' (1869).[16] Lowell's theme is the fading pagan world of the European Old North and the rich Christian promise of the New World in the west. Although the Viking captain Biörn is disappointed that the actuality of the land he sights falls short of his expectations and so never makes landfall,[17] the prophetess of the third section of the poem 'Gudrida's Prophecy' declares:

> There lies the New Land
> Yours to behold it,
> Not to possess it;
> Slowly Fate's perfect
> Fullness shall come.
>
> Then from your strong loins
> Seed shall be scattered,
> Men to the marrow,
> Wilderness tamers,
> Walkers on waves.

This New Land offers the promise of ripe cornfields, peace and open-doored homesteads, free from the jealous old gods and the age of the sword, for,

Walking the New Earth,
Lo, a divine One
Greets all men godlike,
Calls them his kindred,
He, the Divine.

Is it Thor's hammer
Rays in his right hand?
Weaponless walks he;
It is the White Christ,
Stronger than Thor.

Yet Lowell could also see the absurd side to all this fashionable antique musing. In 1862, he published the second series of his satire on US life and politics, *Meliboeus-Hipponax: The Biglow Papers*, in which a certain Rev. Mr Wilbur comes into the possession of a hefty rune stone:

Touching Runick inscriptions, I find that they may be classed under three general heads: 1. Those which are understood by the Danish Royal Society of Northern Antiquities, and Professor Rafn, their Secretary; 2. Those which are comprehensible only by Mr. Rafn; and 3. Those which neither the Society, Mr. Rafn, nor anybody else can be said in any definite sense to understand, and which accordingly offer peculiar temptations to enucleating sagacity. These last are naturally deemed the most valuable by intelligent antiquaries, and to this class the stone now in my possession fortunately belongs.[18]

Wilbur concludes that his runic inscription can be read in any direction to arrive at precisely the same message: 'Here Bjarna Grimolfsson first drank cloud-brother through child-of-land-and-water'. In other words, Bjarni Grimolfsson, a character in *Eiríks saga rauða*, who, it is recounted, sacrifices himself to save a shipmate while journeying from Greenland to Vínland, had actually survived to become the first European to place on record the smoking of tobacco by, in his case, drawing it up through a reed stem.[19]

Miscalculations about, and misrepresentations of, allegedly pre-Columbian artefacts of Nordic origin have continued unabated, with some 52 sites, 73 artefacts and more than 100 inscriptions claiming authenticity. The best-known examples of the triumph of hope over reality have been the allegedly fifteenth-century Vínland Map and the allegedly fourteenth-century Kensington Rune Stone. The map remains controversial and – despite numerous scientific studies – it still has to be explained how chemicals of twentieth-century origin came to be present on it. The Rune Stone, once authoritatively hailed as 'probably the most important archaeological object yet found in North America' is now thought to be the imaginative chiselling of a nineteenth-century Swedish immigrant farmer.[20] Even today, there are those who cling desperately to the belief that these apparent forgeries will turn out to be genuine, not least for reasons of tourism, as in Kensington, Minnesota. Similarly, some pursue equally desperate etymologies with the aim of showing that the name 'America' is of Old Norse origin, rather than the more widespread and likely explanation that it is derived from the name of the late fifteenth-century Italian explorer Amerigo Vespucci (1454–1512).[21]

While the Fireside Poets, as Longfellow, Whittier and Lowell were congenially known,[22] enjoyed considerable success, opinion of the historical status and authority of the Vínland sagas in US scholarly circles in the nineteenth century was divided, just as it was among polemicists with a personal axe to grind. Frequently underlying the various schools of thought, both favouring and denying a Viking foundation of America, were religious values, which among New Englanders usually meant pro-Puritan and which could also signify Teutonic racial supremacy. There were, too, moral questions, whereby some saw the Vikings as noble freedom-lovers, the spiritual, if not physical, ancestors of the Pilgrim Fathers, and others saw them as brutish and barbarous fugitives from their own societies and a demeaning presence on American soil and, perhaps, in American genes. Although there was a gradual, if in some cases begrudging, acceptance that the Vínland sagas were authentic, or at least worthy of due consideration, it is true to say that this particular aspect of the growing interest in Old Norse studies in the United States remained a marginal, if nonetheless frequently overheated, controversy when set beside more mainstream studies of American history.[23]

Yet 'Norsemaniacs', as the Maine historian James Phinney Baxter (1831–1921) once dubbed them,[24] were irrepressible and it was their energy that eventually led to the first statue of Leif Eiriksson being erected amid grand ceremony in Boston in 1887, with much thanks due to the committee service of the Fireside Poets.

Such plans for monuments, commemorative art works, reconstructed longships and theatrical performances celebrating the Viking discovery of America proliferated, with some ten or more statues commemorating the legendary heroics of Leif and his crew, ranging from New England to Seattle, to date. A final and lasting endorsement of the Viking foundation myth occurred in 1964, when Lyndon B. Johnson (1908–73) became the first US president to approve an official Leif Ericson Day to be celebrated annually on 9 October. This was a commemoration that had been urged and gradually adopted at state level since the publication of the bluntly titled *America Not Discovered by Columbus* in 1874, a treatise by the Wisconsin-born professor of Scandinavian Studies Rasmus B. Anderson (1846–1936).[25]

So, whether regarded as an unfortunate incursion, a joyous founding or dubious history, the Viking legacy, as perceived in the nineteenth century, eventually made its way into the political, civic and literary consciousness of Americans. By the early twentieth century, the Vínland voyages had become woven into respectable American history, much as, in 1879, the Georgian poet, musician and scholar, Sidney Lanier (1842–81), had woven them into his epic poetic celebration of America's past, 'Psalm of the West'.[26] Delivering a measure of moral gravitas to Viking enthusiasts was a highly popular trilogy of novels on Vínland themes by Ottilie Liljencrantz (1876–1910): *The Thrall of Leif the Lucky: A Story of Viking Days* (1902), *The Vinland Champions* (1904) and *Randvar the Songsmith: A Romance of Norumbega* (1906). Liljencrantz's overarching intention in her trilogy was to show the Vikings as a crusading master race of high purpose and indomitable spirit, commanded with missionary zeal by the almost saintly Leif Eiriksson. The racial superiority of the Vikings is sharply contrasted with the vulgarity and grotesquery of the natives they encounter, whose underhand tactics and extreme violence eventually lead to the expulsion of the noble white settlers. The Viking leader pronounces this retreat to be a divine punishment brought about due to those among the settlers who failed to contain their animal instincts. Peppered throughout with references to Norse mythology and oaths to Odin and Thor by the, as yet, unenlightened, it is clear that Liljencrantz had done her homework and was intent on delivering a credible commentary on the Christian virtues of America's Scandinavian founding fathers, along with a thinly disguised warning about the perils of miscegenation.[27]

THE VIKINGS ON SCREEN

The Thrall of Leif the Lucky and its sequels heralded a minor although relatively short-lived literary fashion on the subject of Viking derring-do, which could range from the celebratory to the tragic, but perhaps of more significance is that Liljencrantz's novel caught the attention of film-makers. In 1928, Metro-Goldwyn-Mayer studios produced *The Viking* (dir. Roy William Neill) based on *The Thrall of Leif the Lucky*, one of the last silent movies to be made, but one of the first with an accompanying musical soundtrack, as well as being an early colour film using techniques regarded as an important step forward in colour-film technology. Despite its poor timing in cinematic history, and the criticism it received for its indistinguishably bewhiskered males and its 'opéra comique'[28] setting and plot, *The Viking* attracted a large audience. Two years later it was reissued as the sound musical *The Private Life of Leif Ericson*.

The Viking was not the first effort by film-makers to depict the muscular glamour and romance of the Viking Age. Less than 15 years after the Lumière brothers had made the very first motion picture, UK distributors released *The Viking's Bride* (dir. Lewin Fitzhammon, 1907) and in the United States the prolific Vitagraph Company of America presented *The Viking's Daughter: The Story of the Ancient Norsemen* (dir. J. Stuart Blackton, 1908) – both yarns about captured and separated lovers and their eventual happy reunion. The following decade, US audiences could enjoy *The Oath of a Viking* (dir. J. Searle Dawley, 1914) – more lovers' tribulations – and *The Viking Queen* (dir. Walter Edwin, 1915), a tale of anti-feminist skulduggery and the heroine's eventual triumph. For those looking for 'Viking' entertainments somewhat higher up the culture scale, there were silent movies inspired by Wagner's *Ring* cycle, such as the Italian productions *I Nibelunghi* (dir. M. Bernacchi, 1910) and *Siegfried* (dir. Mario Caserini, 1912), although it would not be until Fritz Lang's *Die Nibelungen* of 1924 that filmgoers could savour Wagnerian medieval atmospherics from a director of quite exceptional aesthetic sensibilities.[29]

Conspicuously, Viking films, including anything associated with Wagner, disappeared from the US big screen during the 1930s and did not reappear until the 1950s. The same was largely true in the world of publishing, albeit with two notable non-US exceptions: first, there were the Vínland-themed works by the British author Nevil Shute (1899–1960), whose novel *An Old Captivity* (1940) takes the form of a hallucination by a contemporary narrator, and whose film-script-cum-novel *Vinland the Good* (1946) is delivered as a history lesson on America's founding by a recently demobbed ex-schoolmaster.[30] In Shute's work, Vinland functions variously as a metaphor for Anglo-American relations, for the war effort and for the decline of British imperialism. Second, from Sweden, there was Frans Bengtsson's (1894–1954) exceptionally lyrical novel *Röde Orm* (published in two parts in 1941 and 1945, and later translated as *The Long Ships*).[31] With expert attention to historical detail, *Röde Orm* tells of a kidnapped youth's adventures in Spain, England and Byzantium during the late tenth and early eleventh centuries. Besides these novels, both of which are implicitly critical of fascist ideology, the likely reason behind the dearth of interest in Viking topics in the 1930s and 1940s was Hitler's Germany, which had, so to speak, aggressively cornered the market in Scandinavian myths, legends and history.[32] Seemingly, for the Allies, the Vikings made neither for good box office sales, nor for healthy reading.[33]

One, on the face of it, minor but nonetheless highly noteworthy warning about attaching too much significance to North America's Viking past was delivered in 1952 as a lesson to children. The comic book *Walt Disney's Donald Duck and The Golden Helmet* pits Donald against avaricious descendants of the Viking Olaf the Blue in the search for Olaf's magical helmet. The helmet is clearly a reference to the Tarnhelm that grants Siegfried the power to change shape in Wagner's *Ring* cycle, but, better than this, the owner of Olaf's helmet will also be the master of all he surveys – in this case, the whole of North America. Guided by an ancient map pinpointing the location of the helmet as Labrador, Donald sets out full of dreams of emulating Viking daring on the high seas. Yet, once discovered, it transpires that the helmet turns all who wear it into prospective tyrants, determined to impose their own vision of an ideal United States on the populace. In the end, the helmet is jettisoned and the future of the nation is spared.[34] In *The Golden Helmet*, nostalgia for the past is revealed as dangerously at odds with both Viking Age realities and present security. Although the story's writer Carl Barks (1901–2000) was known to have certain sympathies with Senator Joseph McCarthy (1908–57) and his anti-communist witch-hunt, the target here looks to be the Nazis.[35] Interestingly, in 2006, the Danish Ministry of Culture listed *The Golden Helmet* as a work of significance in Denmark's Cultural Canon, the only non-Danish literature to be granted this status.[36]

The rehabilitation of the Vikings as attractive movie machismo is probably best signalled by the star-studded blockbuster movie *The Vikings* (dir. Richard scher, 1958). While making a serious effort at providing credible *mise en scène*, *The Vikings* runs very much at a tangent to any Scandinavian or English accounts of the Viking conquest of northern England in the ninth century. It is not without merit as entertainment and contains some compellingly saga-like superstitious conjuring, but inevitably the plot is focused on the vexed love interest.[37] Vínland has continued to attract an audience with films such as the factitious *The Norseman* (dir. Charles B. Pierce, 1978), the ethnically sympathetic *Kilian's Chronicle: The Magic Stone* (dir. Pamela Berger, 1995), the back-to-the-woods and evidently right-wing *Severed Ways: The Norse Discovery of America* (dir. Tony Stone, 2007) and the self-consciously mysterious *Valhalla Rising* (dir. Nicolas Winding Refn, 2009).

Apart from these, few film-makers have felt constrained by medieval sources or probabilities, or even good taste in their efforts to please audiences with Viking bravura and Norse mythology; for example: the visually racy but otherwise dull *Viking Women and the Sea Serpent* (dir. Roger Corman, 1957); the misleadingly titled *Thor and the Amazon Women* (originally *Le Gladiatric*; dir. Antonio Leonviola, 1963), where Thor is actually a misogynistic 'Tarzan'; the overtly pornographic *The Long Swift Sword of Siegfried* (dir. Adrian Hoven, 1971); the juvenile and confusing *Erik the Viking* (dir. Terry Jones, 1989); the simplistic goodies versus baddies in *The Tartars* (dir. Richard Thorpe, 1960); and a travesty of Bengtsson's *Röde Orm*, *The Long Ships* (dir. Jack Cardiff, 1963), a film considered by all involved to be 'a disaster and an embarrassment'.[38] These 'dreams' of the Middle Ages were, in most cases, cartoon-like projections of contemporary preoccupations and fantasies, particularly concerning ideas about masculinity.[39] Rather like *The Golden Helmet*, they also suggest a disinclination to attach too much significance to any Nordic inheritance. Back in the late 1950s, one fine and telling example of what was at that time an understandable circumspection about the ideological baggage of Germanic high culture comes not from any popular imaginings about the Nordic past, but as a challenge to the perceived pretensions of its interpreters: the target was Wagner's *Ring* cycle and the missile aimed at it was Bugs Bunny.

Among the educated middle classes, enthusiasm for Wagner's operas had reached cult proportions in Europe and the United States throughout the latter half of the nineteenth century and, as a consequence, Wagnerism had come to be seen by the majority of the public as the embodiment of cultural elitism.[40]

In 1957, cartoonist and screenwriter Chuck Jones (1912–2002) of Warner Brothers produced *What's Opera, Doc?*, his 6-minute take on Wagner's 14-hour tetralogy. Although unique in its exclusive focus on Wagner, some 120 Warner Brothers cartoons had already referenced Wagner's music. The difference with *What's Opera, Doc?* is that it not only references the music, it also parodies the art form. First to take centre stage is the hunter Elmer Fudd, Bugs's arch-enemy. In a clear reference to Thor, Elmer rains lightning bolts down onto the terrain from the mountain tops and then goes in search of his prey chanting 'Kill the wabbit' to the well-known theme of 'The Ride of the Valkyries' (Walkürenritt). Bugs emerges and, determined to bewilder and then beguile the simple-minded Elmer, adopts the guise of the heroine Brünnhilde, a role he first played in the 1945 propaganda cartoon *Herr Meets Hare* (dir. Friz Freleng), a send-up of Hermann Göring and Hitler. Elmer responds by transforming into Siegfried and they sing a love duet. Realizing that he has been duped, Elmer resumes hurling lightning bolts and thereafter finds Bugs lying dead. Overcome with remorse, Elmer cradles Bugs in his arms, at which point Bugs looks to camera and says, 'Well, what did you *expect* in an opera? A happy ending?'[41] With this, the cartoon ends.

As the critic Daniel Goldmark observes, 'Simply placing opera into an animated medium is intrinsically humorous, because it violates cultural tradition – we laugh at the juxtaposition of high and low.'[42] Yet, *What's Opera, Doc?* also has a political subtext, one that Walt Disney Productions had seen fit to avoid in 1941, when, with the United States now at war with Germany, it was decided to omit a Valhalla sequence, accompanied by 'The Ride of the Valkyries', from *Fantasia*.[43] Stereotyped *ad absurdum*, subversive and iconoclastic, Jones's *What's Opera, Doc?* cartoon was intended to signify the triumph of mass taste over elitism, but, more than this, by focusing on Wagner, it also signified the triumph of decent hard-working people who enjoyed simple pleasures, over the arrogant and contemptuous denizens of the citadels of 'higher purpose'; in short, the victory over Germany in World War II.

Whether consciously or unconsciously, the United States' 'ownership' of a Viking legacy, combined with a post-war nervousness of, bordering on antagonism towards, the high-blown rhetoric and artistic posturing that accompanied that legacy, were both part of the cultural zeitgeist behind the conception of The Mighty Thor in 1962. This is perhaps an irony but it was not one without precedent.

THE DEVELOPMENT OF THE 'SUPERMAN' CONCEPT

In the early 1930s, the left-wing activist Joseph Pirincin publicly aired his theories about socialist production methods around his home town of Cleveland, Ohio. He talked of the potential for a 'superabundance' brought about by collectivism that would in turn create a 'veritable superman' of the citizen of a future socialist utopia. Later, he claimed that when he gave this lecture at a local community centre, present in the audience were two young Jewish men. He meant Jerry Siegel (1914–96) and Joe Shuster (1914–92), the creators of the first comic-book superhero Superman.[44] The anecdote may well be apocryphal – in all likelihood it is – but the use of the term 'superman' by a radical left-winger is not in doubt and is, in itself, ironic.

The original meaning of 'superman' comes directly from the translation of Übermensch, a term coined by the German philosopher Friedrich Nietzsche (1844–1900) in his novelistic challenge to Judaeo-Christian morality *Also sprach Zarathustra* (Thus Spoke Zarathustra, 1883). First rendered as 'Superman' by George Bernard Shaw (1856–1950) in the title of his stage play *Man and Superman* (1903), the idea of the Übermensch gained notoriety when it was appropriated by the Nazis as an individuation of the concept of the master race. For the Nazis, the antonym of Übermensch was Untermensch, a denomination translated into German from the title of the pamphlet *The Revolt Against Civilisation: The Menace of the Under Man* (1922), by the American anti-immigrationist, eugenicist and white supremacist Lothrop Stoddard (1883–1950). Untermensch thus came to mean a subhuman, a label that Nazi ideologues thereafter attached to Jews, Gypsies and Slavs; indeed, to anyone not of true Aryan stock and therefore a menace to the future of humankind. The Übermensch or Superman was the person who would transcend false and misleading morality and so vanquish his opposite, the Untermensch. In effect, the Superman was Hitler and all those who shared Hitler's *Weltanschauung*, his worldview.

Exactly how much Siegel, as an aspiring writer of pulp fiction, and Shuster, as an untrained graphic artist, knew or even cared about the etymological history of their superhero's name is difficult to assess but, in various forms, the Übermensch/Untermensch opposition was to become the central dynamic in the violent world of their superhero. Given the racist resonances of the original notion of 'the superman', the fact that the comic-book Superman, as well as just about every other superhero creation, came into being almost entirely as a result of the enterprise of children of late nineteenth-century Jewish immigrants fleeing persecution in Europe might also be considered something of an irony. In this case, the irony was one that became particularly marked during World War II, when Hitler and Mussolini proscribed US comic-book heroes and condemned Superman as a Jew. Even so, the idea of an alien being cast into a strange world, bereft of parents, unable to return home and determined to survive and prosper in his new environment by combating its inequities is an apt metaphor for the immigrant experience, just as the idea of a man with a secret identity and super-powers is a metaphor for the immigrant's wish-fulfilling fantasies.

When the 20-year-old Jerry Siegel first conceived of Superman in 1934, he need not have been a student of German philosophy, for as a keen reader of sci-ence fiction, ideas of a man with superpowers, both directly and indirectly drawn from Nietzsche's Übermensch, were readily available. Tales of lone heroes who triumph over hostile forces that threaten humanity were impressed upon Siegel's imagination through novels by those such as H. G. Wells and Jules Verne, while Edgar Rice Burroughs' *Tarzan of the Apes* (1914) and its 25 sequels were one of the publishing sensations of the time and had been made into a highly popular comic strip in 1929. Addicted, like many others of his generation, to comic-book crime, fantasy and sci-fi, Siegel was struck in particular by stories of men who could transcend their mortal limitations through technological ingenuity or mental and physical discipline.

In August 1928, the teenage Siegel bought the latest issue of *Amazing Stories*, a magazine founded in 1926 by science idealist and 'The Father of Science Fiction' Hugo Gernsback (1884–1967).[45] In this issue there appeared the first instalment of the novel *The Skylark of Space* by Edward Elmer Smith (1890–1965), in which a young boffin invents a device that can fly him into space. Wearing only a skintight red bodysuit and with the device consisting of no more than a belt of cartridges and a handheld joystick attached to a cable, the flying man becomes embroiled in an intergalactic battle against an evil criminal gang, which he helps bring to justice, rescuing his bride to be from their clutches along the way. In the same issue was *Armageddon 2419 A.D.* by Philip Francis Nowlan (1888–1940), in which a World War I veteran, Anthony Rogers, later to be known as Buck Rogers, accidently inhales radioactive gas, falls into a coma and awakes hundreds of years into the future to a time when Americans are living in hiding from a world-dominating Mongolian master race. Rogers is adopted by a technologically inventive fugitive militia and, armed with a ray gun, goes on to lead them to victory over their oppressors. Set together, *The Skylark of Space* and *Armageddon 2419 A.D.* were a departure for the comic-book sci-fi genre and their publication was a landmark event in what would become known as 'scientific utopianism'.[46]

Two years later, in 1930, the Princeton-educated Philip Wylie (1902–71) published his dystopian novel *Gladiator*.[47] Wylie, however, was no pulp-fiction fan; rather, his literary style was indebted to the satires of Henry Fielding and William Makepeace Thackeray, although it was from H. G. Wells that he derived his sci-fi enthusiasms. As for his philosophical inclinations, these came directly from his readings of Nietzsche, as is apparent from the plot of *Gladiator*. Wylie's antihero Hugo Danner is the son of a biologist who, having injected his pregnant wife with a life-transforming serum, fathers Hugo as a physical and intellectual super-being, and raises him to practise a strict code of non-violence. Yet, as a man of vision and integrity, Hugo is vulnerable to those of lesser moral courage. Persecuted by ruffians who want to measure themselves against him, used by women who see him as a sexually fascinating freak, and confounded by unscrupulous politicians, he is finally driven to despair. In desperation, he joins an archaeological expedition to South America, where one stormy night he wanders off alone and passionately beseeches God to show him his life's purpose, but he is struck by lightning and dies. It is an ending that draws not just a little on that suffered by Frankenstein's monster. Unlike Nietzsche's Übermensch, Wylie's 'super-child' is an emotional catastrophe, laid low by the mediocrities of humanity. But for Jerry Siegel, who read *Gladiator* in 1932, Hugo Danner suggested yet another ingredient – biological superiority – for his gradually developing ideas about a new type of hero with exceptional abilities.

A third ingredient was supplied in 1933 when Siegel was browsing his favourite comic book *The Shadow*.[48] In it there figured a new creation, a certain Doc Savage, and in this case the inspiration was explicit. The eponymous hero of *Doc Savage Magazine* has the sobriquet 'Man of Bronze' an obvious prompt for Siegel's 'Man of Steel'. Scientist, inventor, explorer and martial arts expert, Doc Savage was in many ways as much a forerunner to Indiana Jones as he was to Superman, except that Savage has a clear moral mission:

> Let me strive, every moment of my life, to make myself better and better, to the best of my ability, that all may profit by it. Let me think of the right, and lend all my assistance to

those who need it, with no regard for anything but justice. Let me take what comes with a smile, without loss of courage. Let me be considerate of my country, of my fellow citizens and my associates in everything I say and do. Let me do right to all, and wrong no man. [49]

More significant than this, however, was the introductory frame of that first instalment of *Doc Savage*, where, superimposed over Doc Savage wrestling with a gunman, is the word 'SUPERMAN'.

Some months after Siegel first outlined his ideas for Superman, one final basic plot device occurred to him: a dual identity. The idea of a suppressed, hidden or otherwise unrecognized identity is one that has been central to myth and folktale since the earliest times. During the nineteenth century, such ideas became literalized through case studies of personality disorders, emerging psychiatric theories and the fashion for hypnosis. This, in turn, gave rise to fictional notions of a split personality, most dramatically in Robert Louis Stevenson's (1850–94) *Strange Case of Dr Jekyll and Mr Hyde* (1886) and in the gothic tales of Edgar Allan Poe (1809–49). However, while literary and psychoanalytical articulations of the divided self would have been familiar to Siegel, it was Baroness Emmuska Orczy's (1865–1947) more wholesome and heroic account of a concealed identity, *The Scarlet Pimpernel* (1905) that drew his attention. Orczy's protagonist, Sir Percy Blakeney, manages to disguise his role as the liberator of French aristocrats heading for the guillotine, even from his disdainful wife. In December 1934, *The Scarlet Pimpernel* reached a mass market as a lavishly produced movie (dir. Harold Young), starring a smouldering Merle Oberon and a dashing Leslie Howard. All Siegel's ideas now fell into place: Superman would be a crime-busting extraterrestrial with superpowers and a high moral purpose, and, like Sir Percy, have a real-life identity as an innocuous nobody. In Superman's case, this would be the mild-mannered reporter Clark Kent and the unrequited love interest would be Lois Lane – condescending to Clark, her colleague, rival and admirer, but smitten by the abstemious Superman. [50]

It would take almost five frustrating years before *Superman* made it to the magazine stands as a product of the largest comic-book retailer and distributor in the country, DC Comics. Once it did, it sold in millions and by the early 1940s had helped trigger a comic-book craze for a plethora of superheroes, including the rather gothic Batman, vigilante of Gotham City. [51] Alongside DC Comics, was the other main purveyor of superhero fantasies Timely Comics (which later became Marvel Comics), where, using the dual-identity formula, Jack Kirby (Jake Kurtzberg, 1917–94) and Joe Simon (b. 1913) created the hugely successful Captain America in 1941.[52] But the craze also carried in its wake a consumer appetite for the more sleazy magazines that had prospered as an under-the-counter subculture in the 1920s. Images of superheroes bashing German and Japanese war leaders may have been ideal reading for men needing a morale boost in theatres of war, but the comic-book industry was beginning to cause raised eyebrows on the home front. Superheroes, no matter how patriotic, were not exempted. With the turn of the decade, the Golden Age of comic books came to an end.

Concerns expressed during the wartime years about the damaging influence that the comic-book phenomenon was having on the nation's youth turned, in the post-war years, into a widespread moral backlash. The prime targets were the gory excesses and sexual titillations of the horror, crime, detective and 'glamour' comics, but Superman's unregulated violence, often cruelly meted out in his early incarnation, and the dominatrix appearance of characters such as Wonder Woman did not go unremarked. In 1948, the immigrant Jewish-German psychiatrist Fredric Wertham (1895–1981) began a campaign against the comic-book industry that culminated in 1954 with his study *Seduction of the Innocent*. Batman and Robin, he pronounced, signified a homosexual partnership with paedophile characteristics; Wonder Woman was clearly a lesbian; and Superman was a symbol of racial superiority, a fascist in a body stocking, whose trademark 'S', thought Wertham, is fortunate only in so far as it is not 'SS'.[53]

In New York and Chicago, worried parents gathered piles of comic books from their children's bedrooms and held public burnings; the National Congress of Parents and Teachers questioned the freedom of the press; cities across the United States legislated to restrict sales; and the House Committee on Un-American Activities turned its attention on the Jewish comic-book 'racketeers'. With sales plummeting and dozens of bandwagon publishers going out of business, the comic-book industry responded by imposing on itself a code of practice but to little effect. Superman was steadily shifted into radio and television where he was scrupulously laundered. Then, in 1954, the United States Senate Judiciary Subcommittee on Juvenile Delinquency opened an investigation. Wertham was appointed as an expert adviser but, despite his demand for national legislation, the Subcommittee eventually settled for a much tighter code of self-censorship, which was rapidly instituted as the Comics Code Authority. Prurient images, profanities, graphic violence and anything that in any way whatsoever might cause offence to the most upright of citizens was banned.[54]

The comic-book industry did not collapse completely in the 1950s, it merely contracted, went back to the drawing board and rethought its position. As for superheroes, the days of the wham-bam can-do-no-wrong moral crusader and transcendent Nietzschean Übermensch were over. What was required was a new type of superhero, still 'all-American' but sensitive, vulnerable, psychologized, existentially fraught, even victim. There is also little doubt that the Nazi holocaust brought a different perspective to comic-book scriptwriters of a Jewish European background regarding matters of justice and equality.[55] By the end of the decade and on into the 1960s, the reformulated superhero was expressing more subtly than ever before a teenager's angst and his (for comic books have remained a largely male domain) Oedipal struggle for recognition and independence. Either brought out of retirement and appropriately sensitized or given a thorough makeover were heroes such as Captain Marvel, Batman, Wonder Woman and, of course, the indestructible Superman. Alongside them came the comic-book Silver Age new breed, which, during the 1960s at Marvel Comics, included the guilt-ridden alter ego of The Incredible Hulk, the awkwardly introspective Spider-Man, and the product of a highly dysfunctional family, The Mighty Thor.

THE MIGHTY THOR

[H]ow do you make someone stronger than the strongest person?

It finally came to me; don't make him human – make him a god . . . I decided readers were already pretty familiar with the Greek and Roman gods. It might be more fun to delve into the old Norse legends, and fun was always the name of the game. Besides, I pictured the Norse gods looking like Vikings of old, with the flowing beards, horned helmets, and battle clubs . . . One of our established titles, *Journey into Mystery*, needed a shot in the arm, so I picked Thor, the Norse God of Thunder, to headline the book. After writing an outline depicting the story and the characters I had in mind, I asked my brother, Larry, to write the script because I didn't have time . . . and it was only natural for me to assign the penciling to Jack Kirby, who drew it as though he had spent his whole life in Asgard . . . we later took Thor out of *Journey into Mystery* and gave him his own book, and that was when I started having him speak in a pseudo-biblical/Shakespearean manner.[56]

This is how Stan Lee recalls the creation of his Nordic superhero. One mythological character who had been tried out before was Hercules, who had appeared in various DC Comics storylines from as early as 1941, and went on to become a standard with Marvel Comics from 1965, at first as a rival to Thor, then later as his friend and ally as a member of Earth's Mightiest Heroes in *The Avengers* series.[57] Besides Hercules, DC Comics had referenced a number of figures from Graeco-Roman classical and Egyptian mythology in their *Captain Marvel Adventures*, although without any serious intention to develop them.[58] But Thor was a different proposition in a number of ways: first, Thor did not need the concoction of a family group, as this was ready-made in the mythology; second, for the same reason, Thor needed little by way of superpowers to be invented for him; and third, Thor's role as protector and defender of mankind was fundamental to his original mythological purpose. In just about every respect, Thor came pre-packaged and Lee was fortunate in as much as his artist, Jack Kirby, was a keen student of ancient mythologies.[59] Having given Thor the ability to fly by whirling his hammer like a propeller, all that was required was to accommodate him into the Superman dual-identity formula and, given the flawed-personality requirement of the comic-book Silver Age hero, to endow him with a recognizably troublesome psychology.

Thor's 1962 debut in 'Thor the Mighty and the Stone Men from Saturn' (issue 83 of *Journey into Mystery*) established the basic principles. The partially disabled Dr Don Blake is vacationing in Norway when, unseen by him, an alien spaceship lands from which emerge a number of stone men with superpowers. An old fisherman sees the aliens and tries to warn the local village but only Dr Blake gives any credence to his tale and, so, decides to investigate alone. Spotted by the aliens he hides in a cave, where he finds a secret chamber containing a gnarled wooden stick. In his efforts to find an alternative exit, he strikes a large boulder with the stick and is instantly transformed into Thor, while the stick transforms into 'Mjolnir [sic]' bearing an inscription telling Blake of his new identity.[60] In the following issues, Blake/Thor learns to master his weapon and discovers how he can transform from mortal to god and vice versa at will. He subsequently overcomes the aliens after North Atlantic Treaty Organization (NATO) fighter planes from a US airbase come under attack.

Long-running comic-book superhero storylines frequently require a suspension of disbelief that includes having to forget that earlier aspects of a superhero's biography are not consistent with certain later information given about them; or, alternatively, having to accept the most tortuous of explanations about how such discrepancies are not really discrepancies at all. The muddled evolution of The Mighty Thor is a case in point. Whereas Superman is essentially a citizen of Earth disguised as Clark Kent, his planetary home having been destroyed along with his entire family (although he may occasionally access his parents through futuristic technology, for which just about anything is possible), not so with Thor, who inhabits Earth and the alternate universe of Asgard. Exactly how, as both Dr Don Blake, the mortal, and Thor, the immortal, he can live out differing complex social interactions in two separate worlds as two separate beings took some explaining.

The initial proposition was that Thor had been punished by his father, Odin, for showing a lack of humility and, so, was cast into the underground chamber in Norway, without memory of being a god. But this failed to explain how Thor could also be Don Blake, unless being Blake was also part of the punishment. The improvised solution for Marvel's writers was to do exactly this and make being Blake part of Odin's reprimand. Blake, therefore, had always been Thor but was ignorant of this fact. Complicating matters even further is Jane Foster, a nurse and Blake's assistant at his clinic. Blake is deeply enamoured of Jane, thus, so is Thor, an entanglement that prompts Odin to impose further sanctions on his son. For a good while, Blake, Thor and Jane constitute a love triangle, but with an increasing amount of mythological material being drawn from the eddas, along with a very discerning and critical fan base, it eventually had to be acknowledged that Thor had a wife in Asgard: Sif. What is more, in some episodes, he also conducts an affair with an alluring Asgardian mistress with whom he sires a child, something which is also suggested in the eddas. To resolve this problem posed by Jane, she first is made aware that Blake and Thor are the same person, and then is written out of the series and all memory of Thor erased from her mind, only after which can the forlorn Thor be allowed to form a relationship with Sif.[61] In a later attempt to account for the discrepancies between the Norse Thor and The Mighty Thor (such as, the former having red hair and a beard, the latter being blond and clean shaven), it is explained that the old Thor and Odin had died but had been reincarnated in slightly altered form.

Perhaps none of this plot identity crisis mattered that much, for the comic-book Thor is mainly preoccupied with protecting mankind from an evil that he has

inadvertently visited upon it himself; that is to say, Loki, Thor's stepbrother and
the determined agent of his undoing. Loki's mayhem often takes the form of
trying to rob Thor of his hammer – the sexual symbolism of which is more than
a little obvious. And along with Loki, and at his bidding, come Thor's mythological enemies the trolls and the giants, as well as a host of super villains. In
his endless struggle to hold back a swelling tide of monsters, Thor is obliged to
enlist help from a mix of fellow Asgardians and other comic-book superheroes,
either to aid his struggles against Loki's manufactured evils or to combat US
twentieth-century political and military adversaries. In due course, Thor would
go on to be depicted as the one-time enemy of Hitler and the subsequent bane of
all far-right organizations, a bulwark against the Soviet Union and as a combatant
in Vietnam (against another superbeing). Thor also shares Middle America's
social anxieties and is, in the late 1960s, for example, a critic of slothful hippies.
As for his Old Northern devotees, the Vikings, they are rejected for the crime
of massacring Christian monks, and when a longship of zombie Vikings travels
through time and puts ashore in Manhattan, only Thor can deal with them.[62] In
this way, Thor is the embodiment of Viking nobility, while the Vikings themselves
are a depraved subspecies.

Eddic mythology and Wagner's *Ring* cycle have provided an almost endless
supply of ideas for successive writers for *The Mighty Thor*, such as the struggle
for a dangerous Ring of Power in the 'Eye of Odin' sequence, during which Thor
becomes Siegfried and falls in love with Brünnhilde,[63] and episodes in the 1980s
where Thor combats the Midgard Serpent.[64] Yet, as Lee always acknowledged,
the use of any figure from ancient mythologies was secondary to the already
established comic-book mythology of superheroes and super villains, ground out
month after month for the enthusiasts. In this respect, apart from the opportunity
for writers to extemporize on a pre-existing mythico-legendary universe, *The
Mighty Thor* has less to do with Norse myth and more to do with reflecting US
political identity and the mood and mentality of contemporary US life, particularly as it might be perceived by comic-book consumers.[65]

More emphatically than most superheroes, there are two faces to The Mighty
Thor: the public and the private. In his role as a saviour of Earth and Asgard, he
tackles all threats to mortal and immortal life, but he is also capable of terrible
miscalculations, for instance, his plan to correct human failings by enslaving the
Earth's population, just as he is often incapable of summoning his powers when

he most needs them. Thor, in these senses, is a metonym for the responsibilities and anxieties of the most powerful country in the world; more so, in some respects, than Superman. His private life is equally complex. He has a domineering and capricious father, who even after his apparent death and Thor's accession to the throne of Asgard continues to trouble him; he is locked forever into a form of sibling rivalry; and he is incapable of forming a stable sexual relationship. On the one hand, he is a hyperbole of the troubled male breadwinner; on the other, he is a psycho-sexual profile of the suburban geek: unsocialized, unsure of his place in life and resentful of those with authority over him.

Richard Reynolds, an analyst of the comic-book Thor, has remarked that he 'has been fairly ruthlessly cut on the Procrustean bed of the superhero comic – and rarely used as a pretext for expounding Norse mythology', but goes on to conclude that 'Thor has successfully worn its high-culture credentials on its sleeve'.[66] This, surely, is a contradiction. More accurately, one would have to say that the 'cut' of Thor was motivated by an appropriation of high culture for low-culture markets, and that, far from sporting Thor's high-culture credentials, *The Mighty Thor* traded them for dollars. Given where high culture had led Thor in the run-up to World War II, this may not have been such an entirely bad outcome.

From Longfellow to Lee and, so, from myth to Marvel, ideas about Thor and Scandinavian antiquity have generally involved a shift away from the purview of scholars, polemicists and the literati – wrongheaded and prejudicial although some of the those ideas are – and into mass markets, where entertainment substitutes for aesthetics and unbridled imagination substitutes for serious analysis and accuracy. Gerard Jones has summed up the advent of the comic book as 'counter-cultural, lowbrow, idealistic, prurient, pretentious, mercenary, forward-looking, and ephemeral, all in the same instant'.[67] Given the exceptions of the limited circles of scholarly research and analysis, and a continuing fascination with the Norse gods among fantasy and pulp-fiction writers,[68] for Thor, as well as for many other touchstones of national identities and histories, this has meant what would appear to be an irreversible decline into the ersatz, the kitsch and the lowest common denominator.[69] Doubtless the taint of Nazi ideology and the continued promulgation of Nordic supremacist ideas by far-right groups have done much to provoke a counterbalancing trivialization of Norse mythology. Yet, few nowadays would think a second renaissance of the North to be either desirable or even possible.[70] In the final analysis, whatever stance one might adopt concerning the beliefs held by societies long past, and whichever theory one chooses to advance to explain or assess the impact of mass culture, it is possible to conclude that the reception history of the Thunder god is, in any meaningful sense, at an end.

Notes

Notes to Chapter 1: The Giant Killer

1 Jón Jóhannesson, Magnús Finnbogason and Kristján Eldjárn, eds, 'Íslendinga saga', *Sturlunga saga*, 2 vols (Reykjavík: Sturlunguútgáfan, 1946), ch. 151, p. 156.

2 For a useful assessment of Snorri's life and times, see Diana Whaley, *Heimskringla: An Introduction* (Viking Society for Northern Research, 1991), pp. 20–40.

3 Anthony Faulkes, trans., *Snorri Sturluson. Edda* (London: J. M. Dent, 1995), pp. 64–5.

4 Vali's precocious act is also indicated in the account of Baldur's killing in 'The Seeress's Prophecy'.

5 Carolyne Larrington, trans., *The Poetic Edda* (Oxford and New York: Oxford University Press, 1996), v. 45, p. 10.

6 Snorri lists a number of other names for Thor in 'Skáldskaparmál', only a few of which are mentioned elsewhere in the eddas: Atli (The Terrible), Asabrag (Aesir Lord), Biorn (Bear), Eindridi (Lone Rider), Ennilang (Wide Forehead), Hardveur (Strong Archer), Hlorridi (Loud Rider), Rym (Noise), Sonnung (perhaps The True One), Veud (perhaps Shrine Guardian) and Vingthor (perhaps Weapon Shaker).

7 Faulkes, trans., *Edda*, p. 3.

8 Margaret Clunies Ross, 'An interpretation of the myth of Þórr's encounter with Geirrøðr and his daughters', in Ursula Dronke, Guðrún P. Helgadóttir, Gerd Wolfgang Weber and Hans Bekker-Nielsen, eds, *Speculum Norroenum: Norse Studies in Memory of Gabriel Turville-Petre* (Odense: Odense University Press, 1981), pp. 370–91; p. 379.

9   See Per Vikstrand, 'Förkristna sakrala personnamn i Skandinavien', *Studia anthroponymica Scandinavica*, 27 (2009), pp. 5–31.

10 Scholarly speculation about Sif's significance is helpfully summarized in Rudolf Simek, *Dictionary of Northern Mythology*, trans., Angela Hall (Cambridge: D. S. Brewer, 1984), p. 283.

11 Larrington, trans., *The Poetic Edda*, v. 48, p. 75.

12 Faulkes, trans., *Edda*, p.72.

13 Joseph Harris, 'The Masterbuilder Tale in Snorri's *Edda* and two sagas', *Arkiv för nordisk filologi*, 91 (1976), pp. 66–101.

14 Larrington, trans., *The Poetic Edda*, v. 26 and 27, p. 7.

15 H. R. Ellis Davidson, *Pagan Scandinavia* (London: Thames and Hudson, 1967), p. 125.

16 See Martin Arnold, 'Hvat er tröll nema þat? The cultural history of the troll', in Tom Shippey, ed., *The Shadow-Walkers: Jacob Grimm's Mythology of the Monstrous* (Tempe, AZ: Arizona State University; Turnhout: Brepols, 2005), pp. 111–55; pp. 143–55.

17 Peter Hallberg, 'Om Þrymskivða', *Edda*, 58 (1968), pp. 256–70.

18 Larrington, trans., *The Poetic Edda*, v. 18, p. 99.

19 Faulkes, trans., *Edda*, p. 77.

20 Faulkes, trans., *Edda*, p. 77.

21 Faulkes, trans., *Edda*, p. 78

22 Faulkes, trans., *Edda*, p. 73

23 E. O. G. Turville-Petre, *Myth and Religion of the North: The Religion of Ancient Scandinavia* (London: Weidenfield and Nicolson, 1964), p. 78.

24 Faulkes, trans., *Edda*, p. 82.

25 Saxo Grammaticus, *The History of the Danes* (Gesta Danorum): *Books I–IX*, vol. 1, ed. H. R. Ellis Davidson, trans. Peter Fisher (Cambridge: D. S. Brewer, 1996), Book 8, pp. 265–6.

26 Faulkes, trans., *Edda*, p. 37.

27 See Michael Chesnutt, 'The beguiling of Þórr', in Rory McTurk and Andrew Wawn, eds, *Úr Dölum til Dala: Guðbrandur Vigfússon Centenary Essays* (Leeds: Leeds Texts and Monographs, 1989), pp. 35–63.

28 Larrington, trans., *The Poetic Edda*, v. 62, p. 95.

29 Larrington, trans., *The Poetic Edda*, v. 26, p. 73.

30 For this observation and a useful discussion of Thor's role in Norse myth, see Margaret Clunies Ross, *Prolonged Echoes: Old Norse Myths in Medieval Northern Society, Volume 1: The Myths* (Odense: Odense University Press, 1994), pp. 258–68.

31 Faulkes, trans., *Edda*, p. 46.

32 Faulkes, trans., *Edda*, p. 46.

33 Faulkes, trans., *Edda*, p. 47.

34 Larrington, trans., *The Poetic Edda*, v. 38, p. 83.

35 See Preben Meulengracht Sørensen, 'Thor's fishing expedition', in Gro Steinsland, ed., *Words and Objects: Towards a Dialogue between Archaeology and the History of Religion* (Oslo: Norwegian University Press, 1986), pp. 257–78.

36 Larrington, trans., *The Poetic Edda*, v. 56, p. 11.

37 Larrington, trans., *The Poetic Edda*, v. 65, p. 12.

Notes to Chapter 2: Theorizing Thor

1 For a comparative discussion of giants in mythological and legendary traditions, see Randi Eldevik, 'Less than kind: giants in Germanic tradition', in Tom Shippey, ed., *The Shadow-Walkers: Jacob Grimm's Mythology of the Monstrous* (Tempe, AZ: Arizona State University; Turnhout: Brepols, 2005), pp. 83–110.

2 Anthony Faulkes, trans., *Snorri Sturluson. Edda* (London: J. M. Dent, 1995), p. 82

3 Margaret Clunies Ross, *Prolonged Echoes: Old Norse Myths in Medieval Northern Society, Volume 1: The Myths* (Odense: Odense University Press, 1994), p. 261 (see pp. 258–68 for a discussion of Thor in the myths). See also Margaret Clunies Ross, 'An interpretation of the myth of Þórr's encounter with Geirrøðr and his daughters', in Ursula Dronke, Guðrún P. Helgadóttir, Gerd Wolfgang Weber and Hans Bekker-Nielsen, eds, *Speculum Norroenum: Norse Studies in Memory of Gabriel Turville-Petre* (Odense: Odense University Press, 1981), pp. 370–91.

4 For analysis of Thor's role in confronting giantesses, see John McKinnell, 'Fighting the giantess: Þórr', *Meeting the Other in Norse Myth and Legend* (Cambridge: D. S. Brewer, 2005), pp. 109–25.

5   Carolyne Larrington, trans., *The Poetic Edda* (Oxford and New York: Oxford University Press, 1996), v. 17, p. 99. The vernacular reads 'mik muna Æsir *argan* kalla' (my italics).

6   See Martin Arnold, 'Hvat er tröll nema þat? The cultural history of the troll', in Tom Shippey, ed., *The Shadow-Walkers: Jacob Grimm's Mythology of the Monstrous* (Tempe, AZ: Arizona State University; Turnhout: Brepols, 2005), pp. 111–55; pp. 116–24.

7   Larrington, trans., *The Poetic Edda*, v. 41, p. 258.

8   Faulkes, trans., *Edda*, p. 15.

9   Faulkes, trans., *Edda*, p. 15.

10 Larrington, trans., *The Poetic Edda*, v. 52, p. 11.

11 For a discussion of pre-patriarchy, see Ann Heinrichs, '"Annat er várt eðli": The Type of the Pre-Patriarchal Woman in Old Norse Literature', in J. Lindow, L. Lönnroth and G. W. Weber, eds, *Structure and Meaning in Old Norse Literature* (Odense: Odense University Press), pp. 110–40. For a comprehensive discussion of gender valuations in Old Norse literature, see Jenny Jochens, *Old Norse Images of Women* (Philadelphia, PA: University of Pennsylvania Press, 1996).

12 See, for example, Claude Lévi-Strauss, *The Raw and the Cooked*, trans John Weightman and Doreen Weightman from *Le Cru et le Cuit* (1964) (London: Jonathan Cape, 1970).

13 Larrington, trans., *The Poetic Edda*, v. 9, p. 86.

14 Anna Birgitta Rooth, *Loki in Scandinavian Mythology* (Lund: C. W. K. Gleerup, 1961).

15 Larrington, trans., *The Poetic Edda*, v. 24, p. 73.

16 See, for example, Miriam Robbins Dexter and Karlene Jones-Bley, eds, *The Kurgan Culture and the Indo-Europeanization of Europe: Selected Articles from 1952 to 1993 by M. Gimbutas*, Journal of Indo-European Studies Monograph 18 (Washington DC: Institute for the Study of Man, 1997).

17 The Roman Mars and the Greek Ares have also been seen as occupying this function.

18 See Georges Dumézil, *Gods of the Ancient Norsemen* (University of California Press, 1973), ed. Einar Haugen, trans. Francis Charat from *Les Dieux des Germains* (1939); and Georges Dumézil, *The Destiny of the Warrior*, trans.

Alf Hiltebeitel from *Heur et malheur du guerrier: Aspects mythiques de la fonction guerrière chez les Indo-Européens* (1969) (Chicago, IL: University of Chicago Press, 1970).

19 Larrington, trans., *The Poetic Edda*, pp. 246–52.

20 Dumézil, *Gods of the Ancient Norsemen*, pp. 118–25.

21 H. Mattingley, trans., *Tacitus on Britain and Germany: A Translation of the 'Agricola' and the 'Germania'* (Harmondsworth: Penguin, 1948), p. 108.

22 Adam of Bremen, *History of the Archbishops of Hamburg-Bremen*, trans. Francis J. Tschan (New York: Columbia University Press, 1959), pp. 207–8. It has been argued that a twelfth-century tapestry from Skog church, Hälsingland, Sweden, depicts Odin, Thor and Frey in much the same way as Adam describes the disposition of the gods in the Uppsala temple. Other commentators have interpreted the tapestry as representing Olaf Haraldsson (r. 1015–30), Knut IV of Denmark (r. 1080–86) and Erik IX of Sweden (r. 1150–60).

23 Dumézil, *Gods of the Ancient Norsemen*, pp. 71–3. For a further discussion of Thor in the context of Indo-European myth see, for example, Riti Kroesen, 'The great god Þórr: a war god?', *Arkiv för nordisk filologi*, 116 (2001), pp. 97–110.

24 For Ælfric's references to Thor, see Walter W. Skeat, ed. and trans., 'The life of St Martin', *Ælfric's Lives of Saints: Being a Set of Sermons on Saints' Days Formerly Observed by the English Church*, 2 vols (London: Early English Text Society, 1881–85, 1890–1900; repr. Oxford: Oxford University Press for the EETS 1966); and P. Baker, trans., 'De falsis deis' (On the false gods), in John C. Pope, ed., *Homilies of Ælfric: A Supplementary Collection*, 2 vols (London: Early English Text Society, 1967–68), vol. 2, pp. 667–724. For Saxo on Thor, see Saxo Grammaticus, *The History of the Danes* (*Gesta Danorum*): *Books I–IX*, vol. 1, ed. H. R. Ellis Davidson, trans. Peter Fisher (Cambridge: D. S. Brewer, 1996), Book 6, p. 171.

25 Helen Carron, ed. and trans., *Clemens Saga: The Life of St Clement of Rome*, Viking Society for Northern Research Text Series, vol. XVII (London: University College London, 2005), p. 45.

26 For a full examination of the Icelandic saints' lives and their view of the Norse gods, see Simonetta Battista, 'Interpretations of the Roman Pantheon in the Old Norse hagiographic sagas', in Margaret Clunies Ross, *Old*

Norse Myths, Literature and Society (Odense: University Press of Southern Denmark, 2003), pp. 175–97.

27   For a discussion of the origins of the days of the week in the Germanic regions and their Latin correspondences, see James Stephen Stallybrass, trans., *Grimm's Teutonic Mythology*, 4 vols, from Jacob Grimm, *Deutsche Mythologie*, 4th edn (London: George Bell and Sons, 1882–88), vol. 1, pp. 122–30.

28   Ralph T. H. Griffith, trans., *Rig Veda*, (Benares: E. J. Lazarus and Company, 1896), Book 5, Hymn XXXVI.

29   E. O. G. Turville-Petre, *Myth and Religion of the North: The Religion of Ancient Scandinavia* (London: Weidenfield and Nicolson, 1964), p. 104.

30   Dumézil, *The Destiny of the Warrior*, pp. 65–104, esp. 82–95.

31   Saxo Grammaticus, *The History of the Danes*, Books 6 and 8; Hermann Pálsson and Paul Edwards, trans., 'The saga of King Gautrek', *Seven Viking Romances* (Harmondsworth: Penguin Books, 1985), pp. 138–70.

32   For one of many assessments of Dumézil's theories, see J. P. Mallory, *In Search of the Indo-Europeans: Language Archaeology and Myth* (London: Thames and Hudson, 1991), pp. 130–5.

33   Dumézil, *Gods of the Ancient Norsemen*, pp. 68–71.

34   For a discussion of Thor's family roles in this myth, see John Lindow, 'Thor's duel with Hrungnir', *alvíssmál*, 6 (1996), pp. 3–20.

35   Faulkes, trans., *Edda*, p. 38.

36   Larrington, trans., *The Poetic Edda*, v. 30, p. 101.

37   Faulkes, trans., *Edda*, p. 49.

38   For a detailed analysis of Thor's role in initiatory rites, see Jens Peter Schjødt, *Initiation between Two Worlds: Structure and Symbolism in Pre-Christian Scandinavian Religion*, trans. Victor Hansen, The Viking Collection, Studies in Northern Civilisation, vol. XVII (Odense: University Press of Southern Denmark, 2008), pp. 225–51.

39   See Birgit Sawyer, *Viking-Age Rune-Stones; Custom and Commemoration in Early Medieval Scandinavia* (Oxford: Oxford University Press, 2000), pp. 128–9.

40   A near-contemporary runic spell inscribed on a Swedish amulet from Sigtuna has some similarities with the Canterbury charm.

41   Larrington, trans., *The Poetic Edda*, v. 23, p. 73

Notes to Chapter 3: Christ versus Thor

1 Judy Quinn, trans., 'The Saga of the People of Eyri', in Viðar Hreinsson, ed., *The Complete Sagas of the Icelanders*, vol. V (Reykjavík: Leifur Eiríksson Publishing, 1997), pp. 131–218; pp. 133–4.

2 Robert Cook and John Porter, trans, 'The Saga of the People of Kjalarnes', in Viðar Hreinsson, ed., *The Complete Sagas of the Icelanders*, vol. III (Reykjavík: Leifur Eiríksson Publishing, 1997), pp. 305–29; p. 307.

3 See H. R. Ellis Davidson, *Gods and Myths of Northern Europe* (Harmondsworth: Penguin Books, 1964), p. 79. A similar temple to the one at Hof is described as dedicated to Odin in *The Saga of Hákon the Good*; see L. M. Hollander, trans., *Heimskringla; History of the Norwegian Kings*, by Snorri Sturluson (Austin, TX: University of Texas Press, 1964), p. 107.

4 For these observations, see Davidson, *Gods and Myths of Northern Europe*, p. 87, and E. O. G. Turville-Petre, *Myth and Religion of the North: The Religion of Ancient Scandinavia* (London: Weidenfield and Nicolson, 1964), pp. 96–7. The relatively obscure Celtic god Taranis also has associations with thunder and lightning.

5 Quinn, trans., 'The Saga of the People of Eyri', pp. 187–90.

6 See Davidson, *Gods and Myths of Northern Europe*, p. 77, and Michael Swanton, ed. and trans., 'The Peterborough Manuscript', *The Anglo-Saxon Chronicle*, new edn (London: Phoenix, 2000), p. 75.

7 See Hermann Pálsson and Paul Edwards, eds and trans, *The Book of Settlements: Landnámabók* (Winnipeg: University of Manitoba Press, 1972), ch. 85, p. 46; and Quinn, trans., 'The Saga of the People of Eyri', p. 136.

8 Hermann Pálsson and Paul Edwards, eds and trans, *The Book of Settlements: Landnámabók*, ch. 123, pp. 61–2.

9 Keneva Kunz, trans., 'Eirik the Red's Saga', in Viðar Hreinsson, ed., *The Complete Sagas of the Icelanders*, vol. I (Reykjavík: Leifur Eiríksson Publishing, 1997), pp. 1–18; p. 13.

10 E. O. G. Turville-Petre, 'The cult of Óðinn in Iceland', *Nine Norse Studies*, Viking Society for Northern Research Text Series, vol. V (London: University College London, 1972), pp. 1–19.

11 Hermann Pálsson and Edwards, eds and trans, *The Book of Settlements: Landnámabók*, ch. 218, p. 97.

12 Robert Cook, trans., 'Njal's Saga', in Viðar Hreinsson, ed., *The Complete Sagas of the Icelanders*, vol. III (Reykjavík: Leifur Eiríksson Publishing, 1997), pp. 1–220; p. 125.

13 See Siân Grønlie, trans., 'Kristni Saga', *Íslendingabók; Kristni saga: The Book of the Icelanders; The Story of the Conversion*, Viking Society for Northern Research Text Series, vol. XVIII (London: University College London, 2006), pp. 35–74; p. 42.

14 Cook, trans., 'Njal's Saga', p. 124–5.

15 Translation cited in Davidson, *Gods and Myths of Northern Europe*, p. 76.

16 Hollander, trans., 'The Saga of Óláf Tryggvason', *Heimskringla*, pp. 144–244; p. 208.

17 Hollander, trans., 'The Saga of Hákon the Good', *Heimskringla*, pp. 96–127; pp. 110–12.

18 Hollander, trans., 'Saint Óláf's Saga', *Heimskringla*, pp. 245–537; pp. 373–4.

19 Adam of Bremen, *History of the Archbishops of Hamburg-Bremen*, trans. Francis J. Tschan (New York: Columbia University Press, 1959), pp. 97–8.

20 Cited and translated in Davidson, *Gods and Myths of Northern Europe*, p. 81, from Saxo Grammaticus, *Gesta Danorum*, Book XIII.

21 Turville-Petre, *Myth and Religion of the North*, p. 92.

22 Cited in Alfred P. Smyth, *Scandinavian Kings in the British Isles 850–880* (Oxford and New York: Oxford University Press, 1977), p. 115

23 F. M. Stenton, *Anglo-Saxon England*, 3rd edn (Oxford: Oxford University Press, 1971), pp. 98–9.

24 The name 'Saxnot' may mean 'sword friend', but as the name of a deity is otherwise obscure.

25 Dudo of St Quentin, *History of the Normans*, trans. Eric Christiansen (Woodbridge: Boydell Press, 1998), pp. 15–16.

26 Dudo of St Quentin, *History of the Normans*, trans. Eric Christiansen, p. 16.

27 Adam of Bremen, *History of the Archbishops of Hamburg-Bremen*, p. 208.

28 The role of such Thor-related finds in Norway is discussed by Sæbjørg Walaker Nordeide, 'Thor's hammer in Norway: a symbol of reaction against the Christian cross?', in Anders Andrén, Kristina Jennbert and Catharina Raudvere, eds, *Old Norse Religion in Long-Term Perspectives: Origins, Changes, and Interactions* (Lund: Nordic Academic Press, 2006), pp. 218–23.

29 See Elena A. Melnikova, 'Reminiscences of Old Norse Myths, cults and ritu-als in Old Russian literature', in Margaret Clunies Ross, ed., *Old Norse Myths, Literature and Society* (Odense: University Press of Southern Denmark, 2003), pp. 66–86; esp. pp. 67–71.

30 Samuel Hazzard Cross and Olgerd P. Sherbowitz-Wetzor, eds and trans, *The Russian Primary Chronicle: Laurentian Text* (Cambridge, MA: Medieval Academy of America, 1953). For references to Perun, see entries for the following years: 904–07 (p. 65); 945 (p. 74 and 77); 971 (p. 90); 980 (p. 93); and 988 (p. 117).

31 Paul Acker, trans., 'The Saga of the People of Floi', in Viðar Hreinsson, ed., *The Complete Sagas of the Icelanders*, vol. III (Reykjavík: Leifur Eiríksson Publishing, 1997), pp. 271–30; p. 289.

32 Richard Perkins, *Thor the Wind-Raiser and the Eyrarland Image*, Viking Society for Northern Research Text Series, vol. XV (London: University College London, 2001).

33 Adapted from the translation in Perkins, *Thor the Wind-Raiser*, pp. 42–3.

34 For a discussion of the authenticity of Hallfred's verse, see Diana Whaley 'The "Conversion Verses" in *Hallfreðar saga*: Authentic Voice of a Reluctant Christian?', in Margaret Clunies Ross, ed., *Old Norse Myths, Literature and Society* (Odense: University Press of Southern Denmark, 2003), pp. 234–57.

35 Lars Levi Læstadius, *Fragments of Lappish Mythology*, ed. Juha Pentikainen and trans. Borje Vahamaki (Beaverton: Aspasia, 2002), p. 91.

Notes to Chapter 4: Recovering the Past

1 Informing this chapter throughout are Andrew Wawn, 'The post-medieval reception of Old Norse and Old Icelandic literature', in Rory McTurk, ed., *A Companion to Old Norse–Icelandic Literature and Culture* (Malden, MA, Oxford, UK: Blackwell Publishing, 2005), pp. 320–37; and Margaret Clunies Ross and Lars Lönnroth, 'The Norse Muse: report from an international research project', *alvíssmál*, 9 (1999), pp. 3–28; esp. pp. 10–18.

2 Climate conditions recovered during the first half of the fifteenth century but worsened again during the remainder of that century: see Jouko Vahtola,

'Population and settlement', in Knut Helle, ed., *The Cambridge History of Scandinavia: Volume 1; Prehistory to 1520* (Cambridge: Cambridge University Press, 2003), pp. 559–80; p. 571.

3 For the Swedish perspective during this period, see Anthony F. Upton, *Charles XI and Swedish Absolutism* (Cambridge: Cambridge University Press, 1998).

4 This issue is interestingly analysed in Margaret Clunies Ross, 'The measures of Old Norse religion in long-term perspective', in Anders Andrén, Kristina Jennbert and Catharina Raudvere, eds, *Old Norse Religion In Long-Term Perspectives: Origins, Changes, and Interactions* (Lund: Nordic Academic Press, 2006), pp. 412–16; pp. 412–13.

5 Saxo Grammaticus, *Danorum Regum heroumque Historiae* (Gesta Danorum), ed. Christiern Pedersen (Paris: Jodocus Badius, 1514); *Den danske krønicke* (Gesta Danorum), trans. Anders Vedel (Copenhagen: 1575).

6 Extracts were, for example, given in English translation by Samuel Purchas in *Hakluytus Posthumus or Purchas his Pilgrimes: Contayning a History of the World in Sea Voyages and Lande Travells by Englishmen and Others* (1625), vol. 13 (New York: AMS Press, 1965). For an analysis of Arngrímur's linguistic theories, see Gottskálk Jensson, 'The Latin of the north: Arngrímur Jónsson's *Crymogæa* (1609) and the discovery of Icelandic as a classical language', *Renæssanceforum*, 5 (2008). Available online at: www.renaessanceforum.dk/5_2008/gj.pdf (accessed 9 November 2010).

7 See Anthony Faulkes, ed., *Two Versions of Snorra Edda from the Seventeenth Century*, vol. 1, *Edda Magnúsar Ólafssonar* (Laufás Edda) (Reykjavík: Stofnun Árna Magnússonar, 1979).

8 Jordanes' history was in effect a summary of the voluminous historical writings of Cassiodorus, whose study of the Goths has not survived. *Getica* first appeared in print in 1470; Tacitus's *Germania* was printed in 1515.

9 For a biography of the brothers and an assessment of their work, see Kurt Johannesson, *The Renaissance of the Goths in Sixteenth-Century Sweden: Johannes and Olaus Magnus as Politicians and Historians*, ed. and trans. James Larson (Berkeley, CA: University of California Press, 1991). For a contextualization of Johannes Magnus's influence, see Michael Roberts, *The Swedish Imperial Experience: 1560–1718* (Cambridge: Cambridge University Press, 1979), pp. 69–75.

10 Translation of the Latin from the title page.

11 For a discussion of this, see, for example, Herman Richter, *Olaus Magnus: Carta Marina 1539* (Lund: Almquist & Wiksell, 1967).

12 Quoted in Johannesson, *The Renaissance of the Goths*, p. 188.

13 Quoted in Johannesson, *The Renaissance of the Goths*, p. 189.

14 Peder Claussøn Friis, trans., *Snorre Sturlesøns Norske kongers chronica* (1633). Two other Norwegians made translations of *Heimskringla* during the sixteenth century: Laurents Hannsøn (unpublished) and Mattis Størssøn, *Norske kongers krönicke* (1594), the latter being the first printed history of Norway. Friis and Hannsøn were the first scholars outside Iceland to identify Snorri as the author of *Heimskringla*.

15 Walter Charleton, *Chorea Gigantum: Or, the Most Famous Antiquity of Great Britan* [sic], *Vulgarly Called Stone-heng* (London: Henry Herringman, 1663). See also, Rosemary Hill, *Stonehenge* (Profile, 2008).

16 John Dryden, 'Epistle to Dr Charleton', in Walter Charleton, *Chorea Gigantum: Or, the Most Famous Antiquity of Great Britan* [sic], *Vulgarly Called Stone-heng* (London: Henry Herringman, 1663).

17 Quoted in Andrew Wawn, *The Vikings and the Victorians: Inventing the Old North in Nineteenth-Century Britain* (Cambridge: D. S. Brewer, 2000), p. 23.

18 Clunies Ross and Lönnroth, 'The Norse Muse', p. 7. Clunies Ross and Lönnroth perceive this as a shift from the 'pragmatic' to the 'metaphysical', a distinction made by Mats Malm, 'Minervas äpple: Om diktsyn, tolkning och bildspråk inom nordisk göticism' (doctoral dissertation, University of Gothenburg, 1996).

19 Cited in Mats Malm, 'Olaus Rudbeck's *Atlantica* and Old Norse poetics', in Andrew Wawn, *Northern Antiquities: The Post-Medieval Reception of Edda and Saga* (Enfield Lock, London: Hisarlik Press, 1994), pp. 1–25; pp. 9–10.

20 The full text of Thomas Bartholin the Younger's, *Antiquitatum Danicarum de Causis Contemptae a Danis adhuc Gentilibus Mortis* (Heidelberg: Joh. Phil. Bockenhoffer, 1689) is available online at http://books.google.com/books?id=2l8PAAAAQAAJ&printsec=frontcover&source=gbs_ge_summary_r&cad=0#v=onepage&q&f=false (accessed 10 November 2010).

21 These criticisms are made by Lucan in his 'Pharsalia', *De Bello Civili*, Book 1. For a translation, see Susan H. Braund, trans., *Lucan: Civil War* (Oxford: Oxford University Press, 1992). Online translation by Sir Edward Ridley (1896) available at: http://omacl.org/Pharsalia/ (accessed 27 November 2010)

22 Bartholin, *Antiquitatum Danicarum*, p. 550. (Author's own translation).

23 Bartholin, *Antiquitatum Danicarum*, pp. 324–6. (Author's own translation).

24 Eiríkur Benedikz, 'Árni Magnússon', *Saga-Book*, 16 (1962–65), pp. 89–93; p. 89.

25 For a study of Árni's life and work, see Már Jónsson, *Árni Magnússon: Ævisaga* (Reykjavík: Mál og menning, 1998).

26 Ludvig Holberg, *Dannemarks og Norges Beskrivelse* (Copenhagen: Johan Jørgen Høpffner, 1729) and *Dannemarks Riges Historie* (Copenhagen: 1732–35); Olof Dalin, *Svea rikes historia* (History of the Swedish Kingdom), 3 vols (Stockholm: Lars Salvius, 1747).

27 Andrew Wawn draws particular attention to E. J. Biörner's *Nordiska kämpa dater* of 1737, which includes *Friðþjófs saga hins frækna*: see Wawn, 'The post-medieval reception of Old Norse and Old Icelandic literature', p. 325. *Friðþjófs saga* would go on to become a defining text for Romantic views of the Vikings in the nineteenth century. For Wawn's study of the reception of this saga, see *The Vikings and the Victorians*, pp. 117–41.

28 Hickes, George, *Linguarum vett. septentrionalium thesaurus grammatico-criticus et archæologicus* (Oxford: Sheldonian Theatre, Typis Junianis, 1703–05). Hickes's translation was of a poem recorded in the mythico-legendary *Hervarar saga*, which he entitled 'The Waking of Angantýr'. His *Thesaurus* also included an Old Icelandic grammar and a list of Old Norse books and manuscripts. See Richard L. Harris, ed., *A Chorus of Grammars: The Correspondence of George Hickes and his Collaborators on the* Thesaurus Linguarum Septentrionalium (Toronto: Pontifical Institute of Mediaeval Studies, 1992).

29 For a full discussion of the early influence of Norse myth and legend on English scholars, see Christine E. Fell, 'The first publication of Old Norse literature in England and its relation to its sources', in Else Roesdahl and Preben Meulengracht Sørensen, eds, *The Waking of Angantyr: The Scandinavian Past in European Culture; Den nordiske fortid i europæisk kultur*, Acta Jutlandica LXXI: 1, Humanities Series 70 (Aarhus: Aarhus University Press, 1996), pp. 27–57.

30 It is worth noting that folk traditions concerning the Norse gods had remained very much alive; see, for example, the Norwegian ballad, recorded in 1750 and perhaps dating back to the early fifteenth century, 'Thorekarl

of Asgarth', which is loosely based on Thor's humiliation in the eddic lay 'Þrymskivða' (Thrym's Poem): Sven H. Rossel, trans., *Scandinavian Ballads*, Wisconsin Introductions to Scandinavia II, 2 (Madison, WI: Department of Scandinavian Studies, University of Wisconsin-Madison, 1982), pp. 51–2; for a study of ballad traditions in Iceland, see Vésteinn Ólason, *The Traditional Ballads of Iceland: Historical Studies* (Reykjavík: Stofnun Árna Magnússonar, 1982).

31 A further edition of Mallet's *Histoire de Dannemarc* was published in Geneva in 1787.

32 See Thomas Percy's translation of Mallet, *Northern Antiquities: Or, A Description of the Manners, Customs, Religion and Laws of the Ancient Danes, including those of Our Own Saxon Ancestors, with a Translation of the Edda, or System of Runic Mythology, and Other Pieces, from the Ancient Islandic Tongue. Translated from Mons. Mallet's Introduction à l'histoire de Dannemarc, Etc.* (1770), 2 vols (Edinburgh: C. Stewart, 1809), vol. 1, p. 39.

33 Specifically from the *Poetic Edda*, Mallet discusses 'Völuspá' and provides a translation of much of 'Hávamál'. See Percy, *Northern Antiquities*, vol. 2, pp. 151–67.

34 Percy, *Northern Antiquities*, vol. 2, p. xxiv.

35 See Edmund Burke, *A Philosophical Enquiry into the Origin of Our Ideas of the Sublime and Beautiful* (London: R. and J. Dodsley, 1756).

36 See Jean-Jacques Rousseau, *Discours sur l'origine et les fondements de l'inégalité parmi les hommes* (Discourse on the Origin and Basis of Inequality Among Men) (Amsterdam: Marc Michel Rey, 1754).

37 Charles de Secondat, Baron de la Brède et de Montesquieu, *De l'Esprit des Lois* (The Spirit of the Laws), 2 vols (1748) (Geneva: Jacob Vernet, 1748. Originally published anonymously); trans. Thomas Nugent, intro. Franz Neumann, *The Spirit of the Law*, 2 vols (London: J. Nourse and P. Vaillant, 1750). See also Percy, *Northern Antiquities*, vol. 1, pp. 138–9.

38 Percy, *Northern Antiquities*, vol. I, pp. 48–9.

39 Percy, *Northern Antiquities*, vol. 2, p. xvii.

40 Percy, *Northern Antiquities*, vol. 1, pp. 80–2.

41 Percy, *Northern Antiquities*, vol. 2, pp. 98–9.

42 William Lyon Phelps, *The Beginnings of the Romantic Movement: A Study in Eighteenth-Century Literature* (Boston: Ginn and Company, 1893), p. 141.

The impact of Mallet in Britain is discussed at length in Margaret Clunies Ross, *The Norse Muse in Britain: 1750–1820* (Trieste: Edizioni Parnaso, 1998), pp. 41–50.

43 For a discussion of the relationship between Percy's *Reliques* and James Macpherson's *Ossian*, see Philip Connell, 'British identities and the politics of ancient poetry in later eighteenth-century England', *The Historical Journal*, 49/1 (2006), pp. 161–92.

44 Gray's odes were 'The Fatal Sisters' and 'The Descent of Odin', based respectively on 'Darraðarljóð' (recorded in *Njáls saga*) and the eddic lay 'Baldrs draumar', both of which were published in 1768, seven years after their composition. For a discussion of Gray's odes, see Margaret Omberg, *Scandinavian Themes in English Poetry: 1760–1800* (Uppsala: Almqvist & Wiksell, 1976), pp. 36–47; see also Alison Finlay, 'Thomas Gray's Translations of Old Norse Poetry', in David Clark and Carl Phelpstead, eds, *Old Norse Made New: Essays on the Post-Medieval Reception of Old Norse Literature and Culture*, Viking Society for Northern Research (London: University College London, 2007), pp. 1–20.

45 For a discussion of Mallet's reception in France, see François-Xavier Dillman, 'Frankrig og den nordiske fortid – de første etaper af genopdagelsen', in Else Roesdahl and Preben Meulengracht Sørensen, eds, *The Waking of Angantyr: The Scandinavian Past in European Culture; Den nordiske fortid i europæisk kultur*, Acta Jutlandica LXXI: 1, Humanities Series 70 (Aarhus: Aarhus University Press, 1996), pp. 13–26.

46 For a discussion of Ossian, see Omberg, *Scandinavian Themes in English Poetry*, pp. 26–36.

47 See, Paul Barnaby, 'Timeline: European reception of Ossian', in Howard Gaskill, ed., *The Reception of Ossian in Europe* (London and New York: Thoemmes Continuum, 2004), pp. xxi–lxviii.

48 Cited in Magnus Magnusson, *Fakers, Forgers and Phoneys* (Edinburgh: Mainstream Publishing, 2006), p. 340.

49 Both this comment and the quotation from Thomas Warton, *The History of English Poetry* (1774–81), are in Wawn, 'The post-medieval reception of Old Norse and Old Icelandic literature', p. 326. A useful assessment of the Ossian controversy, pitting lovers of literature against lovers of authenticity, is offered by William Sharp, *The Poems of Ossian* (John Grant, 1926),

pp. ix–xxiv. For a more recent assessment, see Fiona J. Stafford, *The Sublime Savage: A Study of James Macpherson and the Poems of Ossian* (Edinburgh University Press, 1990); see also Andrew Wawn, 'Shrieks at the Stones: The Vikings, the Orkneys and the British Enlightenment', in Colleen Batey *et al.*, eds, *The Vikings in Caithness, Orkney and the North Atlantic* (Edinburgh: Edinburgh University Press, 1993), pp. 408–22.

50 John R. Gold and Margaret M. Gold, *Imagining Scotland: Tradition, Representation and Promotion in Scottish Tourism since 1750* (Aldershot: Scholar Press, 1995), pp. 53–9.

51 Omberg, *Scandinavian Themes in English Poetry*, pp. 26–27. Omberg acknowledges the assessment of the Swedish scholar Anton Blanck, *Den nordiska renässansen i sjuttonhundratalets litteratur* (The Scandinavian Renaissance in Eighteenth-Century Literature) (Stockholm: Albert Bonnier, 1911).

52 Omberg, *Scandinavian Themes in English Poetry*, pp. 31–2; and Stefan Thomas Hall, 'James Macpherson's *Ossian*: forging ancient Highland identity for Scotland', in Andrew Wawn, ed., *Constructing Nations, Reconstructing Myth: Essays in Honour of T. A. Shippey* (Turnhout: Brepols, 2007), pp. 3–26; p. 14, n. 50.

Notes to Chapter 5: Thor in Denmark: From Klopstock to Grundtvig

1 Recommending Klopstock to Frederick V was Count Bernstorff (1712–72), who became the Danish Minister of Foreign Affairs in 1751. When Bernstorff fell from grace in 1770, he and Klopstock moved to Hamburg.

2 A detailed study of Klopstock's arrival in, and influence on, Denmark is given by J. W. Eaton, *The German Influence in Danish Literature in the Eighteenth Century: The German Circle in Copenhagen 1750–1770* (Cambridge: Cambridge University Press, 1929), see ch. 2, 'Klopstock in Denmark', pp. 57–88.

3 Although taking no account of Klopstock's enthusiasm for Ossian and the literature of Nordic antiquity, a good study of Klopstock's transformative position between traditional classicism and the Romantic Revival is Kevin Hilliard, *Philosophy, Letters and the Fine Arts in Klopstock's Thought* (London: Institute of Germanic Studies, University of London, 1987).

4   Denis's use of the hexameter meant that his Ossian translations bore little resemblance to the non-metrical verse forms used by James Macpherson.

5   See Eaton, 'Gerstenberg and Danish Literature', *The German Influence in Danish Literature*, pp. 89–117.

6   For a discussion of the extensive impact that Ossianic poetry had on Klopstock and Gerstenberg, see Rudolf Tombo, Jr., *Ossian in Germany: Bibliography, General Survey, Ossian's Influence upon Klopstock and the Bards* (1901) (New York: AMS Press, 1966), pp. 83–119. Tombo also amply demonstrates the widespread enthusiasm for Ossian in his bibliography of translations and related publications in Germany, especially during the last three decades of the eighteenth century.

7   For Klopstock's admiration for Ossian, see, for example, his letter of 5 May 1769, in Klaus Hurlebusch, ed., *Friedrich Gottlieb Klopstock: Briefe 1767–1772* (Berlin and New York: Walter de Gruyter, 1989), vol. VI of Adolf Beck, et al., *Friedrich Gottlieb Klopstock: Werke und Briefe. Historisch-Kritische Ausgabe*, 24 vols (1975–94), pp. 146–9; see also Klopstock's letter of 28 January 1769, pp. 119–20 (same volume) for his desire to see the original Ossian manuscripts.

8   Translated from Eaton, *The German Influence in Danish Literature*, p. 81.

9   August Closs, *The Genius of the German Lyric: An Historical Survey of its Formal and Metaphysical Values* (London: Allen and Unwin, 1938), p. 212.

10   For an assessment of the impact of Ossian in Denmark, see Anna H. Harwell Celenza, 'Efterklange af Ossian: the reception of James Macpherson's *Poems of Ossian* in Denmark's literature, art, and music', *Scandinavian Studies*, 70/3 (1998), pp. 359–96; and, with particular reference to Copenhagen's German circle, see Bo G. Jansson, 'Nordens poetiska reception av Europas reception av det nordiska', in Else Roesdahl and Preben Meulengracht Sørensen, eds, *The Waking of Angantyr: The Scandinavian Past in European Culture; Den nordiske fortid i europæisk kultur*, Acta Jutlandica LXXI: 1, Humanities Series 70 (Aarhus, Denmark: Aarhus University Press, 1996), pp. 192–208.

11   Robert T. Clark Jr., *Herder: His Life and Thought* (Berkeley, CA: University of California Press, 1969), p. 149.

12   S. S. Prawer, *German Lyric Poetry: A Critical Analysis of Selected Poems from Klopstock to Rilke* (London: Routledge, Keegan Paul, 1952), p. 43.

13 See, for example, Alexander Gillies, *Herder und Ossian* (Berlin: Junker und Dünnhaupt Verlag, 1933).

14 Frederick J. Marker and Lise-Lone Marker, *A History of Scandinavian Theatre* (Cambridge: Cambridge University Press, 1996), pp. 97–99.

15 For a survey of the history of Danish studies of Saxo, see Niels Henrik Holmqvist-Larsen, 'Saxo Grammaticus in Danish historical writing and literature', in Brian Patrick McGuire, ed., *The Birth of Identities: Denmark and Europe in the Middle Ages* (Copenhagen: C. A. Reitzel, 1996), pp. 161–88.

16 Ewald reveals his debt to Shakespeare in his presentation of the Iago-like Lok and in scenes where his depiction of the Valkyries recalls the weird sisters of *Macbeth*.

17 See, Johannes Ewald, 'Balders Død', in Hans Brix and V. Kuhr, eds, *Johannes Ewalds Samlede Skrifter efter Tryk og Haandskrifter*, (Copenhagen and Christiania: Gyldendalske Boghandel Nordisk Forlag, 1916), p. 80; and George Borrow, trans., *The Death of Balder from the Danish of Johannes Ewald: 1773* (London: Jarrold and Sons, 1889), p. 38.

18 For an analysis of thematic ambivalences in *Balders Død*, see John L. Greenway, 'The two worlds of Johannes Ewald: *Dyd* vs. Myth in *Balders Død*', *Scandinavian Studies*, 42/4, (1970), pp. 394–409.

19 Galeotti (1733–1816) was of Italian birth but settled in Copenhagen, where he laid the foundations for the Royal Danish Ballet.

20 For a full-length study of the literature inspired by the Arminius legend, see Richard Kuehnemund, *Arminius: Or the Rise of a National Symbol in Literature; From Hutten to Grabbe* (New York: AMS Press, 1966). For the section on Klopstock's contribution, see pp. 73–86.

21 The story of Arminius is recounted in Books I and II of Tacitus's *Annales*; see George Gilbert Ramsay, trans., *The Annals of Tacitus: Books I–IV* (London: John Murray, 1904), esp. pp. 68–183.

22 Herbert W. Benario, 'Arminius into Hermann: history into legend', *Greece and Rome*, 51/1 (2004), pp. 83–94.

23 See Joep Leerssen, *National Thought in Europe: A Cultural History* (Amsterdam: Amsterdam University Press, 2006), pp. 42–4. For a study of both the political and cultural significance of Arminius in Germany, as well as the other 'recovered' Germanic warrior archetype Siegfried, see Christina Lee, 'Children of darkness: Arminius/Siegfried in Germany', in Stephen

O. Glosecki, ed., *Myth in Early Northwest Europe* (Arizona: Arizona Center for Medieval and Renaissance Studies; Turnhout, Belgium: Brepols, 2007), pp. 281–306.

24 See K. A. Schleiden, ed., *Friedrich Gottlieb Klopstock: Ausgewählte Werke* (Munich: Carl Hanser, 1962), pp. 71-2. (Author's own translation.)

25 See Friedrich Gottlieb Klopstock, *Klopstocks Sämmtliche Werke*, 10 vols, vol. 3, (Leipzig: Göschen, 1854) pp. 209-13. (Author's own translation.)

26 For 'Wir und Sie', see Klopstock, *Klopstocks Sämmtliche Werke*, vol. 3, pp. 179-81. (Author's own translation.)

27 Translation adapted from Kuehnemund, *Arminius: Or the Rise of a National Symbol in Literature*, p. 80. For remarks on the cognomens of Klopstock and his circle, see Tombo, *Ossian in Germany*, p. 103. Tombo notes here that Klopstock also adopted the name 'Homer' (*n.* 3).

28 See, for example, Sandro Jung, 'The reception and reworking of *Ossian* in Klopstock's *Hermanns Schlacht*', in Howard Gaskill, ed., *The Reception of Ossian in Europe* (London and New York: Thoemmes Continuum, 2004), pp. 143–55.

29 See analyses and summaries of Klopstock's bardiets in Kuehnemund, *Arminius: Or the Rise of a National Symbol in Literature*, pp. 81-6. See also, Mark Emanuel Amtstätter, ed., *Friedrich Gottlieb Klopstock: Werke und Briefe. Historisch-kritische Ausgabe Abteilung. Werke VI: Hermann-Dramen.* Band 1: Text (Berlin: Walter de Gruyter, 2009).

30 From the early nineteenth-century lament 'Culloden; or Lochiel's Farewell' by John Grieve (1781–1836). Available online at http://www.rampantscotland.com/songs/blsongs_culloden.htm (accessed 29 November 2010).

31 For a discussion of the political implications of Klopstock's Hermann bardiets, see Harro Zimmermann, 'Geschichte und Despotie: Zum politischen Gehalt der Hermannsdramen F. G. Klopstocks', *Text und Kritik* (Klopstock issue) (1981), pp. 97–121.

32 Members of Der Hainbund included H. C. Boie, J. H. Voss, Ludwig Hölty, J. F. Hahn, K. F. Cramer, the Stolberg brothers and J. A. Leisewitz. The group disbanded in 1774.

33 See K. A. Schleiden, ed., *Friedrich Gottlieb Klopstock: Ausgewählte Werke*, pp. 202-07. (Author's own translation.)

34 Leerssen, *National Thought in Europe*, p. 43.

35 Eaton, *The German Influence in Danish Literature*, p. 78.

36 Oehlenschläger acknowledged Klopstock as Ewald's guide in a lecture series he gave in Copenhagen (published 1854).

37 Steffens is usually described as a German philosopher but was born in Norway and largely educated in Denmark. He returned to Germany in 1804 to take up a professorial post at Berlin University after the Danish authorities made it clear that he was unwelcome.

38 Thomas Bredsdorff, 'Oehlenschläger's aesthetics: allegory and symbolism in "The Golden Horns"; and a note on 20th-century eulogy of the allegory', *Edda*, 3 (1999), pp. 211–21; p. 212. Oehlenschläger had already attracted attention as the runner-up in an essay competition set by the University of Copenhagen in 1800, which required competitors to argue for or against the proposition that Scandinavian poets should substitute Norse for Greek mythology. Oehlenschläger's 'yes' came second to the winning 'no'.

39 Holmqvist-Larsen, 'Saxo Grammaticus in Danish historical writing and literature', p. 174.

40 Hallberg Hallmundsson, ed., *An Anthology of Scandinavian Literature from the Viking Period to the Twentieth Century* (New York: Collier, MacMillan, 1965), p. 46.

41 Thomas Bredsdorff, 'Oehlenschläger's aesthetics', p. 213.

42 For all quotes concerning *Nordens Guder*, here and below, see William E. Frye, trans., *Gods of the North: An Epic Poem by Adam Oehlenschlæger* (London: William Pickering; Paris: Stassin and Xavier, 1845), 'Argument of the poem', pp. lxxix–lxxx. For the original, see Adam Oehlenschläger, *Nordens Guder: et episk digt*, Facsimile edn, with commentary by Povl Ingerslev-Jensen ([Copenhagen]: Oehlenschläger Selskabet, 1976), 'Indhold', pp. 10–12.

43 *Gods of the North*, section entitled 'Alphabetical list of proper names', pp. xxxii–lxxv, p. liv.

44 Oehlenschläger had identified Thor as the liberator of Denmark in his novel *Erik og Roller*, his first sortie into the realm of Scandinavian myth and legend in which the hero, Erik, is identified as the god. The novel was withdrawn from publication in 1802 after his 'conversion' by Steffens. It was published posthumously in 1897. For a discussion of the novel's merits, see Kathryn Shailer Hanson, 'Adam Oehlenschläger's *Erik og Roller* and Danish Romanticism', *Scandinavian Studies*, 65/2 (Spring, 1993), pp. 180–95.

45 Hallmundsson, ed., *An Anthology of Scandinavian Literature*, p. 46.

46 Adolph Burnett Benson, *The Old Norse Element in Swedish Romanticism* (New York: AMS Press, 1966), p. 2. See also Peter Graves, 'Ossian in Sweden and Swedish-speaking Finland', in Howard Gaskill, ed., *The Reception of Ossian in Europe* (London and New York: Thoemmes Continuum, 2004), pp. 198–208.

47 Robert William Rix, 'William Blake, Thomas Thorild and Radical Swedenborgianism', *Nordic Journal of English Studies*, 2/1 (2003), pp. 97–128.

48 Benson, *The Old Norse Element in Swedish Romanticism*, p. 39.

49 Benson, *The Old Norse Element in Swedish Romanticism*, p. 32. See also Lars Lönnroth, 'Atterbom och den fornnordiska mytologin', in Tomas Forser and Sverker Göransson, eds, *Kritik och teater: En vänbok till Bertil Nolin* (Goteborg: Graphic Systems, 1992), pp. 7–29.

50 Benson, *The Old Norse Element in Swedish Romanticism*, p. 36.

51 Benson, *The Old Norse Element in Swedish Romanticism*, p. 41.

52 Stjernstolpe's satire was published in *Allmänna Journalen* in 1820. An effective counter-satire was published in the same year by an unknown poet.

53 Benson, *The Old Norse Element in Swedish Romanticism*, p. 39.

54 Benson, *The Old Norse Element in Swedish Romanticism*, p. 32, n. 3.

55 For an English translation of part I of Grundtvig's introduction to *Nordens Mythologi*, see Niels Lyhne Jensen, ed., *A Grundtvig Anthology: Selections from the Writings of N. F. S. Grundtvig (1783–1872)*, trans Edward Broadbridge and Niels Lyhne Jensen (Cambridge: James Clarke; Viby, Denmark: Centrum, 1984), pp. 33–61. For a discussion of the psychodynamics of Grundtvig's ideas on mythology and a comparison with those of Carl Gustav Jung, see Martin Chase, 'True at any time: Grundtvig's subjective interpretation of Nordic myth', *Scandinavian Studies*, 73/4 (Winter, 2001), pp. 507–34.

56 This point, supported by commentary on the censorship that Grundtvig personally had to suffer between 1826 and 1837, is well made by Flemming Lundgreen-Nielsen, 'Grundtvig's Norse mythological imagery: an experiment that failed' in Andrew Wawn, ed., *Northern Antiquity: The Post-Medieval Reception of Edda and Saga* (Enfield Lock, London: Hisarlik Press, 1994), pp. 65–6.

57　Adapted from the fuller schematization of Grundtvig's ideas in Lars Lönnroth, 'The academy of Odin: Grundtvig's political instrumentalisation of Old Norse mythology', in Gerd Wolfgang Weber, ed., *Idee, Gestalt, Geschichte, Festschrift Klaus von See: Studien zur europäischen Kulturtradition* (Odense: Odense University Press, 1988), pp. 339–54; p. 342.

58　Grundtvig preferred the term 'folklighed' which signifies the love of the folk for their country. 'Folk' for Grundtvig meant a common land, common language (only the mother tongue), common history and forefathers, and common culture (especially old ballads, folk dances, folk tale, myth, legend and history): see Vagn Wåhlin, 'Denmark, Slesvig-Holstein and Grundtvig in the 19th Century', in A. M. Allchin, D. Jasper, J. H. Schjørring and K. Stevenson, eds, *Heritage and Prophecy: Grundtvig and the English-Speaking World* (Aarhus: Aarhus University Press, 1993), pp. 243–70, p. 265. For an examination of how Grundtvig and other Danish nationalists helped cultivate jingoism among the ordinary folk, see Hans Kuhn, 'From "Ariebog" to "Folktets Sangbog": the politicizing of Danish song-books in the 19th century', *Scandinavica*, 38/1 (1999), pp. 171–92.

59　Grundtvig's worries about German militarism found lyrical voice in his patriotic ballad 'Niels Ebbesen' (1840), which commemorated the eponymous Danish squire's assassination of Count Gerhard of Holstein in 1340 in his efforts to free Denmark of German oppression.

60　Quotes are taken from two lectures by Grundtvig on 26 and 29 October 1838: see Niels Lyhne Jensen, ed., *A Grundtvig Anthology*, pp. 99–103.

Notes to Chapter 6: Thor in Germany

1　George Stephens, *Thunor the Thunderer, carved on a Scandinavian font of about the year 1000. The first yet found god-figure of our Scando-Gothic forefathers* (London: Williams and Norgate; Copenhagen: H. H. J. Lynge, 1878).

2　Stephens, *Thunor the Thunderer*, p. 16.

3　Stephens, *Thunor the Thunderer*, p. 20.

4　Stephens, *Thunor the Thunderer*, pp. 54–6. *Gastbona*, insists Stephens, does not mean 'ghost killer' but 'giant slayer' and, therefore, Thor.

5　Stephens, *Thunor the Thunderer*, p. 58.

6 Cited from Stephens' 'Cantata' for the University of Copenhagen, in Andrew Wawn, *The Vikings and the Victorians: Inventing the Old North in Nineteenth-Century Britain* (Cambridge: D. S. Brewer, 2000), p. 234.

7 Cited in Wawn, *The Vikings and the Victorians*, p. 238.

8 Johann Gottlieb Fichte, 'What is a People in the Higher Meaning of the Word, and What is Love of Fatherland?' Eighth address in 'Addresses to the German Nation' (1808), in Vincent P. Pecora, ed., *Nations and Identities: Classic Readings* (Malden, MA, and Oxford: Blackwell Publishers, 2001), pp. 114–30.

9 The 1819 edition of *Deutsche Grammatik* was revised in 1822, 1826 and 1840.

10 George Stephens, *The Old-Northern Runic Monuments of Scandinavia and England*, 4 vols (vol. 4 edited by S. O. M. Soderberg) (London: John Russell Smith; Copenhagen: Michaelsen and Tillge, 1866–1901), p. 26, n. 1.

11 Cited in Joep Leerssen, *National Thought in Europe: A Cultural History* (Amsterdam: Amsterdam University Press, 2006), p. 179.

12 Jacob Grimm's political idealism is usefully considered in Frank R. Jacoby, 'Historical method and romantic vision in Jacob Grimm's writings', in Francis G. Gentry, ed., *Studies in Medievalism*, III/4 (Cambridge: D. S. Brewer, 1991), pp. 449–504.

13 Cited in Leerssen, *National Thought in Europe*, p. 183.

14 All quotes from Jacob Grimm, *Deutsche Mythologie*, 3 vols, 4th edn (Berlin: Dümmler, 1875–78) are taken from James Stephen Stallybrass, trans., *Grimm's Teutonic Mythology*, 4 vols, from Jacob Grimm, *Deutsche Mythologie*, 4th edn (London: George Bell and Sons, 1882–88); here, vol. I, p. 10. Stallybrass's translation 'exclusively of' might better be understood as 'exclusive of'.

15 See Tom Shippey, 'A revolution reconsidered: mythography and mythology in the nineteenth century', in Tom Shippey, ed., *The Shadow-Walkers: Jacob Grimm's Mythology of the Monstrous* (Tempe, AZ: Arizona Center for Medieval and Renaissance Studies; Turnhout, Belgium: Brepols, 2005), pp. 1–29, esp. pp. 17–25.

16 In the introduction to the first volume of the fourth edition of *Deutsche Mythologie*, Grimm sets out the eight points of his investigation into 'The antiquity, originality and affinity of the German and Norse mythologies',

including his claims for the 'superiority' of the Gothic, Anglo-Saxon and Old High German dialects over Old Norse, and his expectations of 'distinction and individuality' in the faith of inland Germany (Stallybrass, trans., *Teutonic Mythology*, vol. I, pp. 10–12). An even clearer expression of Grimm's belief that the oldest, most perfect Germanic language and religion of the North existed in inland Germany is given in the preface to the second edition of 1844, prefixed to the fourth German edition, but left in the place it occupied in the second edition (for some reason, in the second volume of that edition) in the English translation (Stallybrass, trans., *Teutonic Mythology*, vol. III, p. vi).

17 Grimm's use of 'Deutsche' in the title was also a worry for Stallybrass, who explains his policy of substituting 'Teutonic' for 'Deutsche' as being 'truer to the facts' in his 'Translator's Preface' (see Stallybrass, trans., *Teutonic Mythology*, vol. I, p. viii). For an elaboration of the Rask/Grimm controversies, see Hans Frede Nielsen, 'Jacob Grimm and the "German" dialects', in Elmer H. Antonsen, ed., *The Grimm Brothers and the Germanic Past* (Philadelphia, PA: John Benjamins, 1990), pp. 25–32. For an excellent survey of the development of Grimm's linguistic science of 'comparative philology' (*vergleichende Philologie*), see Tom Shippey, 'Grimm's law: how one man revolutionised the humanities', *Times Literary Supplement* (7 November 2003), pp. 16–17.

18 Stallybrass, trans., *Teutonic Mythology*, vol. III, p. lv.

19 Stallybrass, trans., *Teutonic Mythology*, vol. I, p. 181.

20 Stallybrass, trans., *Teutonic Mythology*, vol. I, pp. 181–2.

21 Stallybrass, trans., *Teutonic Mythology*, vol. I, pp. 184–5.

22 Stallybrass, trans., *Teutonic Mythology*, vol. I, p. 182.

23 Stallybrass, trans., *Teutonic Mythology*, vol. I, p. 12.

24 Stallybrass, trans., *Teutonic Mythology*, vol. III, p. xix.

25 For a full account of this meeting, see Guðbrandur Vigfússon and F. York Powell, *Grimm Centenary: Sigfred-Arminius and Other Papers* (Oxford: Clarendon Press, 1886), pp. 1–4.

26 Letters A through most of F were completed in three volumes during the Grimms' lifetimes: Jacob and Wilhelm Grimm, *Deutsches Wörterbuch* (Leipzig: S. Hirzel, 1854–62). The full alphabet, comprising 31 volumes, was not completed until 1960. An index was added in 1971.

27 For a survey of Guðbrandur's life and career, including the mixed recep-
    tion of the *Icelandic–English Dictionary*, see B. S. Benedikz, 'Guðbrandur
    Vigfússon: a biographical sketch', in Rory McTurk and Andrew Wawn, eds,
    Úr Dölum til Dala: Guðbrandur Vigfússon Centenary Essays (Leeds: Leeds
    Texts and Monographs, New Series 11, 1989), pp. 11–33.
28 Key poetic expressions of the German medieval revival were the ballads of
    Gottfried August Bürger (1747–94); the folk and fairy tale inspirations of
    Novalis (Friedrich von Hardenberg, 1772–1801) and Ludwig Tieck (1773–
    1853); the eddic verse translations of David Gräter (1768–1830) published in
    'Nordische Blumens' (Nordic Flowers, 1789), and the dramatization of *Das
    Nibelungenlied* in *Sigurd der Schlangentöter, ein Heldenspiel* (Sigurd the Dragon
    Slayer, a Heroic Song) (1808) by Friedrich de la Motte Fouqué (1777–1843).
29 Uhland's first major collection of poetry was published in 1815 under the
    title *Gedichte* (Poems) and was followed in 1817 by *Vaterländische Gedichte*
    (Poems of the Fatherland). For the early nineteenth-century critical recep-
    tion of Uhland's poetry, see Victor Doerksen, *Ludwig Uhland and the Critics*
    (Columbia, SC: Camden House, 1994), pp. 7–24.
30 For all quotes in this paragraph, see Ludwig Uhland, *Der Mythus von
    Thor nach Nordischen Quellen* (Stuttgart and Augsburg: J. G. Cotta'sche
    Buchhandlung, 1836), pp. 44–8. (Author's own translation.)
31 For all quotes in this paragraph, see Uhland, *Der Mythus von Thor nach
    Nordischen Quellen*, pp. 219–23. (Author's own translation.)
32 The full text of Carlyle's collected lectures, *On Heroes, Hero-Worship, and
    the Heroic in History* (London: James Fraser, 1841), is available online at:
    www.online-literature.com/thomas-carlyle/heroes-and-hero-worship/
    (accessed 4 November 2010).
33 For a helpful examination of Arnold's epic poem 'Balder Dead', see Heather
    O'Donoghue, *From Asgard to Valhalla: The Remarkable History of Norse
    Myths* (London; New York: I. B. Tauris, 2007), pp. 157–60. 'Balder Dead' is
    a sanitized, Miltonic rendition of what Arnold gleaned from Thomas Percy's
    Northern Antiquities.
34 For the use of this term and an analysis of 'The Decline of National
    Romanticism', see Margaret Clunies Ross and Lars Lönnroth, 'The Norse
    Muse: report from an international research project', *alvíssmál*, 9 (1999),
    pp. 3–28.

35 Clunies Ross and Lönnroth, 'The Norse Muse', p. 23, note that the Swede Viktor Ryberg (1828–95) also continued to make creative employment of eddic material but to little long-term effect. For a helpful discussion of William Morris's translations of Norse sagas, see David Ashurst, 'William Morris and the Volsungs', in David Clark and Carl Phelpstead, eds, *Old Norse Made New: Essays on the Post-Medieval Reception of Old Norse Literature and Culture*, Viking Society for Northern Research (London: University College London, 2007), pp. 43–62.

36 See Árni Björnsson, *Wagner and the Volsungs: Icelandic Sources of Der Ring des Nibelungen*, Viking Society for Northern Research (London: University College London, 2003). For a consideration of the impact of *Das Nibelungenlied* in the nineteenth century, see Leerssen, *National Thought in Europe*, p. 121.

37 Árni Björnsson, *Wagner and the Volsungs*: for Wagner's debt to Mone, p. 99; to Simrock, p. 101. Mone's analysis of the Volsung legend is in *Untersuchungen zur Geschichte der teutschen Heldensage* (1836). Simrock's translations of the eddas are in *Die Edda, die ältere und jüngere, nebst den mythischen Erzählungen der Skalda* (1851). For Wagner's 'historical' view in 1849 of the Nibelung legend, prior to reading Mone, see Richard Wagner, 'The Wibelungen: world history as told in saga', *Richard Wagner: Stories and Essays*, trans. and ed. Charles Osborne (London: Peter Owen, 1973), pp. 150–87.

38 Barry Millington, *The Master Musicians: Wagner* (Oxford and New York: Oxford University Press, 1984), pp. 191–4.

39 A comprehensive plot analysis of the *Ring*, noting its divergences from Old Norse sources, is given in O'Donoghue, *From Asgard to Valhalla*, pp. 132–46. For Wagner's 1848 original plot, see Árni Björnsson, *Wagner and the Volsungs*, pp. 118–25. See also Gerd Wolfgang Weber, 'Nordisk fortid som chiliastisk fremtid: Den 'norrøne arv' og den cykliske histo- rieopfattelse i Skandinavien og Tyskland omkring 1800 – og senere', in Else Roesdahl and Preben Meulengracht Sørensen, eds, *The Waking of Angantyr: The Scandinavian Past in European Culture; Den nordiske fortid i europæisk kultur*, Acta Jutlandica LXXI: 1, Humanities Series 70 (Aarhus: Aarhus University Press, 1996), pp. 72–119; pp. 74–5.

40 Wagner's debt to Grimm is ubiquitous. See Richard Wagner, *Art and Politics*

(1851), trans. William Ashton Ellis (Lincoln, NE: University of Nebraska Press, 1995), pp. 253–60.

41   For a musicological analysis of this scene, see Warren Darcy, *Wagner's* Das Rheingold (Oxford: Oxford University Press, 1993), pp. 205–9.

42   Bernard Mees, *The Science of the Swastika* (Budapest and New York: Central European University Press, 2008), p. 42.

43   George Webbe Dasent, *Popular Tales from the Norse*, 3rd edn (Edinburgh and New York: David Douglas, 1888), pp. cxxvi–cxxvii.

44   Jón Árnason, *Íslenzkar Þjóðsögur og Æfintýri*, 2 vols (Leipzig: J. C. Hinrich, 1862–64). For a discussion of these nineteenth-century collections, see Martin Arnold, 'Hvat er tröll nema þat? The cultural history of the troll', in Tom Shippey, ed., *The Shadow-Walkers: Grimm's Mythology of the Monstrous* (Tempe, AZ: Arizona State University; Turnhout: Brepols, 2005), pp. 143–55.

45   For an assessment of the learned and literary contexts to Icelandic nationalism, see Jesse L. Byock, 'Modern nationalism and the medieval sagas', in Andrew Wawn, *Northern Antiquities: The Post-Medieval Reception of Edda and Saga* (Enfield Lock, London: Hisarlik Press, 1994), pp. 163–87; also, Jesse L. Byock, 'History and the sagas: the effect of nationalism', in Gísli Pálsson, ed., *From Sagas to Society: Comparative Approaches to Early Iceland* (Enfield Lock, London: Hisarlik Press, 1992), pp. 43–59; and Kirsten Hastrup, *Island of Anthropology: Studies in Past and Present Iceland* (Odense: Odense University Press, 1990), pp. 103–22. For the political situation in Norway, see T. K. Derry, *A History of Modern Norway: 1814–1972* (Oxford: Clarendon Press, 1973); for the folk movement in particular, see ch. 8, 'Norwegian influences abroad: the arts', pp. 237–65.

46   I am grateful to my colleague Professor Peter Wilson (University of Hull) for noting the curious, if limited, continuation of Thor fascination in Scandinavia during this period apparent in the naming of naval crafts: in Sweden, the Odin-class coastal defence ship *Thor* – launched 1898; in Norway, the monitor *Thor* – launched 1870. Equally curious is Professor Wilson's observation that no ship named Thor was in service in Germany from 1848 to the 1950s, although there was an Odin (1894) and two Freyas (1874, 1897).

47   See, for example, Arthur de Gobineau, 'The inequality of human races (1854)' and Houston Stewart Chamberlain, 'Foundations of the nineteenth

century (1899)', in Vincent P. Pecora, ed., *Nations and Identities: Classic Readings* (Malden, MA, and Oxford: Blackwell Publishers, 2001), respectively, pp. 131–41 and pp. 200–4.

48 For a comprehensive study of the ideas and impact of Guido von List, see Nicholas Goodrick-Clarke, *The Occult Roots of Nazism: Secret Aryan Cults and Their Influence on Nazi Ideology* (London and New York: I. B. Tauris, 2005), pp. 33–77; and for the specifically Old Norse context of List's ideas regarding runes, Heather O'Donoghue, 'From runic inscriptions to runic gymnastics', in David Clark and Carl Phelpstead, eds, *Old Norse Made New: Essays on the Post-Medieval Reception of Old Norse Literature and Culture*, Viking Society for Northern Research (London: University College London, 2007), pp. 101–18.

49 See Leerssen, *National Thought in Europe*, p. 234; and Mees, *The Science of the Swastika*, esp. ch. 1, 'The tradition of völkische Germanism', pp. 11–31.

50 Leerssen, *National Thought in Europe*, p. 234.

51 Heather Pringle, *The Master Plan: Himmler's Scholars and the Holocaust* (London: Harper Perennial, 2006), pp. 15–25. See also Bradley F. Smith, *Heinrich Himmler: A Nazi in the Making; 1900–1926* (Stanford, CA: Hoover Institution Press, 1971), passim.

52 Adolf Hitler, *Mein Kampf*, trans. Ralph Manheim (London: Pimlico, 1992), p. 419.

53 From Friedrich Alfred Beck, *Der Aufgang des germanischen Weltalters* (The Rise of the Germanic World-Age) (1944). Cited in Mees, *The Science of the Swastika*, p. 84.

54 Mees, *The Science of the Swastika*, pp. 142–4.

55 O'Donoghue, 'From runic inscriptions to runic gymnastics', p. 116.

56 Goodrick-Clarke, *The Occult Roots of Nazism*, p.187.

57 Cited in Pringle, *The Master Plan*, pp. 46–9.

58 Goodrick-Clarke, *The Occult Roots of Nazism*, p. 177.

59 Pringle, *The Master Plan*, p. 66.

60 Pringle, *The Master Plan*, p. 80. The strange tale of one of Himmler's attempts to uncover the origins of the Aryans is told in Christopher Hale, *Himmler's Crusade: The True Story of the 1938 Nazi Expedition into Tibet* (London: Bantam Books, 2004).

61 Pringle, *The Master Plan*, p. 282. The popular interest in Thor's hammer in Germany is reflected in the adoption of the name 'Mjölnir' by the leading Nazi propaganda artist Hans Schweitzer (1901–80).

62 Niels Lyhne Jensen, ed., *A Grundtvig Anthology: Selections from the Writings of N. F. S. Grundtvig (1783–1872)*, trans Edward Broadbridge and Niels Lyhne Jensen (Cambridge, England: James Clarke; Viby: Centrum, 1984), p. 100.

63 C. J. Jung, 'Wotan', *Civilisation in Transition*, trans. R. F. C. Hull (London: Routledge and Kegan Paul, 1964), pp. 179–93; p. 186.

64 Cited in Stanley Grossman, 'C. G. Jung and National Socialism', in Paul Bishop, ed., *Jung in Contexts: A Reader* (London and New York: Routledge, 1999), pp. 92–121; p. 95.

65 C. G. Jung, 'After the catastrophe', *Civilisation in Transition*, trans. R. F. C. Hull (London: Routledge and Kegan Paul, 1964), pp. 194–217, passim.

Notes to Chapter 7: Thor in America

1 As stated by Lee in Jeff McLaughlin, ed., *Stan Lee: Conversations* (Jackson, MS: University of Mississippi, 2007), p. 91.

2 Preceding the translations of Þormóðr Torfason by just a few years were the partial translations of *Grœnlendinga saga* made by the Swedish scholar Johan Peringskiöld (1654–1720) in his 1697 edition of *Heimskringla*.

3 Geraldine Barnes, *Viking America: The First Millennium* (Cambridge: D. S. Brewer, 2001), pp. 39–41.

4 For a brief examination of the Vínland sagas and the westward voyages of the Vikings, see Martin Arnold, *The Vikings: Culture and Conquest* (London: Hambledon Continuum, 2006), pp. 191–214.

5 This is discussed by Inga Dóra Björnsdóttir, 'Leifr Eiríksson versus Christopher Columbus: the use of Leifr Eiríksson in American political and cultural discourse', in Andrew Wawn and Þórunn Sigurðardóttir, eds, *Approaches to Vínland*, Sigurður Nordal Institute Studies 4 (Reykjavík: Sigurður Nordal Institute, 2001), pp. 220–6.

6 Carl Christian Rafn, *Antiquitates Americanae* (Copenhagen: 1837). Rafn's 'Supplement' of 1841 is available online at: http://books.google.co.uk/books ?id=b1kuAQAAIAAJ&printsec=frontcover&dq=Antiquitates+Americanae

&source=bl&ots=BRERfiLyOw&sig=bQpZP0Cr74KALL_0zhS_cTan X4Y&hl=en&ei=7_rzTMfJMY-GhQfu3YG-DA&sa=X&oi=book_result &ct=result&resnum=2&ved=0CB0Q6AEwAQ#v=onepage&q&f=false (accessed 29 November, 2010).

7   Andrew Wawn, 'Victorian Vínland', in Andrew Wawn and Þórunn Sigurðardóttir, eds, *Approaches to Vínland*, Sigurður Nordal Institute Studies 4 (Reykjavík: Sigurður Nordal Institute, 2001), p. 193, pp. 191–206. Wawn offers a detailed examination of European perspectives and influences on Vínland-related scholarship.

8   Henry Wadsworth Longfellow, 'The Skeleton in Armor' (1841) in *The Poetical Works of Henry Wadsworth Longfellow, with Bibliographical and Critical Notes*, Riverside Edition (Boston and New York: Houghton, Mifflin, 1890), vol. I, p. 55.

9   See Andrew Hilen, *Longfellow and Scandinavia: A Study of the Poet's Relationship with the Northern Languages and Literature* (Hamden, CT: Archon Books, 1970): for Longfellow and Swedish literature, pp. 28–46; for Danish literature, pp. 67–87; for his Scandinavian library, pp. 168–80.

10   Cited in Hillen, *Longfellow and Scandinavia*, p. 63.

11   Henry Wadsworth Longfellow, 'Raud the Strong', part X of 'The Saga of King Olaf' in 'The Musician's Tale', *Tales of a Wayside Inn* (Boston: Ticknor and Fields, 1864), pp. 111–13. Available online at http://books.google.com/ books?id=BBtbAAAAMAAJ&printsec=frontcover&dq=tales+of+a+waysi de+inn&hl=en&ei=WK_pTLjcC-ntnQf_85zsDQ&sa=X&oi=book_result &ct=result&resnum=1&ved=0CC8Q6AEwAA#v=onepage&q&f=false (accessed 22 November 2010).

12   Longfellow, 'The Challenge of Thor', part I of 'The Saga of King Olaf' in 'The Musician's Tale', *Tales of a Wayside Inn*, pp. 71–3.

13   Andrew Wawn, *The Vikings and the Victorians: Inventing the Old North in Nineteenth-Century Britain* (Cambridge: D. S. Brewer, 2000), p. 114 (and same page, n. 104).

14   Cited in Wawn, *The Vikings and the Victorians*, p. 115. Longfellow's semi-autobiographical romantic novel *Hyperion* (1839) also includes some musings on Thor by the novel's chief protagonist, Paul Flemming. Elgar later acknowledged *Hyperion* as key factor in his knowledge of 'the great German nations': Byron Adams, *Edward Elgar and His World* (Princeton:

Princeton University Press, 2007), pp. 64–5. *Hyperion* is available online at http://books.google.co.uk/books?id=-i8fAAAAMAAJ&printsec=frontc over&dq=henry+wadsworth+longfellow,+Hyperion&source=bl&ots=OU jNxCixqv&sig=ivKt9zeSEIPTsqNBYe5SieNIX7M&hl=en&ei=7wr0TIm_ IoOAhAe6oeicCw&sa=X&oi=book_result&ct=result&resnum=3&ved=0 CCkQ6AEwAg#v=onepage&q&f=false (accessed 29 November 2010).

15   John Greenleaf Whittier, *The Complete Poetical Works* (Boston: Houghton Mifflin, 1894): 'The Norsemen, pp. 9–11; 'The Brown Dwarf of Rügen', pp. 138–40; 'The Changeling', pp. 251–3; 'Kallundborg Church', pp. 255–6.

16   James Russell Lowell, 'A Voyage to Vinland', *Under the Willows and Other Poems* (London: Macmillan and Co, 1869), pp. 123–39.

17   Biörn is modelled on Bjarni Herjolfsson, who, according to *Grœnlendinga saga*, was the first European to sight North America but never went ashore.

18   James Russell Lowell, *Meliboeus-Hipponax: The Biglow Papers: Second Series* (1862) (General Books, 2010). See 'No. V: Speech of the Honourable Preserved Doe in Secret Caucus', which is available online at: www.read-bookonline.net/read/title/7223/ (accessed 18 November 2010).

19   This whole tale of Rafn's Viking Tower and Lowell's satire is given in Erik Wahlgren, *The Vikings and America* (London: Thames and Hudson, 1986), p. 105–7.

20   This Smithsonian Institution declaration of 1949 is cited in Wahlgren, *The Vikings and America*, pp. 100–1. For an archaeologist's opinion of the various artefacts of supposed Norse origin, see Birgitta Linderoth Wallace, 'The Vikings in North America: myth and reality', in Ross Samson, ed., *Social Approaches to Viking Studies* (Glasgow: Cruithne Press, 1991), pp. 207–19. For a discussion of the Kensington Stone debate, see Wahlgren, *The Vikings and America*, pp. 111–15.

21   See, for example, Graeme Davis, *Vikings in America* (Edinburgh: Birlinn, 2009), pp. 172–7.

22   The other notable members of this group were Oliver Wendell Holmes Sr. (1809–94) and William Cullen Bryant (1794–1878).

23   For a detailed study of nineteenth-century Vinland controversies in academic and public spheres, see Barnes, *Viking America*, pp. 37–88; for the genetic arguments, see esp. pp. 60–70.

24   Cited in Barnes, *Viking America*, p. 69.

25 Rasmus Anderson, *America Not Discovered by Columbus: an historical sketch of the discovery of America by the Norsemen in the tenth century*, 3rd enlarged edition (Chicago: S. C. Griggs, 1874). The reason for the choice of 9 October was that on that date, in 1825, Norwegian immigrants arrived in New York aboard the *Restauration*, on the first officially organized crossing from Norway.

26 For a discussion of this poem, see Barnes, *Viking America*, pp. 131–4.

27 For a discussion of Liljencrantz's novels and related literature, see Barnes, *Viking America*, pp. 135–44.

28 As reviewed in the *New York Times* by Mordaunt Hall, 'A picture in colors', *New York Times* (29 November 1928), p. 32.

29 For brief plot summaries of all these films and details of the notices they received, see Kevin J. Harty, *The Reel Middle Ages: American, Western and Eastern European, Middle Eastern and Asian Films about Medieval Europe* (London: McFarland and Co, 1999).

30 Nevil Shute, *An Old Captivity* (London: Heinemann, 1940); *Vinland the Good* (London: Heinemann, 1946). For an analysis of Vínland as it was construed in British literature to 1946, see Barnes, *Viking America*, pp. 89–116.

31 Frans Bengtsson, *The Long Ships* (London and New York: HarperCollins, 1984).

32 See, for example, Michael Müller-Wille, 'The political misuse of Scandinavian prehistory in the years 1933–1945', in Else Roesdahl and Preben Meulengracht Sørensen, eds, *The Waking of Angantyr: The Scandinavian Past in European Culture; Den nordiske fortid i europæisk kultur*, Acta Jutlandica LXXI: 1, Humanities Series 70 (Aarhus: Aarhus University Press, 1996), pp. 156–71.

33 For Nazi propaganda on film, see Erwin Leiser, *Nazi Cinema*, trans Gertrud Mander and David Wilson (London: Secker and Warburg, 1974).

34 Carl Barks, *Walt Disney's Donald Duck and The Golden Helmet* (New York: Dell, 1952).

35 More equivocal about the meaning of the cartoon is Alex Service, 'Vikings and Donald Duck', in John Arnold, Kate Davies and Simon Ditchfield, eds, *History and Heritage: Consuming the Past in Contemporary Culture* (Shaftesbury, Dorset: Donhead Publishing, 1998), pp. 117–26.

36   Danish Ministry of Culture, 'Voyage of discovery [Denmark's Cultural Canon]', Ministry of Culture Denmark website (Danish Ministry of Culture: Copenhagen, n.d.). Available online at: http://kulturkanon.kum.dk/en/ (accessed 22 November 2010).

37   *The Vikings* was based on the novel *The Viking* (1951) by Edison Marshall.

38   Harty, *The Reel Middle Ages*, p. 320.

39   For a summary of Umberto Eco's ten re-imaginings or 'dreams' of the Middle Ages, see Harty, *The Reel Middle Ages*, pp. 4–5.

40   For the Wagner cult in America, see Joseph Horowitz, *Wagner Nights: An American History* (Berkeley, CA: University of California Press, 1994).

41   Chuck Jones, dir., *What's Opera, Doc?* (Burbank, CA: Warner Bros. Cartoons, 1957).

42   Daniel Goldmark, *Tunes for 'Toons: Music and the Hollywood Cartoon* (Berkeley and Los Angeles, CA: University of California Press, 2005), p. 134. See ch. 5, '*What's Opera, Doc?* and Cartoon Opera', pp. 132–59.

43   Robin Allan, *Walt Disney and Europe: European Influences on the Animated Feature Films of Walt Disney* (London: John Libbey; Bloomington, IN: Indiana University Press, 1999), pp. 264–5.

44   Cited in Gerard Jones, *Men of Tomorrow: Geeks, Gangsters, and the Birth of the Comic Book* (New York: Basic Books, 2004), p. 81. This section is indebted throughout to Jones's lively and detailed study.

45   Hugo Gernsback was awarded this title by the World Science Fiction Society in 1960.

46   Edward Elmer Smith, *The Skylark of Space*, Parts 1–3, *Amazing Stories* (New York: Experimenter Publishing, August–October 1928); Philip Francis Nowlan, *Armageddon 2419 A.D.*, *Amazing Stories* (New York: Experimenter Publishing, August 1928).

47   Philip Wylie, *Gladiator* (New York: Alfred K. Knopf, 1930). Available online at: http://books.google.com/books?id=jF6oOGPcRTQC&printse c=frontcover&dq=Philip+Wylie,+Gladiator&source=bl&ots=742kt9GT _i&sig=_7-5DSkHJgxh8AF0WFpHf5JAclQ&hl=en&ei=svTqTOfoDYy-s QOphYn6Dg&sa=X&oi=book_result&ct=result&resnum=2&ved=0CCIQ 6AEwAQ#v=onepage&q&f=false (accessed 23 November 2010).

48   See *Doc Savage Magazine: The Man of Bronze*, # 1 (New York: Street and Smith, March, 1933).

49   Cited in Larry Widen, *Doc Savage: Arch Enemy of Evil* (Apple Core Publishing Group, 2006), p. 111. Available online at: http://books.google. com/books?id=ioeYos90eg4C&pg=PA111&dq=the+code+of+doc+sava ge&hl=en&ei=QvrqTOnmKo2-sQO3uMGcDw&sa=X&oi=book_result &ct=result&resnum=1&ved=0CCUQ6AEwAA#v=onepage&q=the%20 code%20of%20doc%20savage&f=false (accessed 23 November 2010).

50   For further discussion of these sources for Superman, see Jones, *Men of Tomorrow*, pp. 75–85 and p. 116.

51   Batman's creator William Finger (1914–74) actually chose the name Gotham City from the New York telephone directory listing for Gotham Jewellers.

52   Marvel Comics did not trade under this name until the 1960s. Kirby worked with Stan Lee for two periods, 1958–70 and 1976–78.

53   Fredric Wertham, *Seduction of the Innocent* (London: Museum Press, 1955), p. 34; for comments on Batman and Wonder Woman, pp. 189–93. The impact of Wertham's campaign is discussed in David Hajdu, *The Ten-Cent Plague: The Great Comic-Book Scare and How It Changed America* (New York: Farrar, Straus and Giroux, 2007), pp. 228–44.

54   Jones, *Men of Tomorrow*, pp. 158–70. For a summary of the Comics Code Authority key points, see Wikipedia, 'Comics code authority', Wikipedia (n.d.). Available online at: http://en.wikipedia.org/wiki/Comics_Code_ Authority (accessed 23 November 2010).

55   See Blair Kramer, 'Superman', Jewish Virtual Library (n.d.). Available at: www.jewishvirtuallibrary.org/jsource/biography/superman.html (accessed 18 November 2010).

56   Stan Lee and George Mair, *Excelsior!: The Amazing Life of Stan Lee* (London: Boxtree, 2002), pp. 157–9.

57   Thor has also appeared in short-lived spin-off comics as, among other things, a woman (*Earth X*), the alter-ego of a seventeenth-century monk (*A-Next*) and as a cannibalistic zombie (*Marvel Zombies*).

58   Richard Reynolds, *Superheroes: A Modern Mythology* (Jackson, MS: University Press of Mississippi, 1994), p. 53.

59   Jordan Raphael and Tom Spurgeon, *Stan Lee and the Rise and Fall of the American Comic Book* (Chicago, IL: Chicago Review Press, 2003), p. 100.

60   Stan Lee, 'Thor the Mighty and the Stone Men from Saturn', *Journey into Mystery*, issue 83 (New York: Marvel Comics, 1962).

61 Plots involving Thor's alter ego Don Blake have largely been abandoned in recent years: see Jeff McLaughlin, ed., *Stan Lee: Conversations*, p. 12.

62 The full Viking zombie series is collected in Garth Ennis, *Thor: Vikings* (Max) (Marvel Comics, 2004). For a biography of Thor, see Marvel Database, 'Thor (Thor Odinson)', Marvel Database (n.d.). Available online at: http://marvel. wikia.com/Thor_(Thor_Odinson) (accessed 23 November 2010).

63 Garth Ennis, 'Eye of Odin', *Thor: Vikings*, vol. 1 (New York: Marvel Comics, 2004), pp. 292–300.

64 See, for example, *Thor* #379–80 (New York: Marvel Comics, May - June 1987).

65 There have been a number of attempts by psychologists to examine this aspect: see, for example, Bryan J. Dik, 'When I grow up I want to be a superhero', in Robin S. Rosenberg with Jennifer Canzoneri, ed., *The Psychology of Superheroes: An Unauthorised Explanation* (Dallas, TX: Benbella Books, 2008), pp. 91–103.

66 Reynolds, *Superheroes*, p. 60.

67 Jones, *Men of Tomorrow*, p. 62.

68 Perhaps the most impressive employment of the Norse gods in recent literary fiction, Thor included, has been Neil Gaiman, *American Gods* (New York: William Morrow, 2001).

69 Now a subject of serious impartial study in such as Tom Morris and Matt Morris, eds, *Superheroes and Philosophy: Truth, Justice, and the Socratic Way* (Chicago, IL: Open Court, 2005). I am grateful to Matthew Croft and Jeannette Ng for drawing my attention to all the Thor merchandise, games, 'lore' and intertext that is available on the internet.

70 These extremist groups and recent fictional renderings of Norse mythology are discussed in Heather O'Donoghue, *From Asgard to Valhalla: The Remarkable History of the Norse Myths* (London and New York: I. B. Tauris, 2007), pp. 163–202.

Bibliography

(*Note: Icelandic patronymics are listed as surnames.*)

Acker, Paul, trans., 'The Saga of the People of Floi', in Viðar Hreinsson, ed., *The Complete Sagas of the Icelanders*, vol. III (Reykjavík: Leifur Eiríksson Publishing, 1997), pp. 271–304.

Adam of Bremen, *History of the Archbishops of Hamburg-Bremen*, trans. Francis J. Tschan (New York: Columbia University Press, 1959).

Adams, Byron, ed., *Edward Elgar and His World* (Princeton, NJ: Princeton University Press, 2007).

Allan, Robin, *Walt Disney and Europe: European Influences on the Animated Feature Films of Walt Disney* (London: John Libbey; Bloomington, IN: Indiana University Press, 1999).

Amtstätter, Mark Emanuel, ed., *Friedrich Gottlieb Klopstock: Werke und Briefe. Historisch-kritische Ausgabe Abteilung. Werke VI: Hermann-Dramen*. Band 1: Text (Berlin: Walter de Gruyter, 2009).

Anderson, Rasmus, *America Not Discovered by Columbus: an historical sketch of the discovery of America by the Norsemen in the tenth century*, 3rd enlarged edition (Chicago: S. C. Griggs, 1874).

Árnason, Jón, *Íslenzkar Þjóðsögur og Æfintýri*, 2 vols (Leipzig: J. C. Hinrich, 1862–64).

Arnold, Martin, 'Hvat er tröll nema þat? The cultural history of the troll', in Tom Shippey, ed., *The Shadow-Walkers: Jacob Grimm's Mythology of the Monstrous* (Tempe, AZ: Arizona State University; Turnhout: Brepols, 2005), pp. 111–55.

— *The Vikings: Culture and Conquest* (London: Hambledon Continuum, 2006).

— '"Lord and Protector of the Earth and its Inhabitants": poetry, philology, politics, and Thor the Thunderer in Denmark and Germany, 1751–1864', in Andrew Wawn, ed., *Constructing Nations, Reconstructing Myth: Essays in Honour of T. A. Shippey* (Turnhout: Brepols, 2007), pp. 27–52.

Ashurst, David, 'William Morris and the Volsungs', in David Clark and Carl Phelpstead, eds, *Old Norse Made New: Essays on the Post-Medieval Reception of Old Norse Literature and Culture*, Viking Society for Northern Research (London: University College London, 2007), pp. 43–62.

Baker, P., trans., 'De falsis deis' (On the false gods), in John C. Pope, ed., *Homilies of Ælfric: A Supplementary Collection*, 2 vols (London: Early English Text Society, 1967–68), vol. 2, pp. 667–724.

Barks, Carl, *Walt Disney's Donald Duck and The Golden Helmet* (New York: Dell, 1952).

Barnaby, Paul, 'Timeline: European reception of Ossian', in Howard Gaskill, ed., *The Reception of Ossian in Europe* (London and New York: Thoemmes Continuum, 2004), pp. xxi–lxviii.

Barnes, Geraldine, *Viking America: The First Millennium* (Cambridge: D. S. Brewer, 2001).

Bartholin, Thomas the Younger, *Antiquitatum Danicarum de Causis Contemptae a Danis adhuc Gentilibus Mortis* (Heidelberg: Joh. Phil. Bockenhoffer, 1689). Available online at http://books.google.com/books?id= 2l8PAAAAQAAJ&printsec=frontcover&source=gbs_ge_summary_r&cad=0 #v=onepage&q&f=false (accessed 10 November 2010).

Battista, Simonetta, 'Interpretations of the Roman Pantheon in the Old Norse hagiographic sagas', in Margaret Clunies Ross, *Old Norse Myths, Literature and Society* (Odense: University Press of Southern Denmark, 2003), pp. 175–97.

Benario, Herbert W., 'Arminius into Hermann: history into legend', *Greece and Rome*, 51/1 (2004), pp. 83–94.

Benedikz, B. S., 'Guðbrandur Vigfússon: a biographical sketch', in Rory McTurk and Andrew Wawn, eds, *Úr Dölum til Dala: Guðbrandur Vigfússon Centenary Essays* (Leeds: Leeds Texts and Monographs, New Series 11, 1989), pp. 11–33.

Benedikz, Eiríkur, 'Árni Magnússon', *Saga-Book*, 16 (1962–65), pp. 89–93.

Bengtsson, Frans, *The Long Ships* (London and New York: HarperCollins, 1984).

Benson, Adolph Burnett, *The Old Norse Element in Swedish Romanticism* (New York: AMS Press, 1966).

Björnsdóttir, Inga Dóra, 'Leifr Eiríksson versus Christopher Columbus: the use of Leifr Eiríksson in American political and cultural discourse', in Andrew Wawn and Þórunn Sigurðardóttir, eds, *Approaches to Vínland*, Sigurður Nordal Institute Studies 4 (Reykjavík: Sigurður Nordal Institute, 2001), pp. 220–6.

Björnsson, Árni, *Wagner and the Volsungs: Icelandic Sources of* Der Ring des Nibelungen, Viking Society for Northern Research (London: University College London, 2003).

Blair, Hugh, *Critical Dissertation on the Poems of Ossian, the son of Fingal* (London: Printed for T. Becket and P. A. De Hondt, 1763).

Blanck, Anton, *Den nordiska renässansen i sjuttonhundratalets litteratur* (The Scandinavian Renaissance in Eighteenth-Century Literature) (Stockholm: Albert Bonnier, 1911).

Borrow, George, trans., *The Death of Balder from the Danish of Johannes Ewald, 1773* (London: Jarrold and Sons, 1889).

Braund, Susan H., trans., *Lucan: Civil War* (Oxford: Oxford University Press, 1992).

Bredsdorff, Thomas, 'Oehlenschläger's aesthetics: allegory and symbolism in "The Golden Horns"; and a note on 20th-century eulogy of the allegory', *Edda*, 3 (1999), pp. 211–21.

Burke, Edmund, *A Philosophical Enquiry into the Origin of Our Ideas of the Sublime and Beautiful* (London: R. and J. Dodsley, 1756).

Byock, Jesse L., 'History and the sagas: the effect of nationalism', in Gísli Pálsson, ed., *From Sagas to Society: Comparative Approaches to Early Iceland* (Enfield Lock, London: Hisarlik Press, 1992), pp. 43–59.

— 'Modern nationalism and the Medieval sagas', in Andrew Wawn, ed., *Northern Antiquities: The Post-Medieval Reception of Edda and Saga* (Enfield Lock, London: Hisarlik Press, 1994), pp. 163–87.

Carlyle, Thomas, *On Heroes, Hero-Worship, and the Heroic in History* (London: James Fraser, 1841). Available online at www.online-literature.com/thomas-carlyle/heroes-and-hero-worship/ (accessed 4 November 2010).

Carron, Helen, ed. and trans., *Clemens Saga: The Life of St Clement of Rome*, Viking Society for Northern Research Text Series, vol. XVII (London: University College London, 2005).

Chamberlain, Houston Stewart, 'Foundations of the nineteenth century (1899)', in Vincent P. Pecora, ed., *Nations and Identities: Classic Readings* (Malden, MA, and Oxford: Blackwell Publishers, 2001), pp. 200–4.

Chamberlain, Timothy J., ed. and trans., *Eighteenth-Century German Criticism* (London: Continuum, 1992).

Charleton, Walter, *Chorea Gigantum: Or, the Most Famous Antiquity of Great Britan [sic], Vulgarly Called Stone-heng* (London: Henry Herringman, 1663).

Chase, Martin, 'True at any time: Grundtvig's subjective interpretation of Nordic myth', *Scandinavian Studies*, 73/4 (2001), pp. 507–34.

Chesnutt, Michael, 'The beguiling of Þórr', in Rory McTurk and Andrew Wawn, eds, *Úr Dölum til Dala: Guðbrandur Vigfússon Centenary Essays* (Leeds: Leeds Texts and Monographs, 1989), pp. 35–63.

Clark, Jr., Robert, T., *Herder: His Life and Thought* (Berkeley, CA: University of California Press, 1969).

Closs, August, *The Genius of the German Lyric: An Historical Survey of its Formal and Metaphysical Values* (London: Allen and Unwin, 1938).

Clunies Ross, Margaret, 'An interpretation of the myth of Þórr's encounter with Geirrøðr and his daughters', in Ursula Dronke, Guðrún P. Helgadóttir, Gerd Wolfgang Weber and Hans Bekker-Nielsen, eds, *Speculum Norroenum: Norse Studies in Memory of Gabriel Turville-Petre* (Odense: Odense University Press, 1981), pp. 370–91.

— *Prolonged Echoes: Old Norse Myths in Medieval Northern Society. Volume 1: The Myths* (Odense: Odense University Press, 1994).

— *The Norse Muse in Britain, 1750–1820* (Trieste: Edizioni Parnaso, 1998).

— 'The measures of Old Norse religion in long-term perspective', in Anders Andrén, Kristina Jennbert and Catharina Raudvere, eds, *Old Norse Religion in Long-Term Perspectives: Origins, Changes, and Interactions* (Lund: Nordic Academic Press, 2006), pp. 412–16.

Clunies Ross, Margaret and Lars Lönnroth, 'The Norse Muse: report from an international research project', *alvíssmál*, 9 (1999), pp. 3–28.

Connell, Philip, 'British identities and the politics of ancient poetry in later eighteenth-century England', *The Historical Journal*, 49/1 (2006), pp. 161–92.

Cook, Robert, trans., 'Njal's Saga', in Viðar Hreinsson, ed., *The Complete Sagas of the Icelanders*, vol. III (Reykjavík: Leifur Eiríksson Publishing, 1997), pp. 1–220.

Cook, Robert and John Porter, trans, 'The Saga of the People of Kjalarnes', in Viðar Hreinsson, ed., *The Complete Sagas of the Icelanders*, vol. III (Reykjavík: Leifur Eiríksson Publishing, 1997), pp. 305–29.

Cross, Samuel Hazzard and Olgerd P. Sherbowitz-Wetzor, eds and trans, *The Russian Primary Chronicle: Laurentian Text* (Cambridge, MA: Medieval Academy of America, 1953).

Dalin, Olof, *Svea rikes historia* (History of the Swedish Kingdom), 3 vols (Stockholm: Lars Salvius, 1747).

Danish Ministry of Culture, 'Voyage of discovery [Denmark's Cultural Canon]', Ministry of Culture Denmark website (Danish Ministry of Culture: Copenhagen, n.d.). Available online at: http://kulturkanon.kum.dk/en/ (accessed 22 November 2010).

Darcy, Warren, *Wagner's Das Rheingold* (Oxford: Oxford University Press, 1993).

Dasent, George Webbe, *Popular Tales from the Norse*, 3rd edn (Edinburgh and New York: David Douglas, 1888).

Davidson, H. R. Ellis, *Gods and Myths of Northern Europe* (Harmondsworth: Penguin Books, 1964).

— *Pagan Scandinavia* (London: Thames and Hudson, 1967).

Davis, Graeme, *Vikings in America* (Edinburgh: Birlinn, 2009).

Dent, Lester, *Doc Savage Magazine: The Man of Bronze*, #1 (New York: Street and Smith, March, 1933).

Derry, T. K., *A History of Modern Norway: 1814–1972* (Oxford: Clarendon Press, 1973).

Dexter, Miriam Robbins and Karlene Jones-Bley, eds, *The Kurgan Culture and the Indo-Europeanization of Europe: Selected Articles from 1952 to 1993 by M. Gimbutas*, Journal of Indo-European Studies Monograph 18 (Washington DC: Institute for the Study of Man, 1997).

Dik, Bryan J., 'When I grow up I want to be a superhero', in Robin S. Rosenberg with Jennifer Canzoneri, ed., *The Psychology of Superheroes: An Unauthorised Explanation* (Dallas, TX: BenBella Books, 2008), pp. 91–103.

Dillman, François-Xavier, 'Frankrig og den nordiske fortid – de første etaper af genopdagelsen', in Else Roesdahl and Preben Meulengracht Sørensen, eds, *The Waking of Angantyr: The Scandinavian Past in European Culture; Den nordiske fortid i europæisk kultur*, Acta Jutlandica LXXI: 1, Humanities Series 70 (Aarhus: Aarhus University Press, 1996), pp. 13–26.

Doerksen, Victor, *Ludwig Uhland and the Critics* (Columbia, SC: Camden House, 1994).

DuBois, Thomas A., *Nordic Religions in the Viking Age* (Philadelphia, PA: University of Pennsylvania Press, 1999).

Dudo of St Quentin, *History of the Normans*, ed. and trans. Eric Christiansen (Woodbridge: Boydell Press, 1998).

Dumézil, Georges, *The Destiny of the Warrior*, trans. Alf Hiltebeitel from *Heur et malheur du guerrier: Aspects mythiques de la fonction guerrière chez les Indo-Européens* (1969) (Chicago, IL: University of Chicago Press, 1970).

— *Gods of the Ancient Norsemen*, ed. Einar Haugen, trans. Francis Charat from *Les Dieux des Germains* (Berkeley, CA: University of California Press, 1973).

Eaton, J. W., *The German Influence in Danish Literature in the Eighteenth Century: The German Circle in Copenhagen, 1750–1770* (Cambridge: Cambridge University Press, 1929).

Eldevik, Randi, 'Less than kind: giants in Germanic tradition', in Tom Shippey, ed., *The Shadow-Walkers: Jacob Grimm's Mythology of the Monstrous* (Tempe, AZ: Arizona State University; Turnhout: Brepols, 2005), pp. 83–110.

Ennis, Garth, *Thor: Vikings* (New York: Marvel Comics, 2004).

Ewald, Johannes, *The Death of Balder from the Danish of Johannes Ewald, 1773*, trans. George Borrow (London: Jarrold and Sons, 1889).

— 'Balders Død', in Hans Brix and V. Kuhr, eds, *Johannes Ewalds Samlede Skrifter efter Tryk og Haandskrifter* (Copenhagen and Christiania: Gyldendalske Boghandel Nordisk Forlag, 1916).

Faulkes, Anthony, trans., *Snorri Sturluson. Edda* (London: J. M. Dent, 1995)

— ed., *Two Versions of Snorra Edda from the Seventeenth Century*, vol. 1, *Edda Magnúsar Ólafssonar* (Laufás Edda) (Reykjavík: Stofnun Árna Magnússonar, 1979).

Fell, Christine E., 'The first publication of Old Norse literature in England and its relation to its sources', in Else Roesdahl and Preben Meulengracht Sørensen, eds, *The Waking of Angantyr: The Scandinavian Past in European Culture; Den nordiske fortid i europæisk kultur*, Acta Jutlandica LXXI: 1, Humanities Series 70 (Aarhus: Aarhus University Press, 1996), pp. 27–57.

Fichte, Johann Gottlieb, 'What is a People in the Higher Meaning of the Word, and What is Love of Fatherland?' Eighth address in 'Addresses to the German Nation' (1808), in Vincent P. Pecora, ed., *Nations and Identities: Classic*

Readings (Malden, MA, and Oxford: Blackwell Publishers, 2001),
   pp. 114–30.

Finlay, Alison, 'Thomas Gray's translations of Old Norse poetry', in David Clark
   and Carl Phelpstead, eds, *Old Norse Made New: Essays on the Post-Medieval
   Reception of Old Norse Literature and Culture*, Viking Society for Northern
   Research (London: University College London, 2007), pp. 1–20.

Friis, Peder Claussøn, trans. *Snorre Sturlesøns Norske kongers chronica*
   (Copenhagen, 1633).

Frye, William E., trans., *Gods of the North: An Epic Poem by Adam
   Oehlenschlæger* (London: William Pickering; Paris: Stassin and Xavier, 1845).

Gaiman, Neil, *American Gods* (New York: William Morrow, 2001).

Gaskill, Howard, ed., and Fiona Stafford, intro., *The Poems of Ossian and
   Related Works* (Edinburgh: Edinburgh University Press, 1996).

Gillies, A., *Herder und Ossian* (Berlin: Junker und Dünnhaupt Verlag, 1933).

— *Herder* (Oxford: Basil Blackwell, 1945).

de Gobineau, Arthur, 'The inequality of human races (1854)', in Vincent P.
   Pecora, ed., *Nations and Identities: Classic Readings* (Malden, MA, and
   Oxford: Blackwell Publishers, 2001), pp. 131–41.

Gold, John R. and Margaret M. Gold, *Imagining Scotland: Tradition,
   Representation and Promotion in Scottish Tourism Since 1750* (Aldershot:
   Scholar Press, 1995).

Goldmark, Daniel, *Tunes for 'Toons: Music and the Hollywood Cartoon*
   (Berkeley and Los Angeles, CA: University of California Press, 2005).

Goodrick-Clarke, Nicholas, *The Occult Roots of Nazism: Secret Aryan Cults and
   Their Influence on Nazi Ideology* (London and New York: I. B. Tauris, 2005).

Graves, Peter, 'Ossian in Sweden and Swedish-speaking Finland', in Howard
   Gaskill, ed., *The Reception of Ossian in Europe* (London and New York:
   Thoemmes Continuum, 2004), pp. 198–208.

Greenway, John L., 'The two worlds of Johannes Ewald: *Dyd* vs. Myth in
   Balders Død', *Scandinavian Studies*, 42/4 (1970), pp. 394–409.

Griffith, Ralph T. H., trans., *Rig Veda* (Benares: E. J. Lazarus and Company, 1896).

Grimm, Jacob, *Deutsche Mythologie*, 3 vols, 4th edn (Berlin: Dümmler,
   1875–78).

Grimm, Jacob and Wilhelm Grimm, *Deutsches Wörterbuch* (Leipzig: S. Hirzel,
   1854–62).

Grimm, Wilhelm C., *Altdänische Heldenlieder, Balladen und Märchen* (Heidelberg: Mohr and Zimmer, 1811).

Grønlie, Siân, trans. *Íslendingabók; Kristni saga: The Book of the Icelanders; The Story of the Conversion*, Viking Society for Northern Research Text Series, vol. XVIII (London: University College London, 2006).

Grossman, Stanley, 'C. G. Jung and National Socialism', in Paul Bishop, ed., *Jung in Contexts: A Reader* (London and New York: Routledge, 1999), pp. 92–121.

Haarder, Andreas, 'Grundtvig and the Old Norse cultural heritage', in Christian Thodberg and Anders Pontoppidan Thyssen, eds, *N. F. S. Grundtvig: Tradition and Renewal*, trans. Edward Broadbridge (Copenhagen: Det Danske Selskab, 1983), pp. 72-86.

Hagland, Jan Ragnar, 'The reception of Old Norse literature in late eighteenth-century Norway', in Andrew Wawn, ed., *Northern Antiquity: The Post-Medieval Reception of Edda and Saga* (Enfield Lock, London: Hisarlik Press, 1994), pp. 27–40.

Hajdu, David, *The Ten-Cent Plague: The Great Comic-Book Scare and How It Changed America* (New York: Farrar, Straus and Giroux, 2007).

Hale, Christopher, *Himmler's Crusade: The True Story of the 1938 Nazi Expedition into Tibet* (London: Bantam Books, 2004).

Hall, Mordaunt, 'A picture in colors', *New York Times* (29 November 1928), p. 32.

Hall, Stefan Thomas, 'James Macpherson's *Ossian*: forging ancient Highland identity for Scotland', in Andrew Wawn, ed., *Constructing Nations, Reconstructing Myth: Essays in Honour of T. A. Shippey* (Turnhout: Brepols, 2007), pp. 3–26.

Hallberg, Peter, 'Om Þrymskviða', *Edda*, 58 (1968), pp. 256–70.

Hallmundsson, Hallberg, ed., *An Anthology of Scandinavian Literature from the Viking Period to the Twentieth Century* (New York: Collier, MacMillan, 1965).

Hanson, Kathryn Shailer, 'Adam Oehlenschläger's *Erik og Roller* and Danish Romanticism', *Scandinavian Studies*, 65/2 (Spring, 1993), pp. 180–95.

Harris, Joseph, 'The Masterbuilder Tale in Snorri's *Edda* and two sagas', *Arkiv för nordisk filologi*, 91 (1976), pp. 66–101.

Harris, Richard L., ed., *A Chorus of Grammars: The Correspondence of George Hickes and his Collaborators on the* Thesaurus Linguarum Septentrionalium (Toronto: Pontifical Institute of Mediaeval Studies, 1992).

Harty, Kevin J., *The Reel Middle Ages: American, Western and Eastern European, Middle Eastern and Asian Films about Medieval Europe* (London: McFarland and Co., 1999).

Harwell Celenza, Anna H., 'Efterklange af Ossian: the reception of James Macpherson's *Poems of Ossian* in Denmark's literature, art, and music', *Scandinavian Studies*, 70/3 (1998), pp. 359–96.

Hastrup, Kirsten, *Island of Anthropology: Studies in Past and Present Iceland* (Odense: Odense University Press, 1990).

Heinrichs, Ann, '"Annat er várt eðli". The type of the pre-patriarchal woman in Old Norse literature', in J. Lindow, L. Lönnroth and G. W. Weber, eds, *Structure and Meaning in Old Norse Literature: New Approaches to Textual Analysis and Literary Criticism* (Odense: Odense University Press, 1986), pp. 110–40.

Hickes, George, *Linguarum vett. septentrionalium thesaurus grammatico-criticus et archæologicus* (Oxford: Sheldonian Theatre, Typis Junianis, 1703-05).

Hilen, Andrew, *Longfellow and Scandinavia: A Study of the Poet's Relationship with the Northern Languages and Literature* (Hamden, CT: Archon Books, 1970).

Hill, Rosemary, *Stonehenge* (London: Profile, 2008).

Hilliard, Kevin, *Philosophy, Letters and the Fine Arts in Klopstock's Thought* (London: Institute of Germanic Studies, University of London, 1987).

Hitler, Adolf, *Mein Kampf*, trans. Ralph Manheim (London: Pimlico, 1992).

Holberg, Ludvig, *Dannemarks og Norges Beskrivelse* (Copenhagen: Johan Jørgen Høpffner, 1729).

— *Dannemarks Riges Historie*, 3 vols (Copenhagen: 1732–35).

Hollander, L. M., trans., *Snorri Sturluson: Heimskringla; History of the Norwegian Kings* (Austin, TX: University of Texas Press, 1964).

Holmqvist-Larsen, Niels Henrik, 'Saxo Grammaticus in Danish historical writing and literature', in Brian Patrick McGuire, ed., *The Birth of Identities: Denmark and Europe in the Middle Ages* (Copenhagen: C. A. Reitzel, 1996), pp. 161–88.

Horowitz, Joseph, *Wagner Nights: An American History* (Berkeley, CA: University of California, 1994).

Hurlebusch, Klaus, ed., *Friedrich Gottlieb Klopstock: Briefe 1767–1772*, vol. VI (Berlin and New York: Walter de Gruyter, 1989), vol. VI of Adolf Beck, et al, *Friedrich Gottlieb Klopstock: Werke und Briefe. Historisch-Kritische Ausgabe*, 24 vols (1975-94).

Jacoby, Frank R., 'Historical method and romantic vision in Jacob Grimm's writings', in Francis G. Gentry, ed., *Studies in Medievalism*, III/4 (1991), pp. 449–504.

Jansson, Bo G., 'Nordens poetiska reception av Europas reception av det nordiska', in Else Roesdahl and Preben Meulengracht Sørensen, eds, *The Waking of Angantyr: The Scandinavian Past in European Culture; Den nordiske fortid i europæisk kultur*, Acta Jutlandica LXXI: 1, Humanities Series 70 (Aarhus: Aarhus University Press, 1996), pp. 192–208.

Jensen, Niels Lyhne, ed., *A Grundtvig Anthology: Selections from the Writings of N. F. S. Grundtvig (1783–1872)*, trans Edward Broadbridge and Niels Lyhne Jensen (Cambridge, England: James Clarke; Viby: Centrum, 1984).

Jensson, Gottskálk, 'The Latin of the north: Arngrímur Jónsson's *Crymogæa* (1609) and the discovery of Icelandic as a classical language', *Renæssanceforum*, 5 (2008). Available online at www.renaessanceforum. dk/5_2008/gj.pdf (accessed 9 November 2010).

Jochens, Jenny, *Old Norse Images of Women* (Philadelphia, PA: University of Pennsylvania Press, 1996).

Jóhannesson, Jón, Magnús Finnbogason and Kristján Eldjárn, eds, *Sturlunga saga*, 2 vols (Reykjavík: Sturlunguútgáfan, 1946).

Johannesson, Kurt, *The Renaissance of the Goths in Sixteenth-Century Sweden: Johannes and Olaus Magnus as Politicians and Historians*, ed. and trans. James Larson (Berkeley, CA: University of California Press, 1991).

Jones, Chuck, dir., *What's Opera, Doc?* (Burbank, CA: Warner Bros. Cartoons, 1957).

Jónsson, Már, *Árni Magnússon: Ævisaga* (Reykjavík: Mál og menning, 1998).

Jones, Gerard, *Men of Tomorrow: Geeks, Gangsters, and the Birth of the Comic Book* (New York: Basic Books, 2004).

Jung, C. J., *Civilisation in Transition*, trans. R. F. C. Hull (London: Routledge and Kegan Paul, 1964).

Jung, Sandro, 'The reception and reworking of *Ossian* in Klopstock's *Hermanns Schlacht*' in Howard Gaskill, ed., *The Reception of Ossian in Europe* (London and New York: Thoemmes Continuum and Athlone Press, 2002).

Klopstock, Friedrich Gottlieb, *Klopstocks Sämmtliche Werke*, 10 vols, vol. 3. (Leipzig: Göschen, 1854).

Kramer, Blair, 'Superman', Jewish Virtual Library (n.d.) Available online at http://www.jewishvirtuallibrary.org/jsource/biography/superman.html (accessed 18 November 2010).

Kroesen, Riti, 'The great god Þórr: a war god?', *Arkiv för nordisk filologi*, 116 (2001), pp. 97–110.

Kuehnemund, Richard, *Arminius: Or the Rise of a National Symbol in Literature (From Hutten to Grabbe)*, (New York: AMS Press, 1966).

Kuhn, Hans, 'From "Ariebog" to "Folkets Sangbog": the politicizing of Danish songbooks in the 19th century', *Scandinavica*, 38/1 (1999), pp. 171–92.

Kunz, Keneva, trans., 'Eirik the Red's Saga', in Viðar Hreinsson, ed., *The Complete Sagas of the Icelanders*, vol. I (Reykjavík: Leifur Eiríksson Publishing, 1997), pp. 1–18.

Læstadius, Lars Levi, *Fragments of Lappish Mythology*, ed. Juha Pentikainen and trans. Borje Vahamaki (Beaverton: Aspasia Books, 2002).

Larrington, Carolyne, trans., *The Poetic Edda* (Oxford and New York: Oxford University Press, 1996).

Lee, Christina, 'Children of darkness: Arminius/Siegfried in Germany', in Stephen O. Glosecki, ed., *Myth in Early Northwest Europe* (Tempe, AZ: Arizona Center for Medieval and Renaissance Studies; Turnhout: Brepols, 2007), pp. 281–306.

Lee, Stan, 'Thor the Mighty and the Stone Men from Saturn', *Journey into Mystery*, issue 83 (New York: Marvel Comics, 1962).

Lee, Stan and George Mair, *Excelsior!: The Amazing Life of Stan Lee* (London: Boxtree, 2002).

Leerssen, Joep, *National Thought in Europe: A Cultural History* (Amsterdam: Amsterdam University Press, 2006).

Leiser, Erwin, *Nazi Cinema*, trans Gertrud Mander and David Wilson (London: Secker and Warburg, 1974).

Lévi-Strauss, Claude, *The Raw and the Cooked*, trans John Weightman and Doreen Weightman from *Le Cru et le Cuit* (1964) (London: Jonathan Cape, 1970).

Liljencrantz, Ottilie, *The Thrall of Leif the Lucky: A Story of Viking Days* (Boston: Small Maynard and Co., 1902)

— *The Vinland Champions* (Boston: D. Appleton and Co., 1904)

— *Randvar the Songsmith: A Romance of Norumbega* (New York: Harper and Brothers, 1906).

Lindow, John, 'Thor's duel with Hrungnir', *alvíssmál*, 6 (1996), pp. 3–20.

— Norse Mythology. *A Guide to the Gods, Heroes, Rituals and Beliefs* (Oxford: Oxford University Press, 2001).

Longfellow, Henry Wadsworth, *Hyperion* (1839). Available online at http:// books.google.co.uk/books?id=-i8fAAAAMAAJ&printsec=frontcover& dq=henry+wadsworth+longfellow,+Hyperion&source=bl&ots=OUjN xCixqv&sig=ivKt9zeSEIPTsqNBYe5SieNIX7M&hl=en&ei=7wr0TIm_ IoOAhAe6oeicCw&sa=X&oi=book_result&ct=result&resnum=3&ved=0CC kQ6AEwAg#v=onepage&q&f=false (accessed 29 November 2010).

— 'The Skeleton in Armor' (1841) in *The Poetical Works of Henry Wadsworth Longfellow, with Bibliographical and Critical Notes*, Riverside Edition (Boston and New York: Houghton, Mifflin, 1890), vol. I, p. 55.

— 'Tegnér's Drapa' (1847) in *By the Fireside*. Available online at http://www. hwlongfellow.org/poems_poem.php?pid=124 (accessed 29 November 2010).

— 'The Saga of King Olaf', 'The Musician's Tale', *Tales of a Wayside Inn* (Boston: Ticknor and Fields, 1864). Available online at http://books.google.com/boo ks?id=BBtbAAAAMAAJ&printsec=frontcover&dq=tales+of+a+wayside+i nn&hl=en&ei=WK_pTLjcC-ntnQf_85zsDQ&sa=X&oi=book_result&ct=r esult&resnum=1&ved=0CC8Q6AEwAA#v=onepage&q&f=false (accessed 22 November 2010).

Lönnroth, Lars, 'The academy of Odin: Grundtvig's political instrumentalisation of Old Norse mythology', in Gerd Wolfgang Weber, ed., *Idee, Gestalt, Geschichte, Festschrift Klaus von See: Studien zur europäischen Kulturtradition* (Odense: Odense University Press, 1988), pp. 339–54.

— 'Atterbom och den fornnordiska mytologin', in Tomas Forser and Sverker Göransson, eds, *Kritik och teater: En vänbok till Bertil Nolin* (Goteborg: Graphic Systems, 1992), pp. 7–29.

Lowell, James Russell, *Meliboeus-Hipponax: The Biglow Papers: Second Series* (1862) (General Books, 2010). Available online at: www.readbookonline.net/ title/7223/ (accessed 18 November 2010).

— *Under the Willows and Other Poems* (London: Macmillan and Co, 1869).

Lundgreen-Nielsen, Flemming, 'Grundtvig's Norse mythological imagery: an experiment that failed', in Andrew Wawn, ed., *Northern Antiquity: The Post-Medieval Reception of Edda and Saga* (Enfield Lock, London: Hisarlik Press, 1994), pp. 41–67.

McKinnell, John, *Meeting the Other in Norse Myth and Legend* (Cambridge: D. S. Brewer, 2005).

McLaughlin, Jeff, ed., *Stan Lee: Conversations* (Jackson, MS: University of Mississippi, 2007).

Macpherson, James, *Fragments of Ancient Poetry Collected in the Highlands of Scotland, and Translated from the Gaelic or Erse Language* (Edinburgh: G. Hamilton & J. Balfour, 1760).

— *Fingal, an Ancient Epic Poem, in Six Books; together with Several Other Poems, Composed by Ossian, the Son of Fingal. Translated from the Galic Language* (London: T. Becket & P. A. De Hondt, 1762).

— *Temora, an Ancient Epic Poem, in Eight Books; together with Several Other Poems, Composed by Ossian, the Son of Fingal. Translated from the Galic Language* (London: T. Becket & P. A. De Hondt, 1763).

Macpherson, James, trans., and William Sharp, intro., *The Poems of Ossian* (Edinburgh: John Grant, 1926).

Magnusson, Magnus, *Fakers, Forgers and Phoneys* (Edinburgh: Mainstream Publishing, 2006).

Mallet, Paul Henri, *Introduction à l'histoire de Dannemarc, où l'on traite de la religion, des loix, des mœurs et des usages des anciens Danois* (Copenhagen: Berling, 1755).

— *Monumens de la mythologie et de la poésie des Celtes, et particulièrement des anciens Scandinave* (Copenhagen: Philibert, 1756).

— *Histoire de Dannemarc* (Geneva: 1763)

Mallory, J. P., *In Search of the Indo-Europeans: Language, Archaeology and Myth* (London: Thames and Hudson, 1991).

Malm, Mats, 'Olaus Rudbeck's *Atlantica* and Old Norse poetics', in Andrew Wawn, ed., *Northern Antiquities: The Post-Medieval Reception of Edda and Saga* (Enfield Lock, London: Hisarlik Press, 1994), pp. 1–25.

— 'Minervas äpple: Om diktsyn, tolkning och bildspråk inom nordisk göticism' (doctoral dissertation, University of Gothenburg, 1996).

Marker, Frederick J., and Lise-Lone Marker, *A History of Scandinavian Theatre* (Cambridge: Cambridge University Press, 1996).

Marvel Database, 'Thor (Thor Odinson)', Marvel Database (n.d.). Available online at: http://marvel.wikia.com/Thor_(Thor_Odinson) (accessed 23 November 2010).

Mattingly, H., trans., *Tacitus on Britain and Germany: A Translation of the 'Agricola' and the 'Germania'* (Harmondsworth: Penguin, 1948).

Mees, Bernard, 'Hitler and Germanentum', *Journal of Contemporary History*, 39 (2004), pp. 255–70.

— 'Germanische Sturmflut: from the Old Norse twilight to the fascist new dawn', *Studia Neophilologica*, 78/ 2 (2006), pp. 184–98.

— *The Science of the Swastika* (Budapest and New York: Central European University Press, 2008).

Melnikova, Elena A., 'Reminiscences of Old Norse myths, cults and rituals in Old Russian literature', in Margaret Clunies Ross, ed., *Old Norse Myths, Literature and Society* (Odense: University Press of Southern Denmark, 2003), pp. 66–86.

Millington, Barry, *The Master Musicians: Wagner* (Oxford and New York: Oxford University Press, 1984).

— ed., *The Wagner Compendium: A Guide to Wagner's Life and Music* (London: Thames and Hudson, 1992).

Montesquieu, Charles de Secondat, Baron de la Brède et de, *De L'Esprit des Lois* (Geneva: Jacob Vernet, 1748. Originally published anonymously); trans. Thomas Nugent, intro. Franz Neumann, *The Spirit of the Law*, 2 vols (London: J. Nourse and P. Vaillant, 1750).

Morris, Tom, and Matt Morris, eds, *Superheroes and Philosophy: Truth, Justice, and the Socratic Way* (Chicago, IL: Open Court, 2005).

Müller-Wille, Michael, 'The political misuse of Scandinavian prehistory in the years 1933–1945', in Else Roesdahl and Preben Meulengracht Sørensen, eds, *The Waking of Angantyr: The Scandinavian Past in European Culture; Den nordiske fortid i europæisk kultur*, Acta Jutlandica LXXI: 1, Humanities Series 70 (Aarhus: Aarhus University Press, 1996), pp. 156–71.

Nielsen, Hans Frede, 'Jacob Grimm and the "German" dialects', in Elmer H. Antonsen, ed., *The Grimm Brothers and the Germanic Past* (Philadelphia, PA: John Benjamins, 1990), pp. 25–32.

Nietzsche, Friedrich, *Also sprach Zarathustra: Ein Buch für Alle und Keinen* (Thus Spoke Zarathustra: A Book for All and None) (Chemnitz: Ernst Schmeitzner: 1883).

Nordeide, Sæbjørg Walaker, 'Thor's hammer in Norway: a symbol of reaction against the Christian cross?', in Anders Andrén, Kristina Jennbert and Catharina Raudvere, eds *Old Norse Religion in Long-Term Perspectives:*

Origins, Changes, and Interactions (Lund: Nordic Academic Press, 2006), pp. 218–23.

Nowlan, Philip Francis, *Armageddon 2419 A.D., Amazing Stories* (New York: Experimenter Publishing, August 1928).

O'Donoghue, Heather, *From Asgard to Valhalla: The Remarkable History of the Norse Myths* (London and New York: I. B. Tauris, 2007).

— 'From runic inscriptions to runic gymnastics', in David Clark and Carl Phelpstead, eds, *Old Norse Made New: Essays on the Post-Medieval Reception of Old Norse Literature and Culture*, Viking Society for Northern Research (London: University College London, 2007), pp. 101–18.

Oehlenschläger, Adam, *Nordens Guder: et episk digt* (1852), Facsimile edn with commentary by Povl Ingerslev-Jensen ([Copenhagen]: Oehlenschläger Selskabet, 1976).

Ólason, Vésteinn, *The Traditional Ballads of Iceland* (Reykjavík: Stofnun Árna Magnússonar, 1982).

Omberg, Margaret, *Scandinavian Themes in English Poetry: 1760–1800* (Uppsala: Almqvist and Wiksell, 1976).

Orczy, Baroness Emmuska, *The Scarlet Pimpernel* (1905).

Pálsson, Hermann and Paul Edwards, eds and trans, *The Book of Settlements: Landnámabók* (Winnipeg: University of Manitoba Press, 1972).

— trans, *Seven Viking Romances* (Harmondsworth: Penguin Books, 1985).

Percy, Thomas, trans., *Five Pieces of Runic Poetry: Translated from the Islandic Language* (London: R. and J. Dodsley, 1763).

—*Reliques of Ancient English Poetry: Consisting of Old Heroic Ballads, Songs, and Other Pieces of Our Earlier Poets, (Chiefly of the Lyric Kind) Together with Some Few of Later Date*, 3 vols (London: R. and J. Dodsley, 1765).

— trans., *Northern Antiquities: Or, A Description of the Manners, Customs, Religion and Laws of the Ancient Danes, including those of Our Own Saxon Ancestors, with a Translation of the Edda, or System of Runic Mythology, and Other Pieces, from the Ancient Islandic Tongue. Translated from Mons. Mallet's Introduction à l'histoire de Dannemarc, Etc.* (1770), 2 vols (Edinburgh: C. Stewart, 1809).

Perkins, Richard, *Thor the Wind-Raiser and the Eyrarland Image*. Viking Society for Northern Research Text Series, vol. XV (London: University College London, 2001).

Phelps, William Lyon, *The Beginnings of the Romantic Movement: A Study in Eighteenth Century Literature* (Boston: Ginn and Company, 1893).

Pope, John C., ed., *Homilies of Ælfric: A Supplementary Collection*, trans. P. Baker, 2 vols (London: Early English Text Society, 259–60, 1967–68).

Prawer, S. S., *German Lyric Poetry: A Critical Analysis of Selected Poems from Klopstock to Rilke* (London: Routledge and Keegan Paul, 1952).

Price, Lawrence M., *The Reception of English Literature in Germany* (Berkeley, CA: University of California Press, 1932).

Pringle, Heather, *The Master Plan: Himmler's Scholars and the Holocaust* (London: Harper Perennial, 2006).

Puhvel, Jaan, *Comparative Mythology* (Baltimore, MD, and London: Johns Hopkins University Press, 1987).

Purchas, Samuel, trans., *Hakluytus Posthumus or Purchas his Pilgrimes: Contayning a history of the world in sea voyages and lande travells by Englishmen and others* (1625), vol. 13 (New York: AMS Press, 1965).

Quinn, Judy, trans., 'The Saga of the People of Eyri', in Viðar Hreinsson, ed., *The Complete Sagas of the Icelanders*, vol. V (Reykjavík: Leifur Eiríksson Publishing, 1997), pp. 131–218.

Rafn, Carl Christian, *Antiquitates Americanae* (Copenhagen: 1837).

Ramsay, George Gilbert, trans., *The Annals of Tacitus: Books I–IV* (London: John Murray, 1904).

Raphael, Jordan and Tom Spurgeon, *Stan Lee and the Rise and Fall of the American Comic Book* (Chicago, IL: Chicago Review Press, 2003).

Rendall, Jane, 'Tacitus engendered: "Gothic feminism" and British histories, c. 1750–1800', in Geoffrey Cubitt, ed., *Imagining Nations* (Manchester: Manchester University Press, 1998), pp. 57–74.

Resen, Peder Hansen, ed., *Edda Islandorum, an. Chr. MCCXV, Islandice, conscripta per Snorronem Sturlæ Islandiæ* (Copenhagen: 1665; Facsimile with intro. Anthony Faulkes. Reykjavík: Stofnun Árna Magnússonar, 1977).

Reynolds, Richard, *Superheroes: A Modern Mythology* (Jackson, MS: University Press of Mississippi, 1994).

Richter, Herman, *Olaus Magnus: Carta Marina, 1539* (Lund: Almquist & Wiksell, 1967).

Rix, Robert William, 'William Blake, Thomas Thorild and Radical Swedenborgianism', *Nordic Journal of English Studies*, 2/1 (2003), pp. 97–128.

Roberts, Michael, *The Swedish Imperial Experience, 1560–1718* (Cambridge: Cambridge University Press, 1979).

Rooth, Anna Birgitta, *Loki in Scandinavian Mythology* (Lund: C. W. K. Gleerup, 1961).

Rossel, Sven H., trans., *Scandinavian Ballads*, Wisconsin Introductions to Scandinavia II, 2 (Madison, WI: Department of Scandinavian Studies, University of Wisconsin-Madison, 1982).

Rousseau, Jean-Jacques, *Discourse on the Origin and Basis of Inequality Among Men* (Discours sur l'origine et les fondements de l'inégalité parmi les hommes) (Amsterdam: Marc Michel Rey, 1754).

Sawyer, Birgit, *Viking-Age Rune-Stones: Custom and Commemoration in Early Medieval Scandinavia* (Oxford: Oxford University Press, 2000).

Saxo Grammaticus, *Danorum Regum heroumque Historiae* (Gesta Danorum), ed. Christiern Pedersen (Paris: Jodocus Badius,1514).

— *Den danske krønicke* (Gesta Danorum), trans. Anders Vedel (Copenhagen: 1575).

— *The History of the Danes* (Gesta Danorum): *Books I–IX*, vol. 1, ed. H. R. Ellis Davidson, trans. Peter Fisher (Cambridge: D. S. Brewer, 1996).

Schjødt, Jens Peter, *Initiation between Two Worlds: Structure and Symbolism in Pre-Christian Scandinavian Religion*, trans. Victor Hansen, The Viking Collection, Studies in Northern Civilisation, vol. XVII (Odense: University Press of Southern Denmark, 2008).

Schleiden, K. A., ed., *Friedrich Gottlieb Klopstock: Ausgewählte Werke* (Munich: Carl Hanser, 1962)

Schmidt, Wolf Gerhard, *'Homer des Nordens' und 'Mutter der Romantik': James Macphersons 'Ossian' und seine Rezeption in der deutschsprachigen Literatur*, 3 vols (Berlin and New York: Walter de Gruyter, 2003).

Service, Alex, 'Vikings and Donald Duck', in John Arnold, Kate Davies and Simon Ditchfield, eds, *History and Heritage: Consuming the Past in Contemporary Culture* (Shaftesbury, Dorset: Donhead Publishing, 1998), pp. 117–26.

Sharp, William, intro. *The Poems of Ossian* (Edinburgh: John Grant, 1926).

Shippey, Tom, 'Grimm's law: how one man revolutionised the humanities', *Times Literary Supplement* (7 November, 2003), pp. 16–17.

— 'A revolution reconsidered: mythography and mythology in the nineteenth century', in Tom Shippey, ed., *The Shadow-Walkers: Jacob Grimm's Mythology of the Monstrous* (Tempe, AZ: Arizona Center for Medieval and Renaissance Studies; Turnhout: Brepols, 2005), pp. 1–29.

Shute, Nevil, *An Old Captivity* (London: Heinemann, 1940).

— *Vinland the Good* (London: Heinemann, 1946).

Simek, Rudolf, *Dictionary of Northern Mythology*, trans. Angela Hall (Cambridge: D. S. Brewer, 1984).

Skeat, Walter W., ed. and trans., *Ælfric's Lives of Saints: Being a Set of Sermons on Saints' Days Formerly Observed by the English Church*, 2 vols (London: Early English Text Society, 1881–85, 1890–1900; repr. Oxford: Oxford University Press for the EETS, 1966).

Smith, Bradley F., *Heinrich Himmler: A Nazi in the Making; 1900–1926* (Stanford, CA: Hoover Institution Press, 1971).

Smith, Edward Elmer, *The Skylark of Space*, Parts 1–3, *Amazing Stories* (New York: Experimenter Publishing, August–October 1928).

Smyth, Alfred P., *Scandinavian Kings in the British Isles, 850–880* (Oxford and New York: Oxford University Press, 1977).

Sørensen, Preben Meulengracht, 'Thor's fishing expedition', in Gro Steinsland, ed., *Words and Objects: Towards a Dialogue between Archaeology and the History of Religion* (Oslo: Norwegian University Press, 1986), pp. 257–78.

Stafford, Fiona J., *The Sublime Savage: A Study of James Macpherson and the Poems of Ossian* (Edinburgh: Edinburgh University Press, 1990).

Stallybrass, James Stephen, trans., *Grimm's Teutonic Mythology*, 4 vols, from Jacob Grimm, *Deutsche Mythologie*, 4th edn (London: George Bell and Sons, 1882–88).

Stenton, F. M., *Anglo-Saxon England*, 3rd edn (Oxford: Oxford University Press, 1971).

Stephens, George, trans., *The Scandinavian Question. Practical Reflections by Arnliot Gellina. Translated from the Swedish Original by an English Scandinavian* (London: John Russell Smith, 1857)

— *The Old-Northern Runic Monuments of Scandinavia and England.* 4 vols (vol. 4 ed. S. O. M. Soderberg) (London: John Russell Smith; Copenhagen: Michaelsen and Tillge, 1866–1901).

— *Thunor the Thunderer, carved on a Scandinavian font of about the year 1000. The first yet found god-figure of our Scando-Gothic forefathers* (London: Williams and Norgate; Copenhagen: H. H. J. Lynge, 1878).

Swanton, Michael, ed. and trans., *The Anglo-Saxon Chronicles*, new edn (London: Phoenix, 2000).

Tombo, Jr., Rudolf, *Ossian in Germany: Bibliography, General Survey, Ossian's Influence upon Klopstock and the Bards* (1901) (New York: AMS Press, 1966).

Turville-Petre, E. O. G., *Myth and Religion of the North: The Religion of Ancient Scandinavia* (London: Weidenfield and Nicolson, 1964).

— *Nine Norse Studies*, Viking Society for Northern Research Text Series, vol. V (London: University College London, 1972).

Uhland, Ludwig, *Der Mythus von Thor nach Nordischen Quellen* (Stuttgart and Augsburg: J. G. Cotta'sche Buchhandlung, 1836).

Upton, Anthony F., *Charles XI and Swedish Absolutism* (Cambridge: Cambridge University Press, 1998).

Vahtola, Jouko, 'Population and settlement', in Knut Helle, ed., *The Cambridge History of Scandinavia: Volume 1; Prehistory to 1520* (Cambridge: Cambridge University Press, 2003), pp. 559–80.

Vigfússon, Guðbrandur and F. York Powell, *Grimm Centenary: Sigfred-Arminius and Other Papers* (Oxford: Clarendon Press; London: Henry Frowde, 1886).

Vikstrand, Per, 'Förkristna sakrala personnamn i Skandinavien', *Studia anthroponymica Scandinavica*, 27 (2009), pp. 5–31.

Wagner, Richard, *Art and Politics* (1851), trans. William Ashton Ellis (Lincoln, NE: University of Nebraska Press, 1995).

— *Richard Wagner: Stories and Essays*, trans. and ed. Charles Osborne (London: Peter Owen, 1973).

Wahlgren, Erik, *The Vikings and America* (London: Thames and Hudson, 1986).

Wåhlin, Vagn, 'Denmark, Slesvig-Holstein and Grundtvig in the 19th Century', in A. M. Allchin, D. Jasper, J. H. Schjørring and K. Stevenson, eds, *Heritage and Prophecy: Grundtvig and the English-Speaking World* (Aarhus: Aarhus University Press, 1993), pp. 243–70.

Wallace, Birgitta Linderoth, 'The Vikings in North America: myth and reality', in Ross Samson, ed., *Social Approaches to Viking Studies* (Glasgow: Cruithne Press, 1991), pp. 207–19.

Wawn, Andrew, 'Shrieks at the stones: The Vikings, the Orkneys and the British enlightenment', in Colleen E. Batey, Judith Jesch and Christopher D. Morris, eds, *The Vikings in Caithness, Orkney and the North Atlantic* (Edinburgh: University of Edinburgh Press, 1993), pp. 408–22.

— *The Vikings and the Victorians: Inventing the Old North in Nineteenth-Century Britain* (Cambridge: D. S. Brewer, 2000).

— 'Victorian Vínland', in Andrew Wawn and Þórunn Sigurðardóttir, eds, *Approaches to Vínland*, Sigurður Nordal Institute Studies 4 (Reykjavík: Sigurður Nordal Institute, 2001), pp. 191–206.

— 'The post-medieval reception of Old Norse and Old Icelandic literature', in Rory McTurk, ed., *A Companion to Old Norse–Icelandic Literature and Culture* (Malden, MA, Oxford, UK: Blackwell Publishing, 2005), pp. 320–37.

Weber, Gerd Wolfgang, 'Nordisk fortid som chiliastisk fremtid: Den 'norrøne arv' og den cykliske historieopfattelse i Skandinavien og Tyskland omkring 1800 – og senere', in Else Roesdahl and Preben Meulengracht Sørensen, eds, *The Waking of Angantyr: The Scandinavian Past in European Culture; Den nordiske fortid i europæisk kultur*, Acta Jutlandica LXXI: 1, Humanities Series 70 (Aarhus: Aarhus University Press, 1996), pp. 72–119.

Wertham, Fredric, *Seduction of the Innocent* (London: Museum Press, 1955).

Whaley, Diana, *Heimskringla: An Introduction*, Viking Society for Northern Research (London: University College of London, 1991).

— 'The "Conversion Verses" in *Hallfreðar saga*: authentic voice of a reluctant Christian?', in Margaret Clunies Ross, ed., *Old Norse Myths, Literature and Society* (Odense: University Press of Southern Denmark, 2003), pp. 234–57.

Whittier, John Greenleaf, *The Complete Poetical Works* (Boston: Houghton Mifflin, 1894).

Widen, Larry, *Doc Savage: Arch Enemy of Evil* (Apple Core Publishing Group, 2006), p. 111. Available online at: http://books.google.com/books?id=ioe Yos90eg4C&pg=PA111&dq=the+code+of+doc+savage&hl=en&ei=Qvrq TOnmKo2-sQO3uMGcDw&sa=X&oi=book_result&ct=result&resnum= 1&ved=0CCUQ6AEwAA#v=onepage&q=the%20code%20of%20doc%20 savage&f=false (accessed 23 November 2010).

Wikipedia, 'Comics code authority', Wikipedia (n.d.). Available at: http:// en.wikipedia.org/wiki/Comics_Code_Authority (accessed 23 November 2010).

Worm, Ole, *RUNIR seu Danica literatura antiquissima* (Runes, or the Most Ancient Danish Literature) (Copenhagen: Martzan,1636; Copenhagen: Holst, 1636; Amsterdam: Janson, 1636).

Wylie, Philip, *Gladiator* (New York: Alfred K. Knopf, 1930). Available online at: http://books.google.com/books?id=jF6oOGPcRTQC&printsec=front cover&dq=Philip+Wylie,+Gladiator&source=bl&ots=742kt9GT_i&sig= _7-5DSkHJgxh8AF0WFpHf5JAclQ&hl=en&ei=svTqTOfoDYy-sQOphYn 6Dg&sa=X&oi=book_result&ct=result&resnum=2&ved=0CCIQ6AEwAQ# v=onepage&q&f=false (accessed 23 November 2010).

Zimmermann, Harro, 'Geschichte und Despotie: Zum politischen Gehalt der Hermannsdramen F. G. Klopstocks', *Text und Kritik* (Klopstock issue) (1981), pp. 97–121.

Index